DATE DUE

DEMCO, INC. 38-2931

FIRMS, CONTRACTS, AND FINANCIAL STRUCTURE

Firms, Contracts, and Financial Structure

OLIVER HART

CLARENDON PRESS · OXFORD

1995

Oxford University Press, Walton Street, Oxford OX2 6DP
Oxford New York
Athens Auckland Bangkok Bombay
Calcutta Cape Town Dar es Salaam Delhi
Florence Hong Kong Istanbul Karachi
Kuala Lumpur Madras Madrid Melbourne
Mexico City Nairobi Paris Singapore
Taipei Tokyo Toronto
and associated companies in
Berlin Ibadan

Oxford is a trade mark of Oxford University Press

Published in the United States
by Oxford University Press Inc., New York

British Library Cataloguing in Publication Data
Data available

Library of Congress Cataloging in Publication Data
Data available
ISBN 0–19–828850–6
ISBN 0–19–828881–6 (Pbk)

Printed in Great Britain
on acid-free paper by
Biddles Ltd, Guildford & King's Lynn

*For Benjamin, Daniel, Rita, Philip
and Ruth*

Acknowledgements

This book has grown out of the Clarendon lectures given at Oxford University in May 1993. Chapters 1, 2, 6, and 7 are based on the lectures themselves; Chapters 3, 4, 5, and 8 represent new material.

I have benefited from the help, suggestions, and encouragement of many people. My greatest debts are to Sandy Grossman, with whom I began much of the work presented here, and to John Moore, with whom I continued it. The ideas in this book could not have been developed without them. John Moore has also provided significant suggestions for improving the book and important psychological support. I owe him a great deal. I would also like to give special thanks to Philippe Aghion, who collaborated with me (and John Moore) on the bankruptcy analysis of Chapter 7, and who provided very useful criticisms of an early draft of the book.

Over the years, I have learned a great deal from talking with some close colleagues about incomplete contracts and the theory of the firm. I would particularly like to thank Patrick Bolton, Mathias Dewatripont, Bengt Holmstrom, Andrei Shleifer and Jean Tirole. They have helped to shape my ideas. Patrick Bolton, Andrei Shleifer, and Jean Tirole also provided detailed comments on a first draft, as did Rabindran Abraham, Raj Aggarwal, Lucian Bebchuk, Maija Halonen, Ilya Segal, and Steve Tadelis. Steve Tadelis, in addition, provided very valuable research assistance.

Discussions with other colleagues, students, and friends have contributed to the development of the ideas in this book. I would like to thank Fabrizio Barca, Morten Bennedsen, Erik Brynjolfsson, Leonardo Felli, Donald Franklin, Martin Hellwig, Henrik Lando, Eric Maskin, Meg Meyer, John Mitchell, Geoffrey Owen, Ying Yi Qian, Matthew Rabin, Charles Sabel, Klaus Schmidt, Lars Stole, Peter Swann, Aaron Tornell, John Vickers, David Webb, Birger Wernerfelt, Chenggang Xu, Xiaokai Yang, Luigi Zingales, and Jeffrey Zwiebel.

I would like to acknowledge those who have helped me in other ways. I have learned a great deal about the art of writing from my wife, Rita Goldberg. She has also given me useful comments on parts of the book. To the extent that this book is well-written, a lot of the credit should go to her. I have also been lucky to have excellent secretarial assistance. Yvonne Zinfon, at Harvard, did a wonderful job of typing the manuscript. She put in extra hours to complete the book on time and managed to keep calm when chaos reigned around her.

Finally, I would like to thank various institutions for their assistance. I started the book when I was on leave at the London School of Economics from MIT, and continued it when I moved to Harvard. I am grateful to all three universities for providing me with a stimulating work environment. I have also received very useful financial support from the National Science Foundation of the United States (Grant No. SBR 9320845), the National Bureau of Economic Research, and British Petroleum (who financed my stay at LSE).

I owe special thanks to Oxford University Press and Oxford University for inviting me to give the Clarendon lectures and for making me realize that this book was possible.

Contents

Introduction

ECONOMISTS have a very well-established theory of market trading and are on the way to possessing a similarly well-developed theory of contractual transactions. The economic analysis of institutions, however, is in a much more rudimentary state.

This book provides a framework for thinking about firms and other kinds of economic institutions. The basic idea is that firms arise in situations where people cannot write good contracts and where the allocation of power or control is therefore important. The book is divided into two parts. Part I is concerned with the boundaries of firms, Part II with the financial structure of firms. In this Introduction I want to sketch out some of the main themes. It is useful to start with a true story.

Recently my wife and I entered into negotiations to buy a piece of land from a contractor, on which the contractor would build us a house. Our first impression of the contractor was favourable; we hope that he felt the same way about us. None the less, it was clear as we talked about how to structure the deal that each of us had legitimate concerns. To mention a few of them, my wife and I were worried that we might spend a lot of money and end up with a house we did not like, or that the house might not be finished on time, or that the contractor might quit in the middle of the project and we would have to hire someone else to complete the house. On the other hand, the contractor was worried that he would build a house designed according to our wishes and we would then not pay for it, or that we would dismiss the contractor in the middle of the project and hire someone else, or that we would choose very expensive kitchen and bathroom fixtures which would raise his costs substantially.

In an ideal world, there would be a simple way to deal with many of these concerns. The three of us would write a binding contract that laid down each person's obligations in every conceivable eventuality and imposed large penalties if anybody failed to live up to them.[1] For example, the contract would provide a description of the house down to the bathroom taps and

---

[1] In an even more ideal world, we would not need a contract at all, since we could simply trust each other and rely on everyone behaving fairly.

light fixtures. It would specify how the price of the house would be altered if my wife and I made any changes—there would be one price for an extra bathroom, another for an extra fitted wardrobe, etc. There would be provisions for how the price of the house would change if the cost of raw materials rose during construction. A completion date would be specified, but extra days would be allowed if there were an unusually severe winter or if the foreman fell ill. And so on.

Unfortunately, it is impossible to write a contract as detailed as this; it is simply too difficult to anticipate all the many things that may happen. The contract we will write (at this point we have not yet agreed on a final contract!) will specify many aspects of the house, but many contingencies will be left out.[2] As the contractor admitted rather disarmingly to us, he is learning how to write contracts as he goes along. The contract he wrote with his last client had many missing provisions; he hopes this one will have fewer.[3]

Given that we will write an incomplete contract, it is clear that revisions and renegotiations will take place. In fact, the contract is best seen as providing a suitable backdrop or starting point for such renegotiations rather than specifying the final outcome. Thus, in thinking about the contract, my wife and I—and I believe the contractor too—have found it useful to imagine worst-case scenarios. We are all looking for a contract that will ensure that, whatever happens, each side has some protection, both against opportunistic behaviour by the other party and against bad luck. For example, here are two contracts that I do *not* think the three of us will sign:

Contract 1: My wife and I pay for the house and the land in advance. The contractor is then obliged to complete the house. He receives no further payment.

---

[2] Needless to say, it will be written in a language that only a lawyer can understand.

[3] An interesting example of an unforeseen contingency is the following. Between the times when the first and second drafts of this book were written, the location of the driveway became an issue. The land is situated between two roads, and my wife and I assumed that the driveway would lead on to the smaller of these. It now turns out that this location may violate town ordinances, and the driveway may have to lead on to a main road. I doubt that any of the three of us could have anticipated this eventuality.

Contract 2: We pay nothing in advance. However, we become the owner of the land immediately. We pay for the house and the land when the house is completed.

It is pretty clear why these contracts are unattractive. With the first one, my wife and I would be concerned that the contractor would disappear after we had paid him the money for the house and land, and we would be left holding only the land—or that, instead of literally disappearing, the contractor might work extremely slowly. With the second one, the contractor would be concerned that we would exclude him from the property that we had just become the owners of, and hire someone else to build the house. (In justification, we might claim that he was doing bad work.)

Instead of these 'extreme' contracts, it seems clear that we will end up writing something closer to the following contract (which is similar to contracts the contractor has used before):

Contract 3: We pay some amount initially which corresponds roughly to the value of the land. We then become the owners of the land. After this we make a series of specified advances to the builder, which are timed to occur when certain parts of the house are finished. (For example, the contractor receives 20 per cent of the price of the house when the foundation is completed, 10 per cent when the chimney is built, and so on.) A final payment is made some time after the house is completed.

The advantage of this kind of contract is that each side has some protection against worst-case scenarios; or, to put it another way, neither side can take too much advantage of the other. If the contractor disappears at any point, we could complete the project without incurring too much additional cost since we have paid an amount roughly commensurate with what we have received from him. On the other hand, if we sack the contractor at some point, he will not suffer too much since he has been paid for the work he has done.

The house story is of course just one example of an economic relationship, but it has two features that I believe are very general. The first is that contracts are incomplete. The second is that, because of this, the *ex post* allocation of power (or control) matters. Here power refers roughly to the position of each party if the other party does not perform (e.g. if the other party behaves opportunistically). It was observed in the house example that contract 3 succeeded in sharing power reasonably between the contractor and my wife and me. In contrast, contract 1 gave the contractor too much power and contract 2 gave my wife and me too much power.[4]

In this book, I will argue that these two ideas—contractual incompleteness and power—can be used to understand a number of economic institutions and arrangements. Before I develop this theme a little further, it is worth pointing out that power is not a standard feature of economic theory. For example, take the frameworks that economists use to analyse the behaviour of economic agents: general equilibrium theory, game theory, mechanism design or principal–agent theory, and transaction cost theory. In general equilibrium theory, it is supposed that trade takes place through anonymous competitive markets and that every agent abides by the terms of any transaction he or she enters into. In such a setting, power is irrelevant. In game theory, agents may have market power, i.e. the ability to affect price. However, market power is not the same as the notion of power used in this book. Market power captures the idea that the contractor can charge my wife and me a lot for our house because there are not many competing contractors around; it says nothing about how we allocate power within our relationship. In mechanism design or principal–agent theory, it is supposed that it is costless to write a contract. An implication is that an optimal contract will be 'comprehensive', in the sense that, like the idealized house contract, it will lay down each person's obligations in every conceivable eventuality and impose large penalties if anybody fails to live up to them. But here again power is irrelevant, since an optimal comprehensive contract will not be breached or renegotiated.

Transaction cost theory comes closest to the framework presented here. However, although transaction cost theory puts a lot

---

[4] There is a sad postscript to the house transaction. Between the time when the second and third drafts of this book were written, the deal fell through. The reason is that the house site adjoined some wetlands and it turned out to be much harder to obtain building permission from the local conservation commission than my wife and I expected (or were led to believe). Both sides lost money, although the contractor appears to have lost more. The conservation issue is another example of an unanticipated contingency—in this case, a critical one.

of emphasis on the costs of writing contracts, and the consequent contractual incompleteness, less attention is paid to the idea that power is important or that institutional arrangements are designed to allocate power among agents.[5]

In the remainder of this introduction, I will try to impart a flavour of how contractual incompleteness and power can be used to understand some important economic phenomena. I will touch on the contents of each chapter except for Chapter 1, which surveys the literature, and Chapter 4, which discusses the foundations of the theory of incomplete contracts.

1. The meaning of ownership

Economists have written a great deal about why property rights are important, and in particular why it matters whether a machine, say, is privately owned or is common property. However, they have been less successful in explaining why it matters *who* owns a piece of private property. To understand the difficulty, consider a situation where I want to use a machine initially owned by you. One possibility is for me to buy the machine from you; another possibility is for me to rent the machine from you. If contracting costs are zero, we can sign a rental agreement that is as effective as a change in ownership. In particular, the rental contract can specify exactly what I can do with the machine, when I can have access to it, what happens if the machine breaks down, what rights you have to use the machine, and so on. Given this, however, it is unclear why changes in asset ownership ever need to take place.

In a world of contracting costs, however, renting and owning are no longer the same. If contracts are incomplete, not all the uses of the machine will be specified in all possible eventualities. The question then arises: who chooses the unspecified uses? A reasonable view is that the owner of the machine has this right; that

---

[5] Given its concern with power, the approach proposed in this book has something in common with Marxian theories of the capitalist–worker relationship, in particular, with the idea that an employer has power over a worker because the employer owns the physical capital the worker uses (and therefore can appropriate the worker's surplus); see e.g. Marx (1867: ch. 7). The connection between the two approaches has not so far been developed in the literature, however.

is, the owner has residual rights of control over the machine, or residual powers. For example, if the machine breaks down or requires modification and the contract is silent about this, the owner can decide how and when it is to be repaired or modified.

It is now possible to understand why it might make sense for me to buy the machine from you rather than to rent it. If I own the machine, I will have more power in our economic relationship since I will have all the residual rights of control. To put it another way, if the machine breaks down or needs to be modified, I can ensure that it is repaired or modified quickly, so that I can continue to use it productively. Knowing this, I will have a greater incentive to look after the machine, to learn to operate it, to acquire other machines that create a synergy with this machine, and so on.

Chapters 2 and 3 develop a formal theory of asset ownership based on these ideas.

2. *The boundaries of firms*

A long-standing issue in organization theory concerns the determinants of the boundaries of firms. Why does it matter if a particular transaction is carried out inside a firm or through the market or via a long-term contract? To put it another way, given any two firms A and B, what difference does it make if the firms transact through an arms-length contract or merge and become a single firm?

It has proved to be difficult to answer these questions using standard theory for the same reason that it is hard to explain why asset ownership matters. If contracting costs are zero, firms A and B can write a contract governing their relationship that specifies the obligations of all parties in all eventualities. Since the contract is all-inclusive, it is unclear what further aspects of their relationship could be controlled through a merger. This is true whether firms A and B are in a vertical relationship—firm A is buying an input from firm B—or in a horizontal or lateral relationship, e.g. where firms A and B sell complementary products and want to save on some duplicative production costs.

Once one recognizes that contracts are incomplete, however, it is possible to explain why a merger might be desirable. Consider the well-known example of Fisher Body, which for many years has supplied car bodies to General Motors. For a long time Fisher Body and GM were separate firms linked by a long-term contract. However, in the 1920s GM's demand for car bodies increased substantially. After Fisher Body refused to revise the formula for determining price, GM bought Fisher out.[6]

Why did GM and Fisher Body not simply write a better contract? Arguably, GM recognized that, however good a contract it wrote with Fisher Body, situations similar to the one it had just experienced might arise again; that is, contingencies might occur that no contract could allow for. GM wanted to be sure that next time around it would be in a stronger bargaining position; in particular, it would be able to insist on extra supplies, without having to pay a great deal for them. It is reasonable to suppose that ownership of Fisher Body would provide GM with this extra power by giving it residual control rights over Fisher Body's assets. At an extreme, GM could dismiss the managers of Fisher Body if they refused to accede to GM's requests.[7]

Of course, although the acquisition increased GM's power and made GM more secure in its relationship with Fisher Body, it arguably had the opposite effect on Fisher Body. That is, Fisher Body may have had more to worry about since the merger. For example, if Fisher Body's costs fall, GM is now in a stronger position to force a reduction in the (transfer) price of car bodies, hence reducing the return to Fisher managers. Anticipating this, Fisher managers may have less incentive to figure out *how* to reduce costs. Thus, there are both costs and benefits from a merger.[8]

Chapters 2 and 3 develop a theory of the firm based on the idea that firm boundaries are chosen to allocate power optimally among the various parties to a transaction. I argue that power is a scarce resource that should never be wasted. One implication of the theory is that a merger between firms with highly

[6] For interesting and informative discussions of the GM–Fisher Body relationship, see Klein *et al.* (1978) and Klein (1988).

[7] There has been some debate about whether GM did in fact increase its power over Fisher Body by buying Fisher Body out; see Coase (1988: 45).

[8] Sometimes the costs of a merger will exceed the benefits. This may explain why GM did not merge with A. O. Smith, which has supplied a significant fraction of its automobile frames for many years. For a discussion of the A. O. Smith case, see Coase (1988: 45–6) and Klein (1988: 205).

complementary assets is value-enhancing, and a merger between firms with independent assets is value-reducing. The reason is as follows. If two highly complementary firms have different owners, then neither owner has real power since neither can do anything without the other. It is then better to give all the power to one of the owners through a merger. On the other hand, if two firms with independent assets merge, then the acquiring firm's owner gains little useful power, since the acquired firm's assets do not enhance his activities, but the acquired firm's owner loses useful power, since she no longer has authority over the assets she works with. In this case, it is better to divide the power between the owners by keeping the firms separate.

3. Financial securities

Debt

Suppose you have an interesting idea for a business venture, but do not have the capital to finance it. You go to a bank to get a loan. In deciding whether to finance the project, the bank is very likely to consider not only the return stream from the project, but also the resale value of any assets you have or will acquire using the bank's funds; in other words, the bank will be interested in the potential collateral for the loan. In addition, the durability of your assets and how quickly the returns come in are likely to determine the maturity structure of the loan. The bank will be more willing to lend long-term if the loan is supported by assets such as property or machines than if it is supported by inventory, and if the returns arrive in the distant future rather than right away.

These observations fit in well with the ideas emphasized in this book. Like the parties in the house transaction, the bank wants some protection against worst-case scenarios. If there is very little collateral underlying the loan, then the bank will worry that you will use its money unwisely or, in an extreme case, disappear with the money altogether. Similarly, if the collateral depreciates rapidly or the returns come in quickly, then the bank would be unhappy with a long-term loan since it would have little protection against your behaving opportunistically when the collateral was no longer worth much or after the project returns had been realized (and 'consumed'). Basically, the bank wants to ensure a rough balance between the value of the debt outstanding and the value remaining in the project, including the value of the collateral, at all times. (Similar considerations made contract 3 in the house example attractive: neither party was in significant deficit or surplus with respect to the other party at any point in the transaction.) Chapter 5 builds a model of debt finance based on these ideas, and derives results about the kinds of project that will be financed.

Equity

Investors who finance business ventures sometimes take equity in the venture rather than debt. Equity, unlike debt, does not have a fixed set of repayments associated with it, with nonpayment triggering default. Rather, equity-holders receive dividends if and when the firm chooses to pay them. This puts equity-holders potentially at the mercy of those running the firm, who may choose to use the firm's profits to pay salaries or to reinvest rather than to pay out dividends. Thus, equity-holders need some protection. Typically, they get it in the form of votes. If things become bad enough, equity-holders have the power to remove those running the firm (the board of directors) and replace them with someone else.

However, giving outside equity-holders voting power brings costs as well as benefits. Equity-holders can use their power to take actions that ignore the (valid) interests of insiders. For example, they might close down an established, family-run business or force the business to terminate long-standing employees. The optimal allocation of power between insiders and outsiders is another of the topics covered in Chapter 5.

4. Dispersed power

So far I have supposed that those with power wield it. That is, I have assumed that an owner will exercise her residual control rights over assets; e.g. an equity-holder will use her votes to replace a bad manager. However, if power is held by many people, then no one of them may have an incentive to be active in exercising this power. It is then important that there exist automatic mechanisms that will achieve what those with power are unable or unwilling to do by themselves.

A leading example of dispersed power is the case of a public company with many, small shareholders. Shareholders cannot run the company themselves on a day-to-day basis and so they delegate power to a board of directors and to managers. This creates a free-rider problem: an individual shareholder does not have an incentive to monitor management, since the gains from improved management are enjoyed by all shareholders, whereas the costs are borne only by those who are active. Because of this free-rider problem, the managers of a public company have a fairly free hand to pursue their own goals: these might include empire-building or the enjoyment of perquisites.

Chapters 6 and 8 explore two 'automatic' mechanisms that can improve the performance of management: debt (in combination with bankruptcy) and take-overs. Debt imposes a hard budget constraint on managers. If a company has a significant amount of debt, management is faced with a simple choice: reduce slack— that is, cut back on empire-building and perquisites—or go bankrupt. If there is a significant chance that managers will lose their jobs in bankruptcy, they are likely to choose the first option.

Take-overs provide a potential way to overcome collective action problems among shareholders. If a company is badly managed, then there is an incentive for someone to acquire a large stake in the company, improve performance, and make a gain on the shares or votes purchased. The threat of such action can persuade management to act in the interest of shareholders.

I derive some implications of these views of debt and take-overs. Chapter 6 shows that the view of debt as a constraining mechanism can explain the types of debt a company issues (how senior the debt is, whether it can be postponed). Chapter 8 shows that the possibility of take-overs can explain why many companies bundle votes and dividend claims together—that is, why they adopt a one share–one vote rule. One share–one vote protects shareholder property rights in the sense that it maximizes the chance that a control contest will be won by a management team that provides high value for shareholders, rather than high private benefits for itself.

Of course, if a company takes on debt, then there is always the chance that it will go bankrupt. If contracting costs were zero, there would be no need for a formal bankruptcy procedure because every contract would specify what should happen if some party could not meet its debt obligations. In a world of incomplete contracts, however, there is a role for bankruptcy procedure. In Chapter 7 I argue that a bankruptcy procedure should have two main goals. The first is that a bankrupt company's assets should be placed in their highest-value use. The second is that bankruptcy should be accompanied by a loss of power for management, so as to ensure that management has the right incentive to avoid bankruptcy. Chapter 7 suggests a procedure that meets these goals, and at the same time avoids some of the inefficiencies of existing US and UK procedures.

5. An omitted topic: public ownership

The book is concerned with the optimal allocation of privately owned assets. A very important topic not considered concerns the optimal balance between public and private ownership. Which assets should be publicly owned and which should be privately owned? This issue has always been a central one in the economic and political debate, but it has attracted new attention in the last few years as major industries have been privatized in the West and the socialist regimes in Eastern Europe and the former Soviet Union have dissolved.

It is natural to analyse public choice versus private choice using the ideas of incomplete contracts and power. If contracting costs are zero, there is no difference between the optimal regulation of a private firm on the one hand, and nationalization or public ownership on the other. In both cases the government will write a 'comprehensive' contract with the firm or its managers that will anticipate all future contingencies. The contract will specify the manager's compensation scheme, how the price of the firm's output should change if costs fall, how the nature of the firm's product should change if there is a technological innovation or a shift in demand, etc.

In contrast, in a world of incomplete contracts, public and private ownership are different, since in one case the government has residual control rights over the firm's assets, while in the other case a private owner does. The public–private case is not a simple extension of the pure private property rights model, however. At least two new questions arise. First, what is the government's objective function? Much existing work views the government as a monolith, but this is unsatisfactory since, even more than in the case of a corporation, the government represents a collection of agents with conflicting goals: civil servants, politicians, and the citizens themselves. Second, what ensures that the government respects an agreed-on allocation of property rights? The government, unlike a private agent, can always change its mind: it can nationalize assets it has privatized or privatize assets it has nationalized.

There is a small, but growing, literature that analyses public versus private ownership in incomplete contracting terms.[9] However, much remains to be done. Developing a satisfactory theory, which deals among other things with the issue of the government's objective function and its commitment to property rights, is a challenging but fascinating task for future research.

---

[9] See, in particular, Schmidt (1990), Shapiro and Willig (1990), Shleifer and Vishny (1994), and Boycko *et al.* (1995).

PART I

Understanding Firms

The first part of the book, Chapters 1–4, is concerned with the nature and extent of the firm, that is, with the determinants of the boundaries of firms in a market economy. Chapter 1 contains a discussion of existing theories of the firm, including the neoclassical, principal–agent, and transaction cost theories. While these theories have proved very useful for some purposes, I shall argue that they cannot by themselves explain the boundaries of firms (or the internal organization of firms). Chapters 2 and 3 describe the more recent incomplete contracting or 'property rights' approach, which can throw some light on firm boundaries. This theory can also explain the meaning and importance of asset ownership. Finally, Chapter 4 provides a discussion of the foundations of the incomplete contracting model used in Part I and, to some extent, throughout the book.

1

Established Theories of the Firm

THIS chapter discusses some of the ways in which economists have looked at firms. I begin with the neoclassical theory of the firm, the standard approach found in all textbooks. I then move on to the principal–agent and transaction cost theories.[1]

1. Neoclassical theory

Neoclassical theory, which has been developed over the last one hundred years or so, views the firm mainly in technological terms. A single-product firm is represented by a production function which specifies the output level Q that is obtained when given levels of n inputs $x_1, \ldots, x_n$ are chosen. It is supposed that the firm is run by a selfless manager, M, who chooses input and output levels to maximize profit. This in turn implies that the manager minimizes costs.

The simplest case is where M purchases the n inputs in a competitive market at given prices $w_1, \ldots, w_n$, so that his total costs are $\sum_{i=1}^{n} w_i x_i$. Let $Q = f(x_1, \ldots, x_n)$ denote the firm's production function. Then, given a target output level Q, M will minimize costs by solving the following problem:

$$\text{Min} \sum_{i=1}^{n} w_i x_i$$

$$\text{s.t.} \quad f(x_1, \ldots, x_n) \geq Q.$$

Solving this for every value of Q generates a total cost curve $C(Q)$, from which can be deduced an average cost curve $C(Q)/Q$ and a marginal cost curve $C'(Q)$. The latter two curves are assumed to have the familiar shape indicated in Figure 1.1.

---

[1] Readers may find it useful to consult some other recent accounts of the theory of the firm, e.g. Holmstrom and Tirole (1989), Milgrom and Roberts (1992), and Radner (1992).

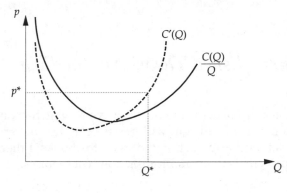

FIG. 1.1

The second stage of M's problem is to decide what level of output to produce. Under the assumption that M is a perfect competitor in the output market and faces price p^*, he maximizes $p^*Q - C(Q)$. This leads to the familiar equality between price and marginal cost, illustrated in Figure 1.1.

The U-shape of the average cost curve is justified as follows. There are some fixed costs of production (plant, machines, buildings) that must be incurred whatever the level of output. As output increases, variable costs increase, but fixed costs do not. Thus, there is a tendency for per-unit costs to fall. However, after a certain point further expansion becomes difficult because some inputs cannot be varied easily with the firm's scale. One of these is managerial talent. As output rises, the manager eventually becomes overloaded and his productivity falls. As a consequence, the firm's average cost begins to rise.[2]

How should one assess this theory of the firm? On the positive side, the theory is surely right to stress the role of technology in general, and returns to scale in particular, as important determinants of the size of firms (see e.g. Chandler 1990: 26–8). In addition, the theory has been very useful for analysing how the firm's optimal production choice varies with input and output prices, for understanding the aggregate behaviour of an industry, and for studying the consequences of strategic interaction between

[2] For a more general account of the neoclassical theory of the firm, see Mas-Colell *et al.* (1995: ch. 5).

firms once the assumption of perfect competition has been dropped (see e.g. Tirole 1988).

At the same time, the theory has several serious weaknesses. First, it completely ignores incentive problems *within* the firm. The firm is treated as a perfectly efficient 'black box', inside which everything operates perfectly smoothly and everybody does what they are told. Even a cursory glance at any actual firm suggests that this is unrealistic. Second, the theory has nothing to say about the internal organization of firms—their hierarchical structure, how decisions are delegated, who has authority. Third, and related, the theory does not satisfactorily pin down the boundaries of the firm. Among other things, it is not clear why managerial talent is a fixed factor: why can't the managerial diseconomies that lie behind the upward-sloping portion of the average cost curve be avoided through the hiring of a second manager?

It is useful to dwell on this last point since it lies at the heart of the first part of this book. Neoclassical theory is as much a theory of division or plant size as of firm size. Consider Figure 1.1 again. Imagine two 'firms' with the same production function f and cost function C, each facing the output price p^* (and both being perfect competitors). Neoclassical theory predicts that in equilibrium each firm produces Q^*. But couldn't one just as well imagine a single large firm operating with each of the smaller firms as divisions, producing $2Q^*$ altogether?

This line of reasoning suggests that it is not enough to argue that a firm will not expand because its manager has special skills and additional managers are inferior. The real issue is why it makes sense for the additional managers to be employed *outside* this firm, rather than within a division or subsidiary operated by this firm. In other words, given the original firm and a second firm employing an alternative manager, why doesn't the first firm expand—possibly laterally—by merging with the second firm?

To put it in stark terms (suggested originally by Coase 1937), neoclassical theory is consistent with there being one huge firm in the world, with every existing firm (General Electric, Exxon, Unilever, British Petroleum, . . .) being a division of this firm. It is also consistent with every plant and division of an existing firm becoming a separate and independent firm. To distinguish between these possibilities, it is necessary to introduce factors not present in the neoclassical story.

2. The agency view

As noted, neoclassical theory ignores all incentive problems within the firm. Over the last twenty years or so, a branch of the literature—principal–agent theory—has developed which tries to rectify this. I shall argue that principal–agent theory leads to a richer and more realistic portrayal of firms but that it leaves unresolved the basic issue of the determinants of firm boundaries.

A simple way to incorporate incentive considerations into the neoclassical model described above is to suppose that one of the inputs, input i say, has a quality that is endogenous, rather than exogenous. In particular, suppose that input i (a widget, say) is supplied by another (owner-managed) 'firm', and that the quality of this input, q, depends on the effort the supplying manager exerts, e, as well as on some randomness outside the manager's control, ϵ:

$$q = g(e, \epsilon).$$

Here ϵ is assumed to be realized after the manager's choice of e.[3]

Assume that quality q is observable and verifiable—it might represent the fraction of widgets that are not defective—but that the purchasing manager does not observe the supplying manager's effort, nor does he observe ϵ.[4] Assume also that the supplying manager dislikes high effort; represent this by a 'cost of effort' function $H(e)$. Finally, suppose (for simplicity) that only one widget is required by the purchaser ($x_i = 1$), that this yields the purchaser a revenue of $r(q)$, and that the supplying manager is risk-averse, while the purchasing manager is risk-neutral.[5]

If the purchaser could observe and verify e, he would offer the supplier a contract of the form: 'I will pay you a fixed amount P^* as long as you choose the effort level e^*.' Here e^* is chosen to be

---

[3] Another version of the principal–agent problem assumes that ϵ is realized before the manager's choice of e; see, e.g. Laffont and Tirole (1993: ch. 1).

[4] The statement that q is observable and verifiable means that the parties can write an enforceable contract on the value of q.

[5] Let the purchasing manager's utility function be $U_p(r(q) - P) = r(q) - P$ and the supplying manager's utility function be $U_s(P,e) = V(P) - H(e)$, where V is concave, and P represents the payment made by the purchasing manager to the supplying manager. The principal–agent problem is interesting only if the supplying manager is risk-averse. Letting the purchasing manager be risk-neutral is a simplifying assumption.

jointly efficient for the purchaser and the supplier and P^* is determined so as to divide up the gains from trade between the two parties, according to the relative scarcity of potential purchasers and suppliers, relative bargaining power, etc.[6]

The advantage of the fixed payment P^* is that it ensures optimal risk-sharing. The purchaser bears all the risk of ϵ realizations, which is efficient since he is risk-neutral and the supplier is risk-averse.

Unfortunately, when e is not observable to the purchaser, the above contract is not feasible, since it cannot be enforced. (The purchaser would not know if the supplier deviated from $e = e^*$.) To put it another way, under the above contract, the supplier would set $e = 0$ if she dislikes working. To get the supplier to exert effort, the purchaser must pay the supplier according to *observed* performance q, i.e. he must offer the supplier an incentive scheme $P = P(q)$. In designing this incentive scheme, the two parties face the classic trade-off between optimal incentives and optimal risk-sharing. A 'high-powered' incentive scheme—that is, one where $P'(q)$ is close to $r'(q)$—is good for supplier incentives since the supplier earns a large fraction of the gains from any increase in e; but it exposes the supplier to a great deal of risk. Conversely, a low-powered scheme protects the supplier from risk but gives her little incentive to work hard.[7]

There is now a vast literature that analyses the form of the optimal incentive scheme under the above circumstances. Moreover, the basic principal–agent problem described has been extended in a number of directions. Among other things, agency theorists have allowed for: repeated relationships, several agents, several principals, several dimensions of action for the agent, career concerns and reputation effects, and so on.[8]

As a result of all this work, a rich set of results about optimal

---

[6] Given the utility functions described in n. 5, and assuming that the supplying manager receives an expected utility of U, it is easy to show that e^* maximizes $E[r(g(e,\epsilon))] - V^{-1}(U + H(e))$, and $P^* = V^{-1}(U + H(e^*))$, where E is the expectations operator. For details, see Hart and Holmstrom (1987).

[7] An optimal incentive scheme solves the following problem:

$\text{Max}_{e,P(\bullet)} \ E[r(g(e,\epsilon)) - P(g(e,\epsilon))]$

s.t. (1) $e \in \text{argmax}_{e'} \{E[V(P(g(e',\epsilon)))] - H(e')\}$,

(2) $E[V(P(g(e,\epsilon)))] - H(e) \geq U$.

For details, see Hart and Holmstrom (1987).

[8] For surveys, see Hart and Holmstrom (1987) and Sappington (1991).

incentive schemes has been obtained. However, although these results can throw important light on the determinants of managerial compensation packages and on certain aspects of the organization of production, the agency approach falls foul of the same criticism that besets neoclassical theory. That is, it does not pin down the *boundaries* of the firm (or say much about the internal organization of firms).

Consider again the incentive problem described above, where the optimal incentive scheme has the form $P(q)$. One interpretation of this situation is that the purchaser and supplier are independent firms linked by the arm's-length contract $P(q)$. For instance, to take an example from the Introduction, the purchaser might be General Motors and the supplier might be Fisher Body, and $P(q)$ might represent the optimal contract written by these firms when they are independent. However, another interpretation is that the purchaser and supplier are divisions of a larger firm and that $P(q)$ represents the incentive scheme that the manager of the supplying division is under. That is, according to this second interpretation, $P(q)$ is the optimal incentive scheme that the managers of the Fisher Body division face after a merger with GM. Agency theory does not distinguish between these two situations, and yet economically they seem quite different. To paraphrase Coase once again, the principal–agent view is consistent with there being one huge firm in the world, consisting of a large number of divisions linked by optimal incentive contracts; but it is also consistent with there being many small, independent firms linked by optimal arm's-length contracts. Clearly, there is something missing from the agency view of firms, just as there is something missing from the neoclassical view. The question is: what is it?

Before moving on, I should mention two possible answers to this question. First, it is sometimes claimed that asymmetries of information are reduced within the firm. For example, if the buyer of input i merges with the seller, he will be able to monitor the supplying manager's effort level better and therefore will be able to devise a better incentive scheme. The trouble with this argument is that it does not explain *why* it is easier to monitor an employee than an independent contractor. Asymmetries of information may indeed diminish within the firm, but if they do it is important to know how and why. Chapters 2 and 3 will present a theory that can throw some light on this issue (see in particular Ch. 3, §8).

Second, it is sometimes argued that cost and/or profit-sharing becomes easier when firms merge; for example, in the above example the buyer can compensate the seller for her costs, including effort, when the buyer and seller are one firm, but not when they are two. Again, the problem with this argument is that it does not explain why cost- and profit-sharing are possible within a single firm, but not between two independent firms.[9] The theory presented in Chapters 2 and 3 will throw some light on this issue too (see in particular Ch. 3, §4).

3. Transaction cost theories

The distinction between comprehensive and incomplete contracts

One important factor missing from the principal–agent view is the recognition that writing a (good) contract is itself costly. This is a theme that lies at the heart of the large transaction cost literature which started with Ronald Coase's famous 1937 paper and has been extensively developed by Oliver Williamson and others (see in particular Williamson 1975, 1985, and Klein *et al.* 1978).

It is worth noting first that agency theory itself already incorporates some contracting costs. In the simple model considered above, it is supposed that managerial effort, e, cannot be made part of an enforceable contract since it is observed only by the agent. Another way of saying this is that the cost of putting e into the incentive contract is infinite. However, this is probably not a very useful way of looking at things. Agency theory ascribes all contracting costs to the cost of *observing* variables. If a variable is observable by both parties, then the theory assumes that it can be contracted on costlessly. But this is not the same as supposing that it is costly to *write* a contract.

This point can be made a little more sharply as follows. Although the optimal contract in a standard principal–agent

---

[9] One possible reason is that profit-sharing between independent firms may be illegal if the firms compete in the same input or output markets. This may explain some mergers.

model will not be first-best (since it cannot be conditioned directly on variables like effort that are observed by only one party), it will be 'comprehensive' in the sense that it will specify all parties' obligations in all future states of the world, to the fullest extent possible. As a result, there will never be a need for the parties to revise or renegotiate the contract as the future unfolds. The reason is that, if the parties ever changed or added a contract clause, this change or addition could have been anticipated and built into the original contract.[10]

It may be worth spelling this out. Consider the simple model of Section 2, but suppose there are two verifiable states of the world, $s = s_1$ and $s = s_2$, and that the value of s affects production quality:

$$q = g(e, \epsilon, s).$$

Assume also that s is learned by both parties at date 1 before production takes place, and that the parties contract at some prior date 0. Then in general it is optimal for the parties to write a state-contingent contract that specifies two incentive schemes, $P(q,s_1)$ and $P(q,s_2)$, one to apply when $s = s_1$ and the other to apply when $s = s_2$.

Now suppose that, after $s = s_1$ is realized, the principal and agent decide that they can do better by replacing the second-period incentive scheme $P(q,s_1)$ by $\hat{P}(q,s_1)$. Then, given that the parties have perfect foresight, they will recognize that the second-period incentive scheme $P(q,s_1)$ will not stand. But, given this, the parties may as well substitute $\hat{P}(q,s_1)$ for $P(q,s_1)$ in the original date 0 contract. In other words, given any contract that is renegotiated on the equilibrium path, there is an equivalent one that is not.[11]

---

[10] One would also not expect to see any legal disputes in a comprehensive contracting world. The reason is that, since a comprehensive contract specifies everybody's obligations in every eventuality, the courts should simply enforce the contract as it stands in the event of a dispute.

[11] In fact, not only does renegotiation not add anything in the standard principal–agent model, but the possibility of it can actually *worsen* matters! See Dewatripont (1989). The argument is subtle, but the following gives a rough idea. In some principal–agent models the presence of inefficiency in later periods can improve the agent's incentives (for truth-telling or exerting effort) in earlier periods so much that the later inefficiency is worthwhile. However, the later inefficiency is not credible: when the future arrives, the parties will renegotiate their contract to eliminate the inefficiency. In a situation like this, the parties would be better off if they could commit not to renegotiate. The problem is that it is not clear how they can achieve this.

The sources of transaction costs

In reality, contracts are not comprehensive and are revised and renegotiated all the time. According to the transaction cost literature, this is a consequence of three factors missing from the standard principal–agent story. First, in a complex and highly unpredictable world, it is hard for people to *think* very far ahead and to plan for all the various contingencies that may arise. Second, even if individual plans can be made, it is hard for the contracting parties to *negotiate* about these plans, not least because they have to find a common language to describe states of the world and actions with respect to which prior experience may not provide much of a guide. Third, even if the parties can plan and negotiate about the future, it may be very difficult for them to *write* their plans down in such a way that, in the event of a dispute, an outside authority—a court, say—can figure out what these plans mean and enforce them. In other words, the parties must be able to communicate not only with each other, but also with outsiders who may have little knowledge about the environment in which the contracting parties operate.[12]

As a result of these three contracting costs, the parties will write a contract that is incomplete. That is, the contract will contain gaps and missing provisions. In particular, it will be silent about the parties' obligations in some states of the world and will specify these obligations only coarsely or ambiguously in other states of the world. For example, the contract might not specify what is to happen if the supplier's factory burns down, because this is not anticipated; or the contract might say that the supplier must always supply one widget, rather than a number of widgets that varies with the state of the world, because it is too costly to distinguish between different states of the world. The contract might also be short-term; that is, it might specify the parties' obligations only up to some date, T.

It is useful to illustrate these points with the General Motors–Fisher Body example from the Introduction. In a constant world, GM and Fisher might find it easy to write a long-term contract specifying the quantity, quality, and price of the car bodies Fisher supplies to GM. For example, it might be optimal for them

---

[12] All of these may be regarded as different forms of 'bounded rationality'. For further discussions, see Coase (1937), Williamson (1985), and Klein *et al.* (1978).

to agree that Fisher should supply 2,000 bodies, of a particular type, each day at a particular price for the foreseeable future.

Now consider the case where the world is changing. The optimal number of car bodies, type of car bodies, and price may depend on a variety of factors, e.g. the demand for General Motors' output, Fisher Body's costs, actions of competitors, new regulations on car pollution, whether a trade agreement is reached with the Japanese, and innovations occurring in car and body production.

It may be prohibitively expensive to write a contract that conditions quantity, quality, and price on all of the external factors just described. This is not just because some of the variables are privately observed, but also because, even if publicly observable, the variables are inherently hard to specify in advance in an unambiguous manner. For example, there may be no objective way of measuring the demand for cars, or the degree of innovation, or the extent of government regulation, or the actions of competitors. Thus, a contract that tries to condition variables on these factors may not be enforceable by a court. In addition, even if it is possible for the parties to anticipate and contract on some of the factors that may be relevant for their relationship, there may be many others that the parties do not anticipate; for example, they may foresee the possibility of a new trade agreement, but not of new regulations on car pollution. Under these conditions, the parties are likely to write an incomplete contract. For example, the contract might be short-term. GM and Fisher may be able to look five years ahead, but not much further. So they might write a contract specifying that Fisher should supply 2,000 bodies per day, of a particular type, at a particular price for the next five years. Both parties realize that towards the end of the five-year period they will have further common information about demand, costs, competitors' strategies, regulations, etc., and that they can then write a new contract for another five years; and so on.

The economic implications of contractual incompleteness

As observed, an incomplete contract will be revised and/or renegotiated as the future unfolds. In fact, given that the parties can fill in the gaps as they go along, one may ask why contractual incompleteness matters. The reason is that the renegotiation process imposes several costs. Some of these are *ex post* costs, incurred at the renegotiation stage itself, and others are *ex ante* costs, incurred in anticipation of renegotiation.[13]

First, the parties may engage in a great deal of haggling over the terms of the revised contract. Argument about division of surplus serves no overall productive purpose and, to the extent that it is time-consuming and wastes resources, it is inefficient.[14]

Second, not only may the process of *ex post* bargaining be costly, but, to the extent that the parties have asymmetric information, they may fail to reach an efficient agreement. Suppose that at the recontracting stage Fisher Body knows the current cost of producing car bodies, but General Motors does not. (It knows only the probability distribution from which costs are drawn.) GM could ensure a supply of bodies by offering Fisher an attractive price (high enough to cover Fisher's costs with probability one). However, this is expensive, since GM is overpaying in states of the world where costs are low. GM may prefer to offer a low price, knowing that in high-cost states Fisher will not supply (even though the cost of bodies is less than their value to GM). In other words, profit-maximizing behaviour by GM leads to absence of profitable trade with positive probability.[15]

It is worth noting at this point that neither of the above *ex post* costs would be significant if the parties could easily switch to new trading partners at the renegotiation stage. Any attempt by Fisher (resp. GM) to haggle for an increased share of surplus would fail if GM (Fisher) could switch to an equally efficient alternative partner. Similarly, asymmetric information does not lead to *ex post* inefficiencies if, after a bargaining breakdown, the parties can (costlessly) start the process again with new identical partners; if GM's low-price offer is turned down, GM will either eventually

---

[13] As will become clear, it is unfair, strictly speaking, to blame these costs on renegotiation *per se*. Given contractual incompleteness, these costs would likely be even greater in the *absence* of renegotiation, i.e. if the parties had to stick to the original incomplete contract.

[14] In addition, there may be costly legal disputes because an incomplete contract will be ambiguous and the parties will look to the courts to resolve the ambiguity.

[15] See e.g. Fudenberg and Tirole (1991: ch. 10) or Myerson and Satterthwaite (1983). The parties may also fail to reach an agreement at the *ex ante* stage of contractual negotiation if there is asymmetric information at this point.

find a low-cost supplier, or, if all suppliers have high costs, GM will learn this and raise its price.

Thus, if the two costs described are high, it must be because there is something binding the partners together and making it difficult for them to switch at the recontracting stage. The leading candidate for that 'something' is an *ex ante relationship-specific investment*, that is, a prior investment, which creates value if the parties' economic relationship extends over time, but does not if the parties split up. In the case of GM and Fisher, examples of relationship-specific investments might be GM's decision to locate a car assembly plant near Fisher's factory, Fisher's decision to locate its factory near GM's assembly plant, GM's decision to spend money on developing cars that rely on the bodies supplied by Fisher, and Fisher's decision to spend money figuring out how to reduce the cost of producing bodies for GM (but not for car manufacturers in general).[16]

Once the existence of relationship-specific investments is recognized, it becomes apparent that there can be a third cost of contractual incompleteness that may dwarf the haggling and *ex post* inefficiency costs discussed so far. Specifically, because contracts are incomplete, the parties may be deterred from making the relationship-specific investments that would be optimal in a 'first-best' world. Suppose it is efficient for Fisher to install machinery that enables it to produce car bodies designed specifically for GM. In a comprehensive contracting world, the contract between GM and Fisher could be structured in such a way that Fisher would have an incentive to make the investment; one way to do this is to have a contract that fixes the body price for the indefinite future, so that the gains from the investment accrue to Fisher.

In an incomplete contracting world, however, such an arrangement may be impossible. Because of the difficulty of specifying quality and quantity very far in advance, both parties recognize that any long-term contract is incomplete and subject to renegotiation. Even if renegotiation proceeds smoothly—that is, if problems due to haggling and asymmetric information do not arise—the division of the gains from trade will depend on the *ex post* bargaining strengths of the parties rather than on what is

---

[16] Insightful discussions about relationship-specific investments may be found in Williamson (1985), Klein *et al.* (1978), and Joskow (1985).

specified in the initial contract or on economic efficiency. As a result, a party may be reluctant to invest because it fears expropriation by the other party at the recontracting stage, i.e. it fears that it will not cover its investment costs.

For example, Fisher will worry that, once it has installed the special machinery, GM will use its bargaining power to set the price of car bodies close to Fisher's variable production costs, thus causing Fisher to make a loss on its initial fixed investment. Alternatively, GM may insist that Fisher's output satisfy very demanding quality criteria. Similarly, GM will worry that, once it has sunk the costs of developing a car that uses Fisher's bodies, Fisher will use its bargaining power to set the price of car bodies close to GM's variable production benefits, thus causing GM to make a loss on *its* initial fixed investment.

Given each party's fear that the other party will 'hold it up' at the renegotiation stage, the parties are likely to make investments that are relatively non-specific.[17] For example, Fisher may decide to install general-purpose machinery that enables it to supply a range of car manufacturers; this way Fisher can play one manufacturer off against the other at the recontracting stage and achieve a higher price for its output. Similarly, GM may decide to develop a car that can use bodies produced by a number of different suppliers, rather than only Fisher bodies. Such decisions sacrifice some of the efficiency benefits of specialization, but, in a world of incomplete contracting, these efficiency losses are more than offset by the security that a general investment provides for each party.

So far I have talked about the costs that plague the relationship between two independent, i.e. non-integrated, firms. The next question to ask is: how would these costs change if the two firms merged and became a single firm? Here transaction cost theory becomes somewhat vaguer. It is often suggested that haggling problems and hold-up behaviour are reduced in a single firm. However, the precise mechanism by which this happens is not usually spelled out. In the discussion of principal–agent theory, I argued that it is unsatisfactory to assume that the informational structure changes directly as a result of a merger. In the same way, it is unsatisfactory to suppose that the agents automatically

[17] For discussions of the hold-up problem, see Williamson (1985) and Klein *et al.* (1978). For formalizations, see Grout (1984) and Tirole (1986*a*).

become less opportunistic. (Also, presumably opportunistic behaviour is not always reduced within the firm, since otherwise it would be optimal to carry out all economic activities within one huge firm.) If there is less haggling and hold-up behaviour in a merged firm, it is important to know *why*. Transaction cost theory, as it stands, does not provide the answer.

2

The Property Rights Approach

ALL the theories discussed in Chapter 1 suffer from the drawback that they do not explain what changes when two firms merge. I now describe a theory—the property rights approach—that tries to address this question head-on.[1] I divide the chapter into three parts. Section 1 provides a verbal description of the property rights approach. Section 2 develops a formal model under a very stylized set of assumptions. Finally, Section 3 discusses what light the theory can throw on actual organizational arrangements.

1. *A general description*

Consider two firms, A and B, and imagine that firm A acquires firm B. Ask the following question: what exactly does firm A get for its money? At least in a legal sense, the answer seems straightforward: firm A acquires, i.e. becomes the owner of, firm B's assets. Included in this category are firm B's machines, inventories, buildings, land, patents, client lists, copyrights, etc.—that is, all of firm B's physical or nonhuman assets. Excluded are the human assets of those people working for firm B; given the absence of slavery, the human capital of these workers belongs to them both before and after the acquisition.

Why does ownership of physical or nonhuman assets matter? The answer is that ownership is a source of power when contracts are incomplete. To understand this, note that an incomplete contract will have gaps, missing provisions, or ambiguities, and so situations will occur in which some aspects of the uses of nonhuman assets are not specified. For example, a contract between General Motors and Fisher Body might leave open certain aspects of maintenance policy for Fisher machines, or might not specify

---

[1] The following is based on Grossman and Hart (1986) and Hart and Moore (1990). The account in the first part of the chapter is drawn from Hart (1989).

the speed of Fisher's production line or the number of shifts per day, or whether GM's production process can be modified to accept Fisher's input more easily.[2]

Given that a contract will not specify all aspects of asset usage in every contingency, who has the right to decide about missing usages? According to the property rights approach, it is the owner of the asset in question who has this right. That is, the owner of an asset has *residual control rights* over that asset: the right to decide all usages of the asset in any way not inconsistent with a prior contract, custom, or law.[3] In fact, possession of residual control rights is taken virtually to be the definition of ownership. This is in contrast to the more standard definition of ownership, whereby an owner possesses the residual income from an asset rather than its residual control rights.[4]

Note that this view of ownership seems to accord with common sense. For example, suppose I rent you my car for six months and during this period you have an urge to install a CD player. It would generally be agreed that, if the contract is silent, you would have to ask my permission to do this; that is, the residual right to change the interior of the car would be mine as owner rather than yours as renter. Furthermore, even if the contract did make provisions for a CD player, there would be many other

[2] In contrast, a comprehensive contract would include a detailed list of the way every asset should be used in every eventuality. For example, the contract might say: machine 1 should be used in the following way (button 1 of machine 1 should be in the 'on' position, button 2 of machine 1 should be in the 'off' position, dial 3 of machine 1 should be in the 45° position, . . .); machine 2 should be used in the following way (button 1 of machine 2 should be in the 'off' position, button 2 of machine 2 should be in the 'on' position, dial 3 of machine 2 should be in the 60° position, . . .); etc. An incomplete contract will not—cannot—contain this much detail.

[3] In the case of a large company such as General Motors, the owner(s) may delegate the residual control rights to management or a board of directors. This chapter ignores the delegation issue and treats firms as if they were owner-managed; however, see Ch. 3, §3, and Chs. 6–8.

[4] For a discussion of the relationship between residual income and residual control rights, see Ch. 3, §4. The idea that an owner has residual control rights seems consistent with the standard view of ownership adopted by lawyers:

But what are the rights of ownership? They are substantially the same as those incident to possession. Within the limits prescribed by policy, the owner is allowed to exercise his natural powers over the subject-matter uninterfered with, and is more or less protected in excluding other people from such interference. The owner is allowed to exclude all, and is accountable to no one. (Oliver Wendell Holmes, *The Common Law 193*, (1963 edn.))

events and actions which would not be covered and with respect to which you would have to ask my permission.[5]

So, in the General Motors–Fisher Body example, if the two companies are separate, GM has the right to decide whether to modify its production process, while Fisher can make the decisions about the speed of its own production line, number of shifts per day, or maintenance of its machines. (This is under the assumption that the contract is silent about these issues.) On the other hand, if GM acquires Fisher, then GM can make all the above decisions. Finally, if Fisher acquires GM, then all the decisions are in the hands of Fisher.

To see the economic implications of different ownership arrangements, it is useful to focus on the third cost of contractual incompleteness described in Chapter 1, the distortion in relationship-specific investments.[6] Suppose GM and Fisher have an initial contract that requires Fisher to supply GM with a certain number of car bodies every day. Imagine that demand for GM's cars now rises and GM requires additional car bodies. Suppose also that the initial contract is silent about this possibility, perhaps because of the difficulty of anticipating the circumstances of the demand increase. If Fisher is a separate company, GM must secure Fisher's permission to increase supply. That is, the status quo point in any contract renegotiation is where Fisher does *not* provide the extra bodies. GM does not have the right to go into Fisher's factory and set the production line to supply the extra bodies; Fisher, as owner, has this residual right of control. This is to be contrasted with the situation where Fisher is a subdivision or subsidiary of GM, so that GM owns Fisher's factory. In this

---

[5] Of course, as renter of my car, you will have *some* residual control rights. For example, it would generally be understood that you can decide where to drive the car or whom to take as a passenger, if the contract is silent about these matters. (However, you would probably have to ask my permission to take the car on safari.) What is important for the analysis that follows is not that the owner has all the residual control rights, but that the owner has some of the most economically significant ones. The fact that renters have some residual rights is consistent with this view. It is also important to note that, to the extent that a rental agreement has a fixed term, the owner of the asset has all the residual control rights concerning actions and events after the agreement ends (and before it begins). So in the car example I can decide where the car is driven and who is a passenger after the six months are up.

[6] Note, however, that a similar analysis could be carried out with respect to the other costs of contractual incompleteness. I will have more to say about this in Ch. 4, §3.

case, if Fisher management refuses to supply the extra bodies, GM has the option to dismiss management and hire someone else to supervise the factory and supply extra bodies. (GM could even run Fisher itself on a temporary basis.) The status quo point in the contract renegotiation is therefore quite different.

To put it very simply, if Fisher is a separate firm, Fisher management can threaten to make both Fisher assets and its own labour unavailable for the uncontracted-for supply increase. In contrast, if Fisher belongs to GM, Fisher management can only threaten to make its own labour unavailable. The latter threat will generally be weaker than the former.[7]

Although the status quo point in the contract renegotiation may depend on whether GM and Fisher are one firm rather than two, it does not follow that the outcomes after renegotiation will differ. In fact, if the benefit to GM of the extra car bodies exceeds the cost to Fisher of supplying them, one would expect the parties to agree that the bodies should be supplied, regardless of the status quo point.[8] However, the divisions of surplus in the two cases will be very different. If GM and Fisher are separate, GM may have to pay Fisher a large sum to persuade it to supply the extra bodies. In contrast, if GM owns Fisher's plant, it may be able to enforce the extra supply at much lower cost since, in this case, Fisher management has much reduced bargaining and threat power.

Anticipating the way surplus is divided, GM will typically be more prepared to invest in machinery that is specifically geared to Fisher bodies if it owns Fisher than if Fisher is independent, since the threat of expropriation is reduced; for example, as noted, GM can always run the Fisher factory itself if Fisher management tries to extract too much surplus. The incentives for Fisher, however, are quite the opposite. Fisher management will generally be more willing to come up with cost-saving or quality-enhancing innovations if Fisher is an independent firm, because Fisher management is more likely to see a return on its activities. If Fisher Body is independent, it can extract some of the surplus from an innovation by incorporating the innovation in bodies it

[7] If current Fisher management is indispensable for the operation of Fisher assets, there is, of course, no difference between the two threats. It is rare, however, that management is completely irreplaceable.

[8] This is an application of the Coase theorem; see Coase (1960).

supplies to another car manufacturer. In contrast, if GM owns Fisher, Fisher management faces partial (or even total) expropriation of the value of an innovation to the extent that GM can deny Fisher management access to the assets necessary to incorporate the innovation (or can even hire a new management team to implement the innovation if the innovation is asset-specific rather than management-specific).[9]

In summary, the benefit of integration is that the acquiring firm's incentive to make relationship-specific investments increases since, given that it has more residual control rights, it will receive a greater fraction of the *ex post* surplus created by such investments. On the other hand, the cost of integration is that the acquired firm's incentive to make relationship-specific investments decreases since, given that it has fewer residual control rights, it will receive a smaller fraction of the incremental *ex post* surplus created by its own investments.[10]

I now present a model that formalizes the above ideas. Before I do so, it is worth noting that so far the discussion of control changes has been restricted to the impact on top management. Workers' incentives will also be affected by changes in ownership, however. I postpone a discussion of worker incentives to Chapter 3. In that chapter I also cover a number of other aspects of the integration decision.

---

[9] One way to protect Fisher managers from expropriation is to provide them with a golden handshake (or parachute). However, while a golden handshake will provide financial security, it may not encourage Fisher management to make relationship-specific investments, since the value of the handshake is unlikely to depend on such investments.

[10] Under some conditions, expropriation problems can be avoided regardless of the structure of ownership. One possibility is for the parties to write an *ex ante* profit-sharing agreement. However, a profit-sharing agreement may be insufficient to encourage *ex ante* investments for two reasons. First, profits may not be verifiable; e.g. one party could inflate costs and claim that profits are low. Second, an *ex ante* agreement that Fisher, a division of General Motors, can receive a share of the profit from an innovation may not mean much if GM—as owner of the Fisher assets—can threaten not to implement the innovation unless Fisher agrees to give up some of its profit share. A second way the parties might overcome expropriation problems is to share investment expenditures. For example, if GM and Fisher are independent, Fisher could compensate GM for its later hold-up power by contributing toward GM's initial Fisher-specific investment. Note, however, that this strategy will work only to the extent that either GM can contractually agree to make the investment (which may be difficult if the investment is hard to describe or verify) or Fisher can make part of the investment on GM's behalf. Otherwise, GM could use an up-front payment from Fisher to make a *non*-relationship-specific investment.

2. *A formal model of the costs and benefits of integration*

In order to develop a formal model, I now abstract from many of the real-world aspects of an economic relationship involving entities such as General Motors and Fisher Body. I focus on a highly stylized situation in which there are just two assets, a1 and a2, and two managers operating them, M1 and M2. Suppose that M2, in combination with a2, supplies a single unit of input—called a widget—to M1. M1, in combination with a1, then uses this widget to produce output that is sold on the output market (see Figure 2.1).

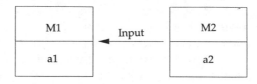

Fig. 2.1

The economic relationship lasts for two dates. *Ex ante* relationship-specific investments are made at date 0, and the widget is supplied at date 1. Assume the assets are already in place at date 0, so that the investments are in making these assets more productive. The parties have symmetric information throughout. Also, there is no uncertainty about the parties' costs or benefits. However, there *is* uncertainty about the type of widget M1 requires. This uncertainty is resolved at date 1; that is, at this time it becomes clear what the relevant widget type is.

The *ex ante* uncertainty about widget type makes an effective long-term contract impossible; the point is that specifying the widget price in advance means nothing, given that the widget type cannot be described.[11] Thus, the parties negotiate about the widget type and price at date 1 from scratch.[12] I shall suppose—and this assumption will be discussed further in Chapter 4—that

---

[11] For further discussion of the no-long-term contract assumption, see Ch. 4, §1.
[12] At date 1 there is no difficulty in writing an enforceable contract about price since the widget type is known and can be described.

the parties have rational expectations about the recontracting process when they make their investments at date 0. In particular, even though the parties cannot write a comprehensive contract, they can make correct calculations about the expected return from any action.

Assume that the parties are risk-neutral and have large (unlimited) amounts of initial wealth, so that each party can purchase any asset it is efficient for her to own. For simplicity, take the interest rate to be zero.

I suppose that it is too costly for the parties to specify particular uses of assets a1 and a2 in a date 0 contract. Thus, whoever owns asset a1 or a2 has not just residual rights of control, but all control rights over the asset. In other words, the owner can use the asset in any way she wants.[13]

For almost all of this section, I will focus on three 'leading' ownership structures:

Non-integration: M1 owns a1 and M2 owns a2.
Type 1 integration: M1 owns a1 and a2.
Type 2 integration: M2 owns a1 and a2.

Other possible ownership structures will be discussed briefly at the end of this section and in Chapter 4.

Investments and payoffs

Denote M1's relationship-specific investment at date 0 by i, where i, a non-negative number, represents the level and cost of the investment. This investment might stand for an expenditure in developing the market for M1's final product. I assume that i will affect M1's revenue both if M1 trades with M2 and if he does not. If trade occurs, M1's revenue is denoted by $R(i)$ and his *ex post* payoff is $R(i) - p$, where p is the agreed widget price. (The investment cost i must be subtracted from this *ex post* payoff to obtain M1's *ex ante* payoff.) If trade does not occur, M1 buys a widget from an outside supplier, that is, a 'non-specific' widget from the spot market at price $\bar{p}$, say. (Alternatively, if M1 has access to a2, he can hire someone to make a widget for him.) This non-specific widget may lead to lower-quality output. Denote M1's revenue in

---

[13] See again Ch. 4 for further discussion.

this case by $r(i;A)$ and his *ex post* payoff by $r(i;A) - \bar{p}$. Here the lower-case r indicates the absence of M2's human capital and the argument A refers to the set of assets M1 has access to in the event that trade does not occur (i.e. A represents the assets M1 owns). (In contrast, if trade does occur, M1 has access to all the assets in the relationship.) So, under non-integration, $A = \{a1\}$; under type 1 integration $A = \{a1,a2\}$; and under type 2 integration $A = \varnothing$. (If M1 has access to a2, he may be able to modify the non-specific widget, which is one reason why r may depend on a2.)

In the same way, denote M2's relationship-specific investment at date 0 by e, where e, a non-negative number, represents the level and cost of the investment. This investment might stand for an expenditure of money or time in making M2's operations more efficient. I assume that e will affect M2's production costs both if M2 trades with M1 and if she does not. If trade occurs, M2's production costs are denoted by $C(e)$ and her *ex post* payoff is $p - C(e)$. (The investment cost e must be subtracted from this *ex post* payoff to obtain M2's *ex ante* payoff.) If trade does not occur, M2 will sell her widget on the competitive spot market for $\bar{p}$, but will have to make some adjustments to turn it into a general-purpose widget. (Alternatively, if M2 has access to a1, she can hire someone to transform her widget directly into final output.) In this case M2's production costs are denoted by $c(e;B)$, so that M2's *ex post* payoff is $\bar{p} - c(e;B)$. Here the lower-case c indicates the absence of M1's human capital and the argument B refers to the set of assets M2 has access to in the event that trade does not occur. So, under non-integration, $B = \{a2\}$; under type 1 integration $B = \varnothing$; and under type 2 integration $B = \{a1,a2\}$.

The total *ex post* surplus if trade occurs is $R(i) - p + p - C(e) = R(i) - C(e)$, and the total surplus if trade does not occur is $r(i;A) - \bar{p} + \bar{p} - c(e;B) = r(i;A) - c(e;B)$. I will assume that there are always *ex post* gains from trade:

(2.1) $R(i) - C(e) > r(i;A) - c(e;B) \geq 0$ for all i and e,
                    and for all A,B,
          where $A \cap B = \varnothing$ and $A \cup B = \{a1,a2\}$.

Condition (2.1) captures the idea that the investments i and e are relationship-specific: they pay off more if trade occurs than if it does not. However, I assume that relationship-specificity also applies in a marginal sense; that is, the marginal return from each investment is greater the more assets in the relationship, human and otherwise, to which the person making the investment has access. In other words, M1's marginal investment return is highest if he has access to both M2's human capital and the assets a1 and a2. If he does not have access to M2's human capital, it is higher if he has access to a1 and a2 than if he has access only to a1, and so on; similarly for M2. Taking into account that C' and c' are negative (an increase in e reduces costs), I write these conditions as:

$$(2.2) \qquad R'(i) > r'(i;a1,a2) \geq r'(i;a1) \geq r'(i;\varnothing)$$
$$\text{for all } 0 < i < \infty,$$

$$(2.3) \qquad |C'(e)| > |c'(e;a1,a2)| \geq |c'(e;a2)| \geq |c'(e;\varnothing)|$$
$$\text{for all } 0 < e < \infty.$$

Here $|x|$ denotes the absolute value of x, and $r'(i;A) \equiv \partial r(i;A)/\partial i$, $c'(e;B) \equiv \partial c(e;B)/\partial e$. I also assume $R' > 0$, $R'' < 0$, $C' < 0$, $C'' > 0$, $r' \geq 0$, $r'' \leq 0$, $c' \leq 0$, $c'' \geq 0$ (i.e., R is strictly concave, C is strictly convex, r is concave, c is convex).[14]

Note that the strict inequalities in (2.2) and (2.3) mean that i is at least partly specific to M2's human capital and e is at least partly specific to M1's human capital. However, the weak inequalities in (2.2) and (2.3) mean that i may or may not be specific to the nonhuman assets a1 and a2. If $r'(i;a1,a2) = r'(i;a1) > r'(i;\varnothing)$, for example, then i is specific to asset a1 but not to asset a2 (in a marginal sense); similarly for e.

Finally, it is supposed that R, r, C, c, and i and e are observable to both parties, but are not verifiable (to outsiders). Thus, they cannot be part of an enforceable contract.[15]

---

[14] In addition, I make the technical assumptions $R'(0) > 2$, $R'(\infty) < 1$, $C'(0) < -2$, $C'(\infty) > -1$. Note that I suppose r to be (weakly) concave and c to be (weakly) convex to allow for the cases where r and c are constants; i.e., the investments i and e do not affect r and c.

[15] The contract, 'I will pay you £1 million if you make the investment i' is not enforceable, since no outsider knows whether it has been fulfilled. Similarly, the parties' revenues and costs cannot be made part of a profit- or cost-sharing agreement. Since the idea that a variable can be observable but not verifiable plays a key role in this book, it is worth giving some examples. One concerns the book itself. The quality of the book is observable, in the sense that anybody can read it. (Of course, some are in a better position to evaluate it than others.) However, it would have been difficult for Oxford University Press and me to have written a contract making my royalties a function of quality, since if a dispute arose it would be hard for either of us to prove that the book did or did not meet some pre-specified

It is worth pointing out that the above formulation implicitly supposes that the investments i and e are investments in human capital rather than in physical capital. To see this, note that under type 1 integration M1's *ex post* payoff in the absence of trade with M2 is $r(i;a1,a2) - \bar{p}$, which is independent of e. If M2's investment were an investment in physical capital, i.e. if it were embodied in asset a2, then one would expect e to affect M1's payoff, given that M1 controls a2. Similarly, M2's type 2 integration payoff in the absence of trade with M1, $\bar{p} - c(e;a1,a2)$, is independent of i, which would not be the case if i were an investment in physical capital embodied in a1.[16]

Ex post division of surplus

Consider what happens at date 1 given particular investment decisions i and e. Take the asset ownership structure as fixed for the moment and suppress i, e, and the sets of assets A and B that M1 and M2 control. So denote M1's revenue and M2's costs by R and C if trade occurs and by r and c if trade does not occur.

According to (2.1), there are *ex post* gains from trade, given by $[(R - C) - (r - c)]$. Moreover, these will not be achieved under the initial contract since the initial contract does not specify the type of widget to be supplied. However, since the parties have symmetric information, it is reasonable to expect them to realize the gains through negotiation. I shall assume that bargaining is such that the *ex post* gains from trade, $[(R - C) - (r - c)]$, are divided

standard. (For this reason my royalties are made to depend on some (more or less) verifiable consequences of quality, e.g. sales.) In other words, quality is not verifiable. A second example is a university tenure decision. In an ideal world the conditions for being granted tenure would be specified in advance in minute detail (quantity and quality of publications, teaching performance, prominence in the profession, etc.). In practice this is impossible to do, and so the criteria are left fairly vague. At the same time, many aspects of a candidate's performance are observable (certainly the publication record is). The difficulty is to prove that someone's work does or does not meet the appropriate standard to justify tenure. In other words, whether the standard is met is not verifiable. For a further discussion of observability and verifiability, see Ch. 4.

[16] The case of investments in physical capital is discussed in §6 of Ch. 3. Note also that it is supposed that type 1 integration does not allow M1 to make M2's investment e on her behalf and type 2 integration does not allow M2 to make M1's investment i on his behalf. That is, M1 always makes the investment i and M2 always makes the investment e, regardless of organizational form. For a further discussion of this, see Ch. 3, §6.

50 : 50, as in the Nash bargaining solution. Then M1 and M2's *ex post* payoffs equal

(2.4) $\quad \pi_1 = R - p = r - \bar{p} + \frac{1}{2}[(R - C) - (r - c)]$

$\qquad\qquad = -\bar{p} + \frac{1}{2}R + \frac{1}{2}r - \frac{1}{2}C + \frac{1}{2}c,$

(2.5) $\quad \pi_2 = p - C = \bar{p} - c + \frac{1}{2}[(R - C) - (r - c)]$

$\qquad\qquad = \bar{p} - \frac{1}{2}C - \frac{1}{2}c + \frac{1}{2}R - \frac{1}{2}r,$

and the widget price is given by

(2.6) $\quad p = \bar{p} + \frac{1}{2}(R - r) - \frac{1}{2}(c - C).$

Notice that M1's payoff function puts equal weight on the variables R and r. The reason is that, if R rises by 1, *ceteris paribus*, then the widget price rises by $\frac{1}{2}$ because of Nash bargaining (half the gains go to M2). Hence M1's profits increase by $\frac{1}{2}$. On the other hand, if r rises by 1, *ceteris paribus*, then the widget price falls by $\frac{1}{2}$ (again by Nash bargaining). Hence M1's profit again increases by $\frac{1}{2}$. Similar considerations explain why M2's payoff function puts equal weight on the variables C and c.[17]

The first-best choice of investments.   Negotiation at date 1 always leads to an efficient *ex post* outcome under any ownership structure. However, as will be seen, the choice of investments may not be efficient. In a first-best world, where the parties could co-ordinate their actions, they would have a joint interest in maximizing the date 0 (net) present value of their trading relationship:

(2.7) $\qquad R(i) - i - C(e) - e.$

The reason is that, given any investments (i,e) that do not maximize (2.7), the parties can always do better by choosing (i,e) to maximize (2.7) and redistributing the increased surplus through lump-sum transfers at date 0. (Recall the assumption that M1 and M2 are both wealthy.) Denote the unique solution to the first-best problem by (i^*,e^*). The first-order conditions for maximizing (2.7) are

---

[17] Note that the bargaining process is assumed to be independent of ownership structure. M1 and M2 still divide the gains from negotiation 50 : 50 even when M2 is an employee of M1 or M1 is an employee of M2. This may seem a strong assumption. In fact, I would argue that it is a weak assumption. It would be *too* easy to obtain a theory of the costs and benefits of integration if it were supposed that the bargaining process changes under integration.

(2.8) $$R'(i^*) = 1,$$
(2.9) $$\mid C'(e^*) \mid = 1.$$

The second-best choice of investments.   Now consider the second-best incomplete contracting world, where the parties choose their investments non-cooperatively at date 0. Suppose that the ownership structure is such that M1 owns the set of assets A and M2 owns the set of assets B. Then from (2.4) and (2.5) M1's and M2's payoffs, net of investment costs, are given by

(2.10) $$\pi_1 - i = -\bar{p} + \tfrac{1}{2} R(i) + \tfrac{1}{2} r(i;A)$$
$$- \tfrac{1}{2} C(e) + \tfrac{1}{2} c(e;B) - i,$$

(2.11) $$\pi_2 - e = \bar{p} - \tfrac{1}{2} C(e) - \tfrac{1}{2} c(e;B) + \tfrac{1}{2} R(i)$$
$$- \tfrac{1}{2} r(i;A) - e.$$

Differentiating (2.10) with respect to i and (2.11) with respect to e yields the following necessary and sufficient conditions for a (Nash) equilibrium:

(2.12) $$\tfrac{1}{2} R'(i) + \tfrac{1}{2} r'(i;A) = 1,$$
(2.13) $$\tfrac{1}{2} \mid C'(e) \mid + \tfrac{1}{2} \mid c'(e;B) \mid = 1.$$

For future reference, it is useful to write out (2.12) and (2.13) for the three 'leading' ownership structures.

Non-integration.   The equilibrium is characterized by
(2.14) $$\tfrac{1}{2} R'(i_0) + \tfrac{1}{2} r'(i_0;a1) = 1,$$
(2.15) $$\tfrac{1}{2} \mid C'(e_0) \mid + \tfrac{1}{2} \mid c'(e_0;a2) \mid = 1.$$
(Here the subscript 0 stands for no integration.)

Type 1 Integration.   The equilibrium is characterized by
(2.16) $$\tfrac{1}{2} R'(i_1) + \tfrac{1}{2} r'(i_1;a1,a2) = 1,$$
(2.17) $$\tfrac{1}{2} \mid C'(e_1) \mid + \tfrac{1}{2} \mid c'(e_1;\varnothing) \mid = 1.$$
(Here the subscript 1 stands for type 1 integration.)

Type 2 Integration.   The equilibrium is characterized by
(2.18) $$\tfrac{1}{2} R'(i_2) + \tfrac{1}{2} r'(i_2;\varnothing) = 1,$$
(2.19) $$\tfrac{1}{2} \mid C'(e_2) \mid + \tfrac{1}{2} \mid c'(e_2;a1,a2) \mid = 1.$$
(Here the subscript 2 stands for type 2 integration.)

Under assumptions (2.2) and (2.3), (2.12) and (2.13) yield the following result about all second-best outcomes.

PROPOSITION 1. Under any ownership structure, there is underinvestment in relationship-specific investments. That is, the investment choices in (2.12) and (2.13) satisfy $i < i^*$, $e < e^*$.

Proof. Suppose i,e satisfy (2.12) and (2.13). Then, by (2.2) and (2.3),

$$R'(i) > \tfrac{1}{2} R'(i) + \tfrac{1}{2} r'(i;A) = 1$$
$$|C'(e)| > \tfrac{1}{2} |C'(e)| + \tfrac{1}{2} |c'(e;B)| = 1.$$

The result follows since $R'' < 0$, $C'' > 0$. $\square$

The intuition for the underinvestment result is as follows. If M1 invests a little more, this increases the gains from trade by $R'(i)$. However, M1's payoff increases only by $\tfrac{1}{2} R'(i) + \tfrac{1}{2} r'(i;A) < R'(i)$; the remaining gains go to M2. Being self-interested, M1 does not take M2's payoffs into account and hence invests too little. A similar argument applies to M2.[18]

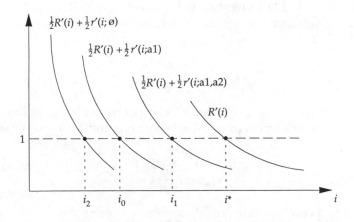

FIG. 2.2

[18] Not all models of ownership yield underinvestment. For example, in Grossman and Hart (1986), overinvestment is possible as well as underinvestment. This is because (2.2) and (2.3) do not hold in the Grossman–Hart model.

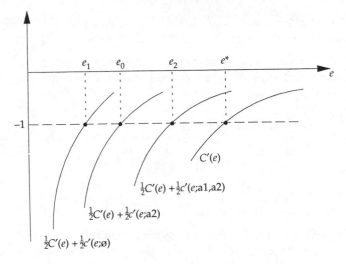

FIG. 2.3

The first-best outcome, and the second-best outcomes under non-integration and type 1 and type 2 integration, are illustrated in Figures 2.2 and 2.3.[19] It is clear from these figures what the effects of integration are. Relative to non-integration, type 1 integration raises M1's investment, but lowers M2's. Relative to non-integration, type 2 integration raises M2's investment, but lowers M1's. That is,

$$(2.20) \qquad i^* > i_1 \geq i_0 \geq i_2,$$

$$(2.21) \qquad e^* > e_2 \geq e_0 \geq e_1.$$

For future reference, note that efficient *ex post* bargaining implies that the total surplus from the relationship under any ownership structure is given by

$$(2.22) \qquad S \equiv R(i) - i - C(e) - e,$$

where i and e satisfy (2.12) and (2.13).[20]

[19] Proposition 1 has been derived under the assumptions that the *ex post* surplus when M1 and M2 trade, given by $T(i,e) \equiv R(i) - C(e)$, is separable in i and e; i.e. $(\partial^2/\partial i\, \partial e)\, T(i,e) = 0$. Proposition 1 can be shown to generalize to the case $(\partial^2/\partial i\, \partial e)\, T(i,e) \geq 0$ (i.e., i and e are complements); see Hart and Moore (1990).

[20] In this model, ownership structure matters because it affects the no-trade payoffs r and c (more particularly, the marginal payoffs r' and c'). Not all bargaining solutions have the property that the equilibrium outcome depends on the

Ex ante division of surplus

Little has been said so far about how the surplus S is divided under a particular ownership structure. Equations (2.10) and (2.11) correspond to the *ex post* division, but, given that lump-sum transfers are possible at date 0, the *ex ante* division may be different. I shall suppose that M1 has many potential trading partners at date 0, but M1 is unique. Then M2 will receive her reservation payoff at date 0, V say, and M1 will get all the gains from the relationship, $S - V$.[21] Nothing depends on this assumption about relative bargaining power, however. In fact, as will be seen, the size of V plays no role in the analysis of optimal ownership structure (as long as $(S - V)$ exceeds M1's date 0 reservation payoff; I assume this in what follows).

The choice of ownership structure

The last step is to determine which ownership structure is best. This is straightforward. Simply compute the total surplus from the various arrangements. (The division of surplus is unimportant since this can always be adjusted using lump-sum transfers at date 0.) In other words, compare the following:

$$
\begin{aligned}
S_0 &= R(i_0) - i_0 - C(e_0) - e_0, \\
S_1 &= R(i_1) - i_1 - C(e_1) - e_1, \\
S_2 &= R(i_2) - i_2 - C(e_2) - e_2.
\end{aligned}
$$

(2.23)

no-trade payoffs. For example, in a bargaining game with outside options, the equilibrium division of surplus is independent of the no-trade payoffs (that is, the outside options) within a certain range (see, e.g., Osborne and Rubinstein 1990). However, what is important for the analysis of ownership is that the no-trade payoffs sometimes matter, not that they always matter. With a reasonable amount of *ex ante* uncertainty about investment returns, the no-trade payoffs will affect the equilibrium division of surplus with positive probability even in a bargaining game with outside options. Thus, the main ideas of the analysis of ownership will continue to be relevant.

[21] More generally, the *ex ante* division of surplus will be determined by the degree of competition in the market for alternative 'M1s' and 'M2s' at date 0, that is, by how many potential trading partners M1 has and how many potential trading partners M2 has. Note that relative bargaining power at date 0 may be very different from relative bargaining power at date 1 since relationship-specific investments have not yet been made at date 0. Williamson (1985) has referred to this as 'the fundamental transformation'.

The theory predicts that the ownership structure that yields the highest value of S will be chosen in equilibrium. For example, if at the starting point of their relationship M1 owns a1 and M2 owns a2, and $S_1 > \text{Max}(S_0, S_2)$, then M1 will buy a2 from M2 at some price that will make them both better off. (In fact, given the assumptions about relative bargaining power, the price will be such that M2's final payoff is V.)

Analysis of the optimal ownership structure

I now consider in greater detail what forces favour one ownership structure over another. Before I start, it is worth making a simple observation. As is clear from (2.12)–(2.13), any change in ownership structure that increases $r'(i;\cdot)$ (resp., increases $|c'(e;\cdot)|$) without decreasing $|c'(e;\cdot)|$ (resp., decreasing $r'(i;\cdot)$), or more generally that increases i or e without decreasing the other, is good. The reason is that, since both parties (always) underinvest (see Proposition 1), such a change moves the parties closer to the first-best and so total surplus given by $R(i) - i - C(e) - e$ rises.

It is useful to introduce some definitions.

> DEFINITION 1. M1's investment decision will be said to be *inelastic* in the range $\frac{1}{2} \le \rho \le 1$ if the solution to $\text{Max}_i\, \rho\, R(i) - i$ is independent of ρ in this range. Similarly, M2's investment decision will be said to be *inelastic* in the range $\frac{1}{2} \le \sigma \le 1$ if the solution to $\text{Min}_e\, \sigma\, C(e) + e$ is independent of σ in this range.[22]
>
> DEFINITION 2. M1's investment will be said to become *relatively unproductive* if $R(i)$ is replaced by $\theta R(i) + (1 - \theta)i$, and $r(i;A)$ is replaced by $\theta r(i;A) + (1 - \theta)i$ for all $A = $ a1, (a1,a2) or $\varnothing$, where $\theta > 0$ is small. M2's investment will be said to become *relatively unproductive* if $C(e)$ is replaced by $\theta C(e) - (1 - \theta)e$, and $c(e;B)$ is replaced by $\theta c(e;B) - (1 - \theta)e$ for all $B = $ a2, (a1,a2) or $\varnothing$, where $\theta > 0$ is small.
>
> DEFINITION 3. Assets a1 and a2 are *independent* if $r'(i;a1,a2) \equiv r'(i;a1)$ and $c'(e;a1,a2) \equiv c'(e;a2)$.

---

[22] For M1's investment decision to be inelastic, it must be the case that, for some $\hat{\imath}$, $R'(i) > 2$ for $0 < i < \hat{\imath}$, $R'(i) < 1$ for $i > \hat{\imath}$; and for M2's investment decision to be inelastic, it must be the case that, for some $\hat{e}$, $|C'(e)| > 2$ for $0 < e < \hat{e}$ and $|C'(e)| < 1$ for $e > \hat{e}$. In Definition 1, therefore, the assumption that R'' and C'' exist everywhere is relaxed.

DEFINITION 4. Assets a1 and a2 are *strictly complementary* if either $r'(i;a1) \equiv r'(i;\varnothing)$ or $c'(e;a2) \equiv c'(e;\varnothing)$.

DEFINITION 5. M1's human capital (resp., M2's human capital) is *essential* if $c'(e;a1,a2) \equiv c'(e;\varnothing)$ (resp., $r'(i;a1,a2) \equiv r'(i;\varnothing)$).

These definitions are intuitive. The first one guarantees that M1 (resp., M2) will choose the same level of i, $\hat{i}$ say, (resp., the same level of e, $\hat{e}$ say) in any one of the ownership structures with 50 : 50 bargaining.

In the second definition, the net social return from M1's (resp., M2's) investment, $R(i) - i$, becomes $\theta(R(i) - i)$ (resp., $C(e) + e$ becomes $\theta(C(e) + e)$), which is small when θ is small. In other words M1's (resp., M2's) investment becomes unimportant relative to M2's (resp., M1's).

The third definition says that a1 and a2 are independent if access to a2 will not increase M1's marginal return from investment given that he already has access to a1; and if access to a1 will not increase M2's marginal return from investment given that she already has access to a2.

The fourth definition says that a1 and a2 are strictly complementary either if access to a1 alone has no effect on M1's marginal return from investment (M1 needs a2 as well), or if access to a2 alone has no effect on M2's marginal return from investment (M2 needs a1 as well).

Finally, the fifth definition says that one party's human capital is essential if the other party's marginal return from investment is not enhanced by the presence of the assets a1 and a2 in the absence of the first party's human capital.

Proposition 2 makes use of the above definitions.

PROPOSITION 2. (A) If M2's investment decision (resp., M1's investment decision) is inelastic, then type 1 integration (resp., type 2 integration) is optimal.

(B) Suppose M2's investment (resp. M1's investment) becomes relatively unproductive, and $r'(i;a1,a2) > r'(i;a1)$ for all i (resp. $|c'(e;a1,a2)| > |c'(e;a2)|$ for all e). Then, for θ small enough, type 1 integration (resp., type 2 integration) is optimal.

(C) If assets a1 and a2 are independent, then non-integration is optimal.

(D) If assets a1 and a2 are strictly complementary, then some form of integration is optimal.

(E) If M1's (resp., M2's) human capital is essential, then type 1 (resp., type 2) integration is optimal.

(F) If both M1's human capital and M2's human capital are essential, then all ownership structures are equally good.

Proof. (A) Suppose M2's investment decision is inelastic. Then (2.3) and (2.13) imply that M2 sets $e = \hat{e}$ under all ownership structures. Thus, it is best to give all the control rights to M1. Conversely, if M1's investment decision is inelastic, it is best to give all the control rights to M2.

(B) Suppose that M2's investment is relatively unproductive. Then M2's first-order condition under any ownership structure becomes (see (2.13)):

$$\tfrac{1}{2}\theta \,|\,C'(e)\,| + \tfrac{1}{2}\,(1 - \theta) + \tfrac{1}{2}\theta\,|\,c'\,(e;B)\,| + \tfrac{1}{2}(1 - \theta) = 1,$$

which simplifies to

$$\tfrac{1}{2}\,|\,C'(e)\,| + \tfrac{1}{2}\,|\,c'(e;B)\,| = 1.$$

In other words, M2's investment decision is independent of θ. However, net surplus, given by

$$\begin{aligned} S &= R(i) - i - \theta\, C(e) + (1 - \theta)\, e - e \\ &= R(i) - i - \theta\,(C(e) + e) \\ &\rightarrow R(i) - i \text{ as } \theta \rightarrow 0. \end{aligned}$$

Thus, for θ small, what matters is M1's investment decision. Hence it is optimal to give all the control rights to M1. The same argument shows that M2 should have all the control rights if M1's investment is relatively unproductive.

(C) Note that, by the definition of independence, the solutions to (2.14) and (2.16) are the same; that is, $i_1 = i_0$. Since $e_1 \le e_0$, non-integration dominates type 1 integration. Also, the solutions to (2.15) and (2.19) are the same; that is, $e_2 = e_0$. Since $i_2 \le i_0$, non-integration dominates type 2 integration.

(D) Suppose first that $r'(i;a1) \equiv r'(i;\varnothing)$. Then the solutions to (2.14) and(2.18) are the same; that is, $i_0 = i_2$. Since $e_0 \le e_2$, type 2 integration dominates non-integration. The same argument shows that, if $c'(e;a2) \equiv c'(e;\varnothing)$, type 1 integration dominates non-integration.

(E) Note that, if M1's human capital is essential, then the solutions to (2.15), (2.17), and (2.19) are all the same; that is,

$e_0 = e_1 = e_2$. Since $i_1 \geq i_0 \geq i_2$, type 1 integration is optimal. The same argument shows that, if M2's human capital is essential, type 2 integration is optimal.

(F) This follows from the fact that, if M1 and M2's human capital are both essential, the solutions to (2.14), (2.16), and (2.18) are all the same and so are the solutions to (2.15), (2.17), and (2.19); that is, $i_0 = i_1 = i_2$ and $e_0 = e_1 = e_2$. Thus, organizational form is irrelevant. $\square$

Most of Proposition 2 is very intuitive. Part (A) says that there is no point giving ownership rights to a party whose investment decision is not responsive to incentives. Part (B) says that there is no point giving ownership rights to a party whose investment is unimportant. Parts (C)–(F) are a little more striking, and it is worth saying a bit more about them.

To understand (C), start with non-integration and consider transferring control of a2 from M2 to M1. This has no effect on M1's marginal return from investment in the event that the parties fail to reach agreement since a1 is no more useful with a2 than without; but transferring control to M1 may have a significantly negative effect on M2's marginal investment return, since without a2 M2 may be able to achieve very little. Thus, the effect of the control transfer is to keep i constant but reduce e, which reduces total surplus. A similar logic applies if we transfer control of a1 from M1 to M2: e stays constant, but i may fall significantly. Thus, when the assets are independent, both forms of integration are dominated by non-integration.

Consider next (D). Start with non-integration. If a1 and a2 are strictly complementary, then transferring control of a2 from M2 to M1 weakly increases M1's marginal return from investment (his return from investment absent an agreement with M2 rises), but it has no effect on M2's marginal return. The reason is that a2 is useless without a1 and so giving up a2 does not change M2's return absent an agreement with M1. Thus, moving from non-integration to integration yields benefits but no costs. A similar logic applies as one moves from non-integration to type 2 integration; hence type 2 integration also is superior to non-integration. Thus, when the assets are strictly complementary, some form of integration is better than non-integration, but without further information (about, say, the importance of M1's investment relative to M2's) it is not possible to rank type 1 integration against type 2 integration.

To understand (E), note that, if M1's human capital is essential, then transferring assets from M2 to M1 has no effect on M2's investment incentives, since M2's no-trade payoff does not depend on the assets she has in the absence of M1's human capital (at the margin). Thus, there is no cost of the control transfer. However, there may be a benefit, since if M1 has all the assets this is likely to increase his incentive to invest.

Note that (B) and (E) together can be summarized as saying that a party with an important investment or important human capital should have ownership rights.

Finally, (F) says that, if both M1 and M2 have essential human capital, then ownership structure does not matter since neither party's investment will pay off in the absence of agreement with the other.

Two observations are worth making. First, the argument showing that complementary assets should be owned together also shows that joint ownership of an asset is suboptimal. Suppose a1 is owned by both M1 and M2. What this means is that if negotiations break down neither M1 nor M2 has access to a1 independently (since any asset usage must be agreed by both). However, such an arrangement is equivalent to dividing a1 in two and assigning one half to M1 and the other half to M2. Since it is clear that the two halves are strictly complementary, an argument similar to that in the proof of Proposition 2(D) tells us that such an outcome is dominated by one in which all of a1 is assigned to either M1 or M2. (This is true whoever is the owner of a2.)[23]

A caveat is important here. I have supposed that the investments *i* and *e* are embodied in M1 and M2's human capital, in the sense that M1 does not obtain the benefit of *e* unless he reaches agreement with M2, and M2 does not obtain the benefit of *i* unless she reaches agreement with M1. As will be seen in Chapter 3, if investments are embodied in physical assets rather than human assets, it is no longer clear that strictly complementary assets

[23] This argument assumes that an asset cannot be used by two people independently. However, for some assets joint usage is possible. For example, a patent can be developed and marketed by two separate firms. In such a case, joint ownership may be optimal. See Aghion and Tirole (1994) and Tao and Wu (1994).

should be owned by the same person (or that assets should not be jointly owned).[24]

Second, it should be noted that there is another ownership arrangement that has not been considered: 'reverse' non-integration, in which M1 owns a2 and M2 owns a1. It is easy to rule this arrangement out, however. Since a1 is the primary asset M1 works with and a2 is the primary asset M2 works with, one would expect M1 to be more productive with a1 than with a2 and M2 to be more productive with a2 than with a1. In other words, one would expect $r'(i;a2)$—the marginal return on M1's investment if he has access only to a2—to be less than $r'(i;a1)$, and $|c'(e;a1)|$—the marginal return on M2's investment if she has access only to a1—to be less than $|c'(e;a2)|$. It follows immediately from this that non-integration dominates this fourth ownership arrangement.[25]

3. *Simple things the theory can tell us about the world*

To conclude this chapter, I would like to consider whether the theory's predictions match up with the actual organizational arrangements observed. Unfortunately, there has to date been no formal testing of the property rights approach, and so in what follows I do not attempt to go beyond what is impressionistic.

One very simple implication of the theory is that, *ceteris paribus*, a party is more likely to own an asset if he or she has an important investment decision (where the investment decision might represent figuring out how to make the asset more productive or looking after the asset). As an example of this, consider the fact

[24] It is also not clear that Proposition 2(D) generalizes to the case where contracts are partially, but not totally, incomplete, i.e. where long-term contracts have some role to play. The reason is that Proposition 2(D) depends on the idea that allocating a2 to M2, say, in the absence of a1 does not increase M2's marginal return if bargaining breaks down (since a2 is useless without a1), but does lower M1's marginal return. However, if a long-term contract is in place, then disagreement corresponds to sticking to the original contract. In this case, a2 may have value to M2 under the original contract, even if M2 does not own a1, and there may therefore be some gain from allocating a2 to M2.

[25] I have also ignored stochastic ownership structures, i.e. arrangements in which, say, M1 owns a2 with probability σ and M2 owns a2 with probability $(1 - \sigma)$. These are discussed further in Ch. 4.

that it is usually thought efficient for someone to own the house they live in or the car they drive (as long as they can afford to; wealth constraints are not part of the present story, but see Chapter 5).[26] Presumably the reason is that the person with most influence on the house's or car's value is the user; giving anybody else ownership or control rights in the asset would dilute the incentives of the user, with no compensating gains since this other person has no effect on asset value. So in the above model it would be like making M2 the owner of a1 and a2 when $C' = 0$.[27]

Another stylized fact consistent with this implication of the theory is that lower-level employees in an organization usually do not have significant ownership or control rights in the organization. Arguably the reason is that lower-level employees carry out (relatively) routine tasks.[28] Motivating such employees by giving them ownership rights may not therefore achieve very much in terms of increased productivity. (It is as if R' or $|C'|$ is small in the above model.) It makes more sense to allocate the scarce ownership rights so as to motivate key higher-ups, whose actions (usually) have a greater effect on company value (Proposition 2(B)) or whose human capital is very important (Proposition 2(E)).[29]

A second implication of the theory is that highly complementary assets should be under common ownership. There are many instances of this in practice (some trivial): a window of a house and the house itself are usually owned together; so are a lock and a key, the engine of a truck and its chassis; a list of clients' names and the list of their addresses.[30] There are also less obvious and more significant examples. Joskow (1985) has investigated the ownership arrangements governing electricity generating plants

[26] I am also ignoring taxes. Tax considerations can sometimes cause parties to lease an asset, say, rather than own it.

[27] An investment in a house or a car might correspond more closely to a physical capital investment than to a human capital investment. However, the same logic applies. On this, see also Ch. 3, §6.

[28] Wealth constraints could also be a factor here.

[29] In large companies, ownership and control rights are often in the hands of outside shareholders rather than key employees. It might be thought that this contradicts the theory presented here since outside shareholders do not take important actions or have essential human capital. However, shareholders make a financial investment in the company and need some protection against this investment being expropriated; ownership and control rights can be seen as providing this protection. Financial investment is discussed further in Chs. 5–8.

[30] For a discussion of examples like these, see Klein *et al.* (1978).

that site next to coal mines. Such assets are highly complementary, and not surprisingly he finds a high incidence of common ownership in the form of vertical integration. Stuckey (1983) has investigated the case of aluminium refineries that site next to bauxite mines. In this situation, the degree of complementarity is arguably even greater, since, not only are the two entities located next to each other, but also the refinery installs equipment that is specific to the particular bauxite mine. Stuckey finds that vertical integration occurs in essentially every case.

Related to the idea that complementary assets should be owned together is the idea that increasing returns to scale should lead to the formation of large firms. Under increasing returns to scale, one large asset is more productive than two assets of half the size. In a first-best world one large asset would be chosen, although, as was argued in Chapter 1, it is not clear that one can interpret this outcome as corresponding to a firm. In a second-best world the choice of the large asset is less clear, since moving from two assets to one may have undesirable incentive consequences. (M2 may invest less if she loses ownership rights.) However, if the technological returns to scale are strong enough—a limiting case is where the smaller assets are completely unproductive—then the large asset outcome will be second-best optimal. Since, according to Proposition 2(D), it makes no sense to allocate ownership of different parts of a single asset to different people, one can interpret this outcome as corresponding to a single, large firm.

Just as the theory predicts that complementarities—otherwise known as synergies—make integration more likely, so it predicts the opposite: independent assets should be separately owned. This advice is not always heeded by companies considering acquisitions—consider for example the conglomerate merger wave of the 1960s in the USA and the UK—but, at least in the 1990s, it seems to command considerable support. And, of course, there are so many instances of independent assets under separate ownership that this might be said to be the leading case empirically.

An interesting application of the idea that independent assets should be separately owned is the case of a standard competitive spot market where there are many buyers trading with many sellers. It is usually thought that non-integration is an efficient arrangement in such a market. The theory supports this. Consider a typical non-integrated buyer M1 and a typical non-integrated seller M2. For example, M1 might be Oxford University and M2 might be Apple Computers, which, say, supplies Oxford with computers. If Oxford and Apple fail to reach agreement about the price and quality of computers, each can fairly easily switch to another partner. In other words, $R'(i) \simeq r'(i;a1)$ and $C'(e) \simeq c'(e;a2)$, and so non-integration yields approximately the first-best. In contrast, if Oxford University bought Apple, Oxford could extract some of the returns from innovative activity by Apple management (and possibly Apple workers) and so Apple would underinvest in such activity. ($|c'(e;\varnothing)|$ may be much less than $|C'(e)|$.) Thus, in the case of Oxford University and Apple—and more generally in the case of competitive buyers and sellers—integration yields considerable costs but almost no benefits.

The conclusions about strictly complementary and independent assets can throw light on a well-known idea due to Stigler (1951). Stigler argues that an industry in an early stage of development will be characterized by integration, since the industry will be too small to support specialized supply services, which are subject to increasing returns to scale. Hence firms will make their own inputs. As the industry expands, however, specialist suppliers will eventually be able to set up, and, since they are more efficient, non-integration will become optimal. The analysis is consistent with this. When the industry contains a small number of firms (possibly just one), complementarities between the purchaser(s) of input and supplier(s) of input are great, since there are few alternative trading partners. Proposition 2(D) then implies that integration is optimal. However, when the market is large enough to support many purchasers and suppliers, complementarities between any single purchaser and supplier become smaller, and Proposition 2(C) implies that non-integration is then optimal.[31]

The cases of strictly complementary assets (one buyer and one seller, who have no alternative trading partners) and independent assets (many buyers and sellers, each of whom can switch to an alternative trading partner at date 1) are both quite special. Another interesting situation is where a single seller supplies

---

[31] This argument implicitly assumes that as the industry expands the number of producers grows (i.e. that a few purchasers do not dominate the market). This is discussed further at the end of the section.

many buyers with input. To the extent that each buyer is worried about the possibility of hold-up, it may want to acquire ownership rights in the seller. Since it is impossible for every buyer to own 100 per cent of the seller, the best arrangement may be to give each buyer a share of the seller, with attached voting rights (and to adopt some sort of majority voting rule). An example of this in practice is an oil pipeline that is collectively owned by the oil refineries that use it (see Klein *et al.* 1978). Other examples may be various kinds of partnerships, including law firms (the partners of the law firm may all use a common input consisting of administrative services plus the law firm's name); or consumer, worker, and producer co-operatives (see Hansmann 1996). For more details on the theory behind this case, see Hart and Moore (1990).[32]

The simple model of this chapter may also help us to understand changes in organizational structure over time. A number of commentators have argued that a trend toward de-integration has occurred in the 1980s and 1990s.[33] This trend is often traced to the fact that the large factories of the past are being replaced by smaller-scale, more flexible technologies, causing a reduction in lock-in effects; and to the fact that, because of advances in information technology, agents who were previously engaged in routine tasks need to be motivated to make wise decisions on the basis of the increasing amount of information at their disposal.[34]

The model in Section 2 can explain why the above factors could be responsible for a trend toward de-integration. The increased flexibility in technology means that assets are becoming less complementary. (An asset can more easily be modified to be suitable

[32] It is worth noting that a partnership or co-operative is different from joint ownership (which, I argued above, is suboptimal). Under two-party joint ownership, both parties have a veto, which means that each party can hold up the other. In contrast, under a partnership or co-operative, decisions are (typically) made by majority rule, which means that no fixed subset of the parties has a veto. For more on the theory of co-operatives, see Hart and Moore (1994*b*).

[33] See e.g. *Business Week* (22 October 1993, Special Issue, 'Enterprise: How Entrepreneurs are Reshaping the Economy and What Big Companies can Learn'); *The Economist* (5 March 1994, 'Management Focus', 79); *Wall Street Journal* (19 December 1994, 'Manufacturers Use Supplies to Help Them Develop New Products', 1). The de-integration trend often goes under the name of 'contracting out' or 'out-sourcing'.

[34] For an interesting discussion of the impact of information technology on the size of firms, see Brynjolfsson (1994).

for a new trading partner.) The importance of individual initiative means that M1's and M2's investment decisions are both significant. According to Proposition 2(B) and (C), both forces suggest that non-integration is more likely to be optimal than before (on this, see also Brynjolfsson 1994).

It might be thought that another explanation for de-integration is that advances in information technology have reduced the costs of writing contracts. However, the theory developed here does *not* predict that non-integration is more likely the lower are contracting costs. I argued in Chapter 1 that in a zero-transaction-cost world organizational form does not matter, i.e. that non-integration and integration are equally efficient. On the other hand, this chapter has considered the case where transaction costs are so large that long-term contracts cannot be written at all. It has been shown that under these conditions non-integration and integration can both be optimal depending on the circumstances. It follows that a simple monotonic relationship between transaction costs and integration does not exist.[35]

Finally, it is worth returning to the traditional U-shaped average cost diagram in Figure 1.1. I argued that it is hard for neoclassical theory to justify this figure. The property rights approach may have an easier time. At small scales of production, a firm uses assets that are highly complementary (two machines located next to each other or several rooms of a building), or assets that exhibit increasing returns to scale, and Proposition 2(D) tells us that hold-up problems would be increased if these assets were not under common ownership. In other words, initially the average cost of carrying out activities within the firm is declining. However, when the firm extends beyond a certain point, synergies between assets may fall. In particular, the manager and assets at the centre will become less important with regard to operations at the periphery, in the sense that investments at the periphery are unlikely to be specific either to the manager or to the assets at the centre. (In a large firm, the centre and the periphery may for many purposes operate almost independently.) In addition, investments at the centre are unlikely to be enhanced very much by the existence of the periphery.

---

[35] Also, it is not clear empirically that contracting costs *have* fallen as a result of advances in information technology; see Brynjolfsson (1994) and the references therein.

According to Proposition 2(C), the average cost of carrying out activities within the firm starts to rise.

In a rough sense, then, the theory developed in this chapter is consistent with the story about firm size found in every standard microeconomics textbook.[36]

---

[36] Throughout this chaper, I have ignored the effect of imperfect competition. That is, I have supposed that any contract M1 and M2 enter into, including a change in ownership, has a negligible impact on any other parties, including consumers. This assumption is clearly very restrictive, but I have made it because I wanted to focus on the 'efficiency' reason for firms and for integration. In practice, of course, not all integration decisions are made for efficiency reasons. Firms integrate horizontally to raise prices to consumers. Firms integrate vertically to foreclose on rival purchasers and suppliers. There is a huge industrial organization literature on mergers, although very little of it has taken an incomplete contracting approach. (For a discussion of the literature, see Tirole (1988); two papers that do take an incomplete contracting approach are Bolton and Whinston (1993) and Hart and Tirole (1990).) The theory developed in this book should be a useful ingredient in future work in this area.

3

Further Issues Arising from the Property Rights Approach

THIS chapter touches on a number of issues omitted from the simple property rights approach presented in Chapter 2. These include the nature of authority, worker incentives, delegation, the role of reputation, investment in physical capital, and information dissemination within firms.

1. *The role of nonhuman assets and the nature of authority*

The two crucial features of the theory described in Chapter 2 are (i) that contracts are incomplete and (ii) that there are some significant nonhuman assets in the economic relationship. I have already explained in Chapter 1 why contractual incompleteness is important. I now provide some justification for the idea that (at least some) nonhuman assets are an essential feature of a theory of the firm. These might be 'hard' assets such as machines, inventories, and buildings, or 'softer' assets such as patents, client lists, files, existing contracts, or the firm's name or reputation.[1]

To understand better the role of nonhuman assets, consider a situation where 'firm' 1 acquires 'firm' 2, which consists entirely of human capital. Ask the following question: what is to stop firm 2's workers from quitting, possibly *en masse*? In the absence of any physical assets—e.g. buildings—firm 2's workers would not even have to relocate physically. For example, if they are linked by telephone or computer terminal (assets which they own themselves), they could simply announce one morning that they have become a new firm.

[1] A qualification is in order. It is fairly straightforward to extend the model of Ch. 2 to the case of patents, client lists, or files, but less straightforward to include assets such as existing contracts, or the firm's name or reputation. A more elaborate analysis—probably a dynamic one—is required to explain why a firm's name or reputation has value. This is a fascinating topic for future research.

For firm 1's acquisition of firm 2 to make any economic sense, there must be some source of firm 2 value over and above the workers' human capital, i.e. some 'glue' holding firm 2's workers in place. This source of value may consist of as little as a place to meet; the firm's name, reputation, or distribution network;[2] the firm's files, containing important information about its operations or its customers;[3] or a contract that prohibits firm 2's workers from working for competitors or from taking existing clients with them when they quit.[4] The source of value may even just represent the difficulty firm 2's workers face in co-ordinating a move to another firm. But without something holding the firm together, the firm is just a phantom.

A firm's nonhuman assets, then, simply represent the glue that keeps the firm together, whatever this may be.[5]

The concept of nonhuman assets is also helpful in clarifying the notion of authority. Ronald Coase, in his pioneering 1937 article, argued that the distinguishing feature of the employer–employee relationship is that an employer can tell an employee what to do, whereas one independent contractor must bribe another independent contractor to do what he or she wants. Herbert Simon made a similar observation in his 1951 article. However, as Alchian and Demsetz (1972) point out, it is unclear what is the source of an employer's authority over an employee. It is true that an employer can tell an employee what to do, but it is also true that one independent contractor can tell another independent contractor what to do. The interesting question is why the employee pays attention whereas the independent contractor (perhaps) does not.[6]

---

[2] This might be relevant for newspapers, journals, or publishing houses.

[3] This might be relevant for insurance companies or law firms.

[4] This might be relevant for accounting firms, public relations firms, advertising agencies, or R&D laboratories, as well as for law firms.

[5] It is important to stress that there is no inconsistency between defining a firm in terms of nonhuman assets and recognizing that a large part of a firm's value derives from human capital. Suppose firm 2 consists of one nonhuman asset a2 and one worker W2. Assume that W2 can make $300,000 a year using a2 and only $200,000 in its absence, and suppose that W2 is the only person who knows how to operate a2 and that the scrap value of a2 is zero. Then, under the assumption of Nash bargaining, asset a2 is worth $50,000 to an acquirer since the acquirer will be able to obtain 50% of W2's incremental $100,000 by threatening to deny W2 access to the asset. That is, the value of the firm to an acquirer is significant even though the value of a2 in its next-best use (its scrap value) is zero.

[6] As Alchian and Demsetz put it, just as an employer can tell an employee what

When nonhuman assets are present, it is not difficult to under-stand the difference between the employer–employee situation and the independent contractor situation. In the former case, if the relationship breaks down, the employer walks away with all the nonhuman assets, whereas in the latter case each independent contractor walks away with some nonhuman assets. This differ-ence gives the employer leverage. Individual i is more likely to do what individual j wants, if j can exclude i from assets that i needs to be productive than if i can take these assets with her, or than if someone else—k, say—owns these assets (in which case i is likely to do what k wants). *In other words, control over nonhuman assets leads to control over human assets.* This is discussed further in Section 2 below.[7]

The above views on the role of nonhuman assets can be sum-marized as follows. On the one hand, in many firms—even those without obvious 'physical' equipment—some significant nonhu-man assets can be identified. On the other hand, if such assets do not exist, then it is not clear what keeps the firm together, or what defines authority within the firm.[8] One would expect firms with-out at least some significant nonhuman assets to be flimsy and

tasks to carry out, so can a customer tell her greengrocer what to do (what veg-etables to sell at what prices). Moreover, the sanction for non-performance is (at least superficially) the same in the two cases: a refusal will likely lead to a termi-nation of the relationship, a dismissal. In the case of the greengrocer, this means that the consumer shops at another greengrocer.

[7] Masten (1988) has argued that there are also legal differences between the employer–employee and independent contractor situations. Specifically, an employee owes her employer duties of loyalty and obedience that one indepen-dent contractor does not owe another independent contractor.

[8] Even the notion of replacement or dismissal is hard to make sense of in the absence of nonhuman assets. To give someone the sack and replace them with someone else means that the first person is in some physical sense removed from the job they were doing and the second person is substituted. This makes sense if there are nonhuman assets: the first person is excluded from these nonhuman assets, while the second person is given access to them. In contrast, if all assets are human, it is not clear what dismissal and replacement mean (or how they are enforced).

Kreps (1990) and Wernerfelt (1993) have developed theories of authority based on the idea that an employee agrees to accept the authority of an employer as part of an implicit contract. There is undoubtedly a lot of truth in this idea. However, the approach does not explain why authority is transferable, i.e. why, if firm 1 buys firm 2, firm 2's workers will transfer their allegiance—and implicit con-tract—from the owner of firm 2 to the owner of firm 1. Thus, it is not clear that the implicit contract view of authority can explain the motivation for integration (although the view may be useful in explaining other things).

unstable entities, constantly subject to the possibility of break-up or dissolution. My impression is that the (casual) evidence is not inconsistent with this view.[9]

2. *Worker incentives*

The model of Chapter 2 focused on how ownership affects the incentives of top managers. However, workers' incentives will also be affected by changes in ownership and this can influence the costs and benefits of integration.

A full treatment of this issue would require extending the analysis of Chapter 2 to the multi-agent–multi-asset case (on this, see Hart and Moore 1990). However, the main idea can be illustrated using the following example. Consider the model of Chapter 2, but assume now that there is only *one* nonhuman asset, a2, and that neither M1 nor M2 has an investment, i.e. $R' \equiv C' = 0$. Suppose a worker W can, by incurring a (non-verifiable) cost of x, acquire a productive skill. This skill, in conjunction with some combination of a2 and managers M1 and M2, yields (non-verifiable) income equal to Y at date 1, where $Y > x$.[10] For simplicity, assume that the worker's investment is discrete: he can acquire the skill or not. Assume that a2 is essential for this skill to pay off (i.e. the skill is asset-a2-specific). For simplicity, start with the polar case where M1's human capital is essential, but M2's human capital is irrelevant. (M2 can be costlessly replaced.) Also,

[9] The recent and much publicized departures of Maurice Saatchi from Saatchi and Saatchi and Steven Spielberg from MCA are instructive in this regard. It seems that some of the most important assets of the two firms were the human capital of the departing individuals (plus a few colleagues) rather than nonhuman assets. For this reason, the departures caused considerable instability. See *New York Times* (16 October 1994, 'Hollywood Beckoned, Leading Japanese Astray', Week in Review); *Financial Times* (12 January 1995, 'Saatchi's Soap Opera Has Only Just Begun', 17). Another example in a somewhat different context is provided by the World Chess Championship of 1993. Gary Kasparov and Nigel Short decided not to play in the official (FIDE) tournament because they were dissatisfied with the terms, and instead set up the Professional Chess Association, which ran its own championship. The asset, consisting of the right to hold the official World Chess Championship, did not seem to mean much under the circumstances.

[10] As in Ch. 2, I assume that M1 and M2 cannot reimburse W directly for acquiring the skill (since x is non-verifiable).

confine attention to just two ownership arrangements: M1 ownership and M2 ownership. (Suppose that wealth constraints, say, prevent W from owning asset a2 himself.)

Consider W's incentive to acquire the skill under M2 ownership. If W does acquire the skill, then at date 1 he needs to bargain with both M1 and M2 about the division of the income Y. The reason is that M1 is critical to the bargaining because his human capital is essential; while M2 is critical because W requires access to a2, which M2 owns. Under the (reasonable) assumption that the parties split the surplus equally, W will receive $(Y/3)$. Thus, under M2 ownership W will invest if and only if

(3.1) $$\frac{Y}{3} \geq x.$$

Consider next M1 ownership. Now M2 is irrelevant to the bargaining process, since M2's human capital can be replaced and she no longer owns a2. Thus, W will be in a two-way bargaining situation with M1 at date 1. Under the assumption that W and M1 split the income Y equally, the condition for W to invest becomes

(3.2) $$\frac{Y}{2} \geq x.$$

A comparison of (3.1) and (3.2) shows that W's incentive to invest is stronger under M1 ownership than under M2 ownership.

Obviously the results of the example would be reversed if M2's human capital were essential and M1's human capital were irrelevant. In this case, W's incentive to invest would be greater if M2 owned a2 than if M1 did.

The main lesson to be drawn from the example is that changes in control affect the incentives of those who do not have control rights either before or after the change. When M1 has essential human capital it is better for M1 to own asset a2 since this reduces hold-up problems: W has to bargain only with M1 to realize the income Y as opposed to having to bargain with M1 and M2. The opposite is the case if M2 has essential human capital. The example thus confirms the thrust of Proposition 2(E), that assets should reside in the hands of those with important human capital. In fact, the example strengthens Proposition 2(E) in the sense that it shows that an additional benefit of concentrating ownership of assets in the hands of those with important human capital is that worker incentives will be improved.

The example can easily be extended to illustrate how worker incentives are affected by a merger of firms with complementary, or independent, assets. Suppose that M1 owns asset a1. Then, if a1 and a2 are strictly complementary, it is as if M1 has essential human capital. (He is a critical player because he owns a1.) Therefore, W's incentive to invest is stronger if M1 owns a2 as well as a1, than if a2 and a1 are separately owned. On the other hand, if a1 and a2 are independent and M1's human capital is irrelevant, while M2's is significant, then W's incentive to invest is stronger if M2 owns a2. (The reason is that W has to bargain only with M2 about the return from his investment, rather than with M1 and M2. For details, see Hart and Moore (1990).)

Thus, the example also confirms the thrust of Proposition 2(D), that highly complementary assets should be owned together. In fact, the example again strengthens Proposition 2(D), in the sense that it shows that an additional benefit of concentrating ownership of highly complementary assets is that worker incentives are improved.

Finally, the example can be used to shed some light on the discussion about authority in Section 1. If M1's human capital is essential, one can interpret W's investment as being specific to M1, in the sense that M1 is necessary for the investment to pay off. The example shows that the identity of W's employer matters: W is more likely to undertake an M1-specific investment if M1 is W's employer (M1 owns the asset a2 that W works with) than if M2 is W's employer. In other words, the example shows how control over nonhuman assets can lead to authority over human assets, in that employees will tend to carry out actions or investments that are of interest to their boss.

3. Delegation and other forms of intermediate ownership

The theory developed in Chapter 2 applies most directly to closely held or owner-managed firms, in the sense that it has been supposed that those who own an asset actually exercise residual control rights over the asset. In reality, the owners of a company—particularly a large one—often cannot run the company themselves on a day-to-day basis and so they delegate power to a board of directors and to managers. This delegation creates potential conflicts of interest, which will be the subject of Chapters 6–8. In particular, managers may have their own reasons for merging, which have little to do with profit: for example, they may wish to build a bigger empire. Thus, some mergers may be carried out that do not increase value (for the companies concerned).

Even though there are important differences between the owner-managed and large company cases, the main insights of the property rights approach continue to be relevant. It is still useful to think of a large company as consisting of nonhuman assets. It is also helpful to analyse a merger in terms of a change in residual control rights. Prior to a merger, some residual control rights are delegated to the board of the acquiring company and some to the board of the company that is to be acquired; after the merger, all the residual control rights are delegated (in the first instance) to the board of the acquiring company. An interesting topic for further research is to extend the model of Chapter 2 to the case of public companies.

Just as the shareholders of a public company delegate power to the board of directors and managers, so top managers delegate power to subordinates, who delegate power to their subordinates, and so on down the line. It is hard to make sense of this process in a comprehensive contracting world, because even the concept of authority is difficult to define. What does it mean to put someone 'in charge' of an action or decision if all actions can be specified in a contract? Thus, the incomplete contracting framework is a natural one for studying authority.

An interesting recent paper that analyses authority from an incomplete contracting perspective is Aghion and Tirole (1995). These authors make a distinction between real authority and formal (legal) authority.[11] They argue that someone with superior information may have effective power, even though he does not have legal power, because those with legal power—owners—may follow his suggestions. In fact, it may be in the interest of

---

[11] This distinction has also been made in the sociology and organization behaviour literature; see Weber (1968: 215) and Barnard (1938: 164–5).

owners to *create* an asymmetry of information, so that subordinates can wield power, and can thereby be rewarded for making relationship-specific investments. The cost of such an arrangement is that the subordinates will sometimes take actions that are not in the interest of the owner. Aghion and Tirole use these ideas to develop a theory of information acquisition and the optimal span of control within the firm.[12]

4. Residual control versus residual income

I have emphasized the connection between ownership and residual control rights. However, it is often argued that a key characteristic of ownership is that the owner of an asset is entitled to the residual income from that asset. I now consider the relationship between these two concepts.

A problem that one faces when discussing the notion of residual income is that in many contexts it is not well defined. For example, if two parties enter into a profit-sharing agreement, whereby party A receives $\log(\pi + 1)$ and party B receives $\pi - \log(\pi + 1)$, where π is total profit, then who is the residual income (or profit) claimant? The answer is that both parties are. Given that profit-sharing contracts are not in principle costly to write if profits are verifiable (and it is unclear how residual income is to be allocated if profits are not verifiable), the conclu-

[12] Delegated authority or control can be seen as an intermediate form of authority lying somewhere between no control (the employee case) and full control (the owner case). There are other kinds of intermediate control or ownership. If firm A buys firm B and converts it into a wholly owned subsidiary, then it is often argued that the managers of firm B have more control and authority ('independence') than if firm A merges with firm B. Similarly, if firm A enters into a long-term contract, whereby B rents or leases some assets from A (possibly owning others itself), then the managers of B probably have more authority than if they are employees of A, but less authority than if they are owners. Among other things, B's managers may be able to decide who works with the assets they have leased from A, even if they cannot make physical alterations to these assets. (One of the assets may be the company name, in which case one has something close to a franchising arrangement.) The literature has by and large not used the property rights approach to analyse intermediate forms of ownership, but this is an interesting topic for future research. For papers that make some progress in this direction, see Holmstrom and Tirole (1991) (on the comparison of the U-form and M-form structures within firms) and Burkart *et al.* (1994).

sion is that residual income may not be a very robust or interesting theoretical concept. (For more on this, see Hart 1988.)[13]

In practice, complicated profit-sharing agreements are often not written, and some party (or set of parties) *can* be identified as the residual claimant for a particular asset. The question then arises, will this party also hold the residual control rights? The answer is, not necessarily: residual income and residual control do not have to be bundled together on a one-to-one basis. One example is given by publicly traded companies that have several classes of shares with different voting rights (so the ratio of income rights to control rights varies across investors)—such an arrangement is rare in the USA and UK but common in many other countries. A second example is given by joint ventures, where it sometimes happens that two parties share control 50 : 50 but have differential profit shares. A third example is given by any situation where a manager or worker is on a profit-based incentive or bonus scheme: the employee is in some sense a residual claimant, but may not have any voting rights.

The above examples are somewhat special. I now present some theoretical arguments as to why in many cases one might expect the holder of residual control rights to have significant residual income rights, that is, why residual control and residual income should often go together.

First, if residual income and residual control are separated, then this creates a hold-up problem. Assume that M1 has the control rights for asset a1 and M2 has most of the income rights (where income is verifiable). Then M1 will have little incentive to develop an idea for a profitable new use of a1 since most of the gains go to M2. Similarly, M2 has little incentive to develop an idea for operating a1 more efficiently since she must negotiate with M1 for the right to implement the idea. To put it simply, control rights and income rights are highly complementary and so,

[13] The same difficulty does not arise regarding the definition of residual control rights. Residual control rights are not divisible in the same way as residual income rights. For example, if there are two parties and one asset, then it is reasonable to suppose that one party or the other has residual control rights: it would be difficult if not impossible to allocate 80 per cent of the residual control rights to party A and 20 per cent to party B. (However, see Ch. 4 for a discussion of more flexible ownership arrangements.)

by Proposition 2(D), it makes sense to allocate them to the same person.[14]

Second, in some situations it may not be possible to measure (or verify) all aspects of an asset's return stream.[15] For example, suppose return is composed of two parts: 'short-term' income from current activities and 'long-term' income, that is, changes in the asset's value. Arguably, (most of) the latter will accrue to whomever has control rights, possibly because this person can decide when or even whether to sell the asset. Now suppose the former return—short-term income—is allocated to a worker who operates the asset, as part of a 'high-powered' incentive contract. (The worker does not have control rights.) Then the worker will maximize current output, without regard to the asset's long-term value; for example, he might not repair the asset, he might misuse it, etc. This may lead to a very inefficient outcome. It might be better to give the worker low-powered incentives, that is, to bundle the short-term income rights with the control rights. This way, even though the worker may not work very hard, at least he will be prepared to balance his time between activities that increase current output and those that increase the resale value of the asset.[16]

Third, in some cases it may not even be *feasible* to separate residual income and residual control rights. Consider a widget producer, A, who enters into an *ex ante* contract with B, whereby A agrees to hand over all the future profit from widget production to B. Then, whatever the contract says, A may be able to use his *ex post* power as the owner to direct much of the profit from the widgets to himself. One way for A to do this is to refuse to sell any widgets until B agrees to give up a significant part of her profit share.[17] Another possibility is for A to sell the widgets for a nominal amount in return for purchasers compensating A in some other way; for example, prospective buyers could be required to buy something else from A at an inflated price. In both cases, the outcome is that A receives much of the profit from

---

[14] This example is drawn from Boycko *et al.* (1995: ch. 2).

[15] The following is based on Holstrom and Milgrom (1991, 1994).

[16] Holmstrom and Milgrom (1994) have extended this idea to explain why employees not only have limited ownership rights and low-powered incentives, but also are subject to direct controls with respect to their actions.

[17] There may be some doubt as to whether such a threat is credible, however.

widget sales by virtue of his possession of the residual control rights.[18]

Chapter 8 will provide another reason why residual income and residual control rights should be bundled together. It will be shown that unbundling residual income rights from residual control rights can lead to inefficiencies in the market for corporate control. In particular, unbundling—that is, a departure from one share–one vote—may allow a management team with high private benefits but low total value to win a take-over contest against a management team that has low private benefits, but that creates higher value for shareholders overall.

The above results can be used to understand an idea briefly mentioned in Chapter 1. I noted there that it is often assumed— particularly in the industrial organization literature—that profit-sharing is easier within a single firm than between independent firms. I observed that it is hard to make sense of this idea in a comprehensive contracting world, since the independent firms could always write a profit-sharing contract. However, in an incomplete contracting world, those who possess residual rights of control may end up receiving the firm's profit, given their power to direct profit to themselves. As a result, if firm A buys firm B the owner-manager of A may receive both A and B's profit; that is, profit-sharing may occur. In contrast, when the firms are separate, B's profit may be diverted to the owner-manager of B; that is, whatever any profit-sharing agreement may say, profit-sharing will not actually occur.

5. *The effects of reputation*

Nothing so far has been said about the effects of reputation. This is restrictive since it is often argued that reputation can overcome many of the problems of opportunism identified in this book. For example, if one takes the static model of Chapter 2 and repeats it infinitely often, then the first-best can be achieved if the interest

---

[18] In a similar vein, Williamson (1985) has argued that the owner of a firm can divert profit to herself by manipulating the accounting system. Williamson uses this idea to explain why incentive schemes within a firm will be low-powered and incentive schemes between firms will be high-powered.

rate is not too high. One way to do this is for the parties to agree in advance to co-operate, with this outcome being sustained by the threat that if one party deviates the other party will refuse to trade with it any more.[19]

There are two reasons why reputation has been put to one side, in spite of its obvious importance. First, as discussed in Chapter 1, in a first-best world firms don't matter at all, since the optimum can be sustained under any organizational form. Thus, to develop a theory of the firm, one must analyse a situation where the first-best cannot be guaranteed, i.e. where reputational forces are not strong enough to eliminate all problems of opportunism. As a first step, therefore, it does not seem unreasonable to consider the static model of Chapter 2, where reputation plays no role at all.

Second, it is not clear that—even in an infinitely repeated relationship—reputation will eliminate all the problems of opportunism that have been described. In some cases, although the trade is repeated, it is reasonable to suppose that the parties' relationship-specific investments are made only once. However, this means that the gains from breaching a co-operative agreement are sizeable even if a breach marks the end of the relationship. The point is that the deviating party gets a huge one-time gain from expropriating the other party's specific investment. Thus, it may be the case that the repeated version of the model exhibits problems of opportunism similar to those of the static model. [20]

In spite of these comments, I believe that the general issue of the influence of reputation on organizational form is a fascinating one. An interesting recent analysis is Halonen (1994) (see also Garvey 1991). Halonen considers the infinitely repeated version of the static model of Chapter 2, where the relationship-specific investment is made each period. She finds that for one range of parameters repetition makes joint ownership of assets optimal. (Joint ownership is never optimal in the static model of Chapter 2.) The reason is that joint ownership, by maximizing hold-up problems, minimizes the parties' payoffs if co-operation breaks down and therefore makes it easier to sustain co-operation. In

[19] This is a well-known result from game theory; see e.g. Fudenberg and Tirole (1991: ch. 5).

[20] To be more precise, a very low interest rate may be necessary to support the co-operative outcome. For a formal analysis of a situation like this, see Thomas and Worrall (1994).

contrast, for a second range of parameters she finds that the basic results of the static model apply; that is, either non-integration or (some type of) integration is optimal. However, integration is less likely to be optimal in a repeated relationship than in the static case.

6. *Investments in physical capital*

The model of Chapter 2 supposes that all investments are investments in human capital. What this means is that, if M1 invests i, this creates a return from operating a1 and a2 of $R(i)$, but only if M1 is a party to the transaction. In effect, M1 is acquiring an asset-specific skill that is not transferable to others in his absence.

In practice, the return from many investments is embodied, at least partially, in a piece of physical capital rather than in the human capital of the person making the investment. The main ideas of the property rights approach generalize to the case where investments are embodied in physical capital, but some of the details change. In particular, it is no longer clear that strictly complementary assets should be owned together or that joint ownership is never optimal.

It will be useful to illustrate this point. Suppose there is a *single* asset a* and two agents M1 and M2 who can each increase the asset's value. For simplicity, take the investments to be *discrete*: M1 can make an investment that costs i and increases the value of a* by R; and M2 can make an investment that costs $\hat{\imath}$ and increases the value of a* by $\hat{R}$. (As in Chapter 2, increases in value and investment expenditures are observable but not verifiable.) Assume that each investment is embodied entirely in the physical capital, i.e. that once the investment is made neither M1 nor M2 is necessary to realize the value increase. Suppose also that $R > i$, $\hat{R} > \hat{\imath}$, so that both investments would be made in a first-best world.[21]

---

[21] Even though the investments are embodied in physical capital, it does not follow that the investments are themselves physical. They may represent the efforts taken by M1 and M2 at date 0 to make a* more profitable (e.g., to increase the size of the market for a*'s product). The difference from Chapter 2 is that it is now supposed that the increases in value, R or $\hat{R}$, can be enjoyed at date 1 in the absence of M1 or M2.

Consider a second-best world where M1 owns a* (that is, M1 enjoys the full value of the asset a*). Then M1 will certainly invest since he receives the full increase in value R for himself. However, M2 will not invest since any increase in the value of the asset goes to M1 and not to her. (Once M2 has made her investment M1 does not need M2 any more.) The opposite is true if M2 owns a*: now M2 invests but M1 does not.

Joint ownership may be an improvement here. Under joint ownership—where M1 and M2 each have veto power over the use of the asset—any increase in value will be shared 50 : 50 under Nash bargaining (since agreement by both is necessary to realize the increase in value, e.g. through a sale). Therefore, M1 and M2 will both invest if and only if

$$\tfrac{1}{2}R \geq i,$$
$$\tfrac{1}{2}\hat{R} \geq \hat{\imath}.$$

If R and $\hat{R}$ are large, the above inequalities will be satisfied and so joint ownership will yield a more efficient outcome than single ownership.

Similar examples can easily be constructed to show that strictly complementary assets should sometimes be separately owned. However, a word of caution is appropriate. There are other ways than joint ownership to provide agents with incentives to invest in physical capital. In the above example the same outcome could be achieved with a *stochastic* ownership scheme, whereby M1 and M2 each own a* with probability $\tfrac{1}{2}$.[22] (Also, instead of separating ownership of complementary assets, one could allocate joint or stochastic ownership in an overall asset consisting of the complementary assets combined.) At this stage little is known in general about the relative advantages of joint ownership and stochastic ownership when there are many assets and many agents. Thus, it is not clear that the above discussion provides an explanation for joint ownership in practice (e.g. the fact that joint ventures are often owned 50 : 50 by the companies setting them up).[23]

[22] However, joint ownership will be more attractive than stochastic ownership if the parties are risk-averse.

[23] In this section, I have continued to assume that the investments i and $\hat{\imath}$ are non-transferable, in the sense that M1 must make the investment i and M2 must make the investment $\hat{\imath}$. However, many physical capital investments are not specific to a particular individual; for example, under type 1 integration M1 may be

7. *Formation of assets*

Chapter 2 assumed that the assets were already in place. The analysis generalizes, however, to the case where they need to be constructed. It is useful to distinguish between two situations. In the first the construction costs are verifiable; e.g. the asset is purchased from a manufacturer at a (verifiable) price P. Under these conditions, the ownership decision can be separated from the construction decision. That is, suppose the model of Chapter 2 predicts that it is efficient for M1 to own a1 in the absence of construction. Then it will also be efficient for M1 to own a1 in the presence of construction—the only issue is how the construction cost should be divided between M1 and M2 and this will depend on who gains more from the presence of a1 and on M1 and M2's relative date 0 bargaining positions. For example, if M1 gains greatly from a1, then M1 may pay most of P, whereas if M2 gains greatly from the economic relationship with M1—e.g. from her ability to hold M1 up—then M2 will pay most of P.

The second case is when construction costs are themselves hard to verify. Under these conditions, construction is somewhat similar to the physical capital investments discussed in Section 6; in particular, because these construction costs are not verifiable, they cannot be shared. (If I agree to pay half the costs, you could spend my share on 'inappropriate' construction.) Given this, the ownership and construction decisions become interlinked. Specifically, if I am going to own the asset, it may make sense for me also to build it, since if you build it I can hold you up at the completion stage.

---

able to make the investment $\hat{i}$ as well as the investment i (e.g. M1 could install new machines in the 'a2' plant or build an extension to the 'a2' plant). Ownership still matters in this case since it determines who has the *right* to make the investment. (M1 would not be able to make the investment $\hat{i}$ under non-integration without M2's permission.) The allocation of rights in turn affects the *ex post* division of surplus and hence the incentives to make prior relationship-specific investments. Thus, the allocation of ownership will be determined by the same factors that applied in Chapter 2.

8. *Integration, information dissemination and co-operation*

As noted in Chapter 1, it is sometimes argued that a benefit of carrying out activities within the firm is that information is exchanged more readily and parties are more willing to co-operate. In fact, some parts of the literature take the defining property of integration to be that informational asymmetries are removed within the firm.[24]

The incomplete contracting approach can provide some foundations for this idea. First, as observed in Section 2, an employer has more leverage over an employee than one independent contractor has over another, since the employer owns the assets the employee needs to be productive. Applying this idea to the case of information dissemination, one may conclude that an employee has a strong incentive to provide the information that an employer wants, if only so that the employee can establish himself as reliable, thereby increasing his future value to the employer (and hence possibly his wage).

Second, Section 4 showed that employees' incentives within firms are likely to be low-powered, since employees do not have residual control rights. A disadvantage of this is that employees may have limited incentives to work hard or have good ideas because they do not receive the return from such activities. However, precisely because of this, they may be prepared to co-operate more. That is, someone with a low-powered incentive scheme may, say, be willing to help a fellow worker make an additional sale to a customer, or provide the information that makes such a sale possible, because she has little to lose. In contrast, someone on a higher-powered incentive scheme may not be prepared to help her fellow worker because she would prefer to make the sale herself.[25]

Each of these effects can go the other way, however. In some cases an employee may be *less* willing to supply information than

---

[24] See e.g. Arrow (1975), Riordan (1990), and Schmidt (1990). In Cremer (1994), integration endogenously affects the flow of information.

[25] Williamson (1985: ch. 6) has argued forcefully that a benefit of integration is that employees will receive low-powered incentives, which will foster co-operation. For analyses of the relationship between incentives and co-operation in a comprehensive contracting framework, see Laffont and Tirole (1993: ch. 4), Holmstrom and Milgrom (1990), Itoh (1991), and Lazear (1989).

an independent contractor, since, given that the employee has no control rights, his employer can use the information to take advantage of him (see e.g. Aghion and Tirole 1995). Similarly, two employees may compete rather than co-operate to the extent that only one of them will receive a promotion, and the employer as possessor of the residual control rights can decide which one it will be. (For a related phenomenon, see Milgrom 1988.)

Thus, it is more accurate to say that integration *changes* the incentives of parties to reveal information and co-operate, rather than to say that it improves them.

4

A Discussion of the Foundations of the Incomplete Contracting Model

IN this chapter I provide a discussion of the foundations of the incomplete contracting model used in Chapter 2. The discussion will be informal. I will not try to provide firm foundations for the model—this is unfortunately too difficult at this stage. Instead, I will consider some natural ways to get round the incompleteness of contracts, and explain why in many cases they won't work. For a very interesting recent paper that adopts a more rigorous approach to some of the same issues, see Segal (1995).[1]

The chapter is divided into three parts. First, the hold-up problem is considered in more detail.[2] Next, a more general class of asset ownership structures than those in Chapter 2 is analysed. The chapter concludes with a consideration of how important the hold-up problem is for the property rights theory of the firm.

1. Discussion of the hold-up problem

In Chapter 2 the existence of a hold-up problem was established under the assumption that the parties could not write a long-term contract. This section re-examines this assumption.[3]

It is useful to consider a simplified one-sided version of the

---

[1] Also, for an excellent discussion and summary of the current state of incomplete contract theory, which complements that in this chapter, see Tirole (1994).

[2] Grout (1984) contains one of the first formalizations of the hold-up problem.

[3] There have been a number of recent papers that derive the incompleteness of contracts from first principles, although not necessarily in the context of a hold-up problem; see, e.g. Allen and Gale (1992), Bernheim and Whinston (1995), and Spier (1992). In recent work, Anderlini and Felli (1994) have derived the incompleteness of contracts from the assumption that, to be enforceable, a contract must be *formal*. In turn, formality means that the mapping between states of the world and prescribed outcomes is 'general recursive', or, equivalently, is computable by a Turing machine. Anderlini and Felli's approach is considerably more general than the one described here, but does not deal directly with the hold-up problem.

investment story. Suppose M1 requires a widget from M2 at date 1, which yields a gross return of $R(i)$ if M1 has made a prior investment of i (at date 0). M2's supply costs are C^* (a fixed number). M1 has no alternative supplier and M2 has no alternative purchaser at date 1 (so $r \equiv 0$, $c \equiv \infty$). Assume that $R(0) > C^*$, $R'(0) > 2$, $R'(\infty) < 1$, $R'(i) > 0$, and $R''(i) < 0$ for all i. (The first of these assumptions implies that there are always gains from trade.) Suppose also that both parties are risk-neutral and that the rate of interest is zero. Ignore issues of asset ownership. The timeline is given in Figure 4.1.

Fig. 4.1

Start with the case considered in Chapter 2 where the parties do not write a long-term contract at date 0. Instead, they wait until date 1 and bargain then about the type and price of the widget. Given Nash bargaining, the parties split the *ex post* surplus 50 : 50, and so the widget price is

(4.1) $p = \tfrac{1}{2}R(i) + \tfrac{1}{2}C^*$

and M1's net return is

(4.2) $\tfrac{1}{2}R(i) - \tfrac{1}{2}C^* - i.$

At date 0 M1 chooses i to maximize (4.2), the first-order condition for which is

(4.3) $\tfrac{1}{2}R'(i) = 1.$

In contrast, the first-best choice of i maximizes total (net) surplus, $R(i) - i - C^*$, and is characterized by

(4.4) $R'(i^*) = 1.$

Clearly, $\hat{i} < i^*$; that is, M1 underinvests in the absence of an effective long-term contract.

The question is: can the parties write a date 0 contract to solve this hold-up problem? In two simple cases, the answer is yes.

Case 1. The widget type can be described in advance. Under these conditions it is easy for M1 and M2 to write a specific performance contract. The contract states that M2 must supply M1 with a date 1 widget with the appropriate characteristics (specified in the contract) at a predetermined price p^*, where p^* is chosen somewhere between C^* and $R(i^*) - i^*$; moreover, M2 pays large damages if she fails to perform. (Recall the assumption that both parties are wealthy.) With a contract like this, M1's net return is

$$(4.5) \qquad R(i) - p^* - i,$$

and, maximizing this, M1 will choose $i = i^*$.

Case 2. The investment can be verified. A second possibility is for the parties to contract on M1's date 0 investment rather than on the date 1 widget. The reason M1 does not invest in the absence of a contract is that 50 per cent of the gains from investment go to M2. M2 could compensate M1 for this by sharing in M1's investment costs. In particular, M1 and M2 could write a contract stating that, in return for M1's investing i^*, M2 will make a payment to M1 of somewhere between $i^* - \frac{1}{2}R(i^*) + \frac{1}{2}C^*$ and $\frac{1}{2}R(i^*) - \frac{1}{2}C^*$. (If M1 does not invest i^*, he pays a large penalty.) This cost-sharing arrangement ensures that M1 at least breaks even on his investment and so the first-best is again achieved.

Cases 1 and 2 are fairly restrictive for two reasons. First, in practice, it may be difficult to specify the type and quality of input M1 requires in advance. The reason is that the nature of the input may depend on a number of factors occurring between dates 0 and 1 (see below).[4] Second, it may be hard to specify M1's investment obligations unambiguously in a contract. The investment M1 is meant to carry out may be hard to describe; it may be multidimensional and involve the expenditure of time and effort (say, in skill acquisition) as well as the expenditure of money (on physical capital). Given this, it may be hard for a court to determine whether M1 has fulfilled his contractual responsibilities. Note that, even if all expenditure is monetary, it is not enough for the court to look at M1's expenses since M1 could have spent the money in the wrong way.

---

[4] It may also be difficult to specify the *quantity* of input M1 requires in advance, since this too may depend on a number of factors occurring between dates 0 and 1. I will not deal with the quantity issue here; however, see Aghion *et al.* (1994c), Chung (1991), Hart and Moore (1988) and Noldeke and Schmidt (1995).

Note also that M2 cannot simply hand M1 a payment at date 0 and *hope* that M1 carries out his first-best investment. A lump-sum payment does not affect M1's investment incentive; that is, given (4.1) and (4.2), M1 will accept the payment and set $i = \hat{i}$.

It is useful to provide a (partial) formalization of the idea that the widget type cannot be specified in advance. Suppose that there are a very large number of equally likely states of the world S and a very large number of possible widgets, and in each state a different type of widget is required by M1. Moreover, the wrong widget is useless for M1; that is, widget s in state s yields $R(i)$, whereas widget t yields nothing for all $t \neq s$.[5] In addition, the production cost of each widget is C^*.[6]

Ideally, the parties would write a contingent contract, stating which widget should be supplied in each state of the world. However, unless there is a shorthand for describing a type-s widget, this contract would have to consist of a list of S statements of the following form: in state 1, a widget with the following characteristics should be supplied . . . ; in state 2, a widget with the following (different) characteristics should be supplied . . . ; etc. If S is very large and there is some cost of writing each statement (this could be just the cost of the paper used), then such a contract would be prohibitively expensive. Note also that, although the parties could reduce costs by indicating only what should happen in some states of the world—e.g. in the first 100 states—there is little point in doing this if S is very large since the probability that one of these states will be relevant is negligible.

The fact that the parties cannot write a contingent contract does not mean that they cannot achieve the first-best. Consider the following contract:

> CONTRACT (A). M1 specifies the widget he wants at date 1. If M2 agrees to supply it, she receives p_1. If she does not, she receives p_0.

Here p_0 is a transfer that M1 makes to M2 if trade does not occur. p_0 could be positive or negative (or zero). If it is negative, then it

---

[5] So there is no notion of some widgets being closer than others.

[6] The analysis generalizes straightforwardly to the case where $R(i)$ and C^* are random variables as of date 0, whose realizations become known to both M1 and M2 at date 1.

can be interpreted as a damage payment made by M2 to M1 for non-delivery.[7]

The first-best can be achieved by setting $p_0 \geq 0$, $p_1 = p_0 + C^*$. If state s occurs, M1 will ask for a type-s widget. M2 is prepared to supply the widget since she breaks even. (It is possible to make M2 strictly prefer to supply by setting p_1 just above $p_0 + C^*$.) M1's return is $R(i) - C^* - i - p_0$, and this is maximized by setting $i = i^*$.

The trouble with this solution to the hold-up problem is that it is extremely sensitive to the timing.[8] Contract (A) works well if M1's request for M2 arrives just before production occurs. Suppose, however, that there is a period of time after M2 receives M1's widget proposal, but before production occurs. Then M2 can turn down M1's request, and renegotiate to supply the widget under better terms. Assume that the renegotiation game proceeds as follows: with probability $\frac{1}{2}$, M1 can make an offer to M2, who can accept or reject it, and, with probability $\frac{1}{2}$, M2 can make an offer to M1, who can accept or reject it. If M1 gets to make an offer, he will continue to suggest $p_0 + C^*$. On the other hand, if M2 gets to make an offer, she will suggest $p_0 + R(i)$. Thus, the (expected) price M1 pays under renegotiation is

$$(4.6) \qquad \hat{p}_1 = p_0 + \tfrac{1}{2}R(i) + \tfrac{1}{2}C^*.$$

But this means that there is again a hold-up problem: M1's net return is

$$(4.7) \qquad R(i) - \hat{p}_1 - i = \tfrac{1}{2}R(i) - \tfrac{1}{2}C^* - i - p_0,$$

which is maximized at $i = \hat{\imath}$.[9]

Equation (4.6) was derived under the assumption that $p_1 = p_0 + C^*$. However, a similar argument shows that (4.6) holds generally when renegotiation is possible. That is, whatever prices (p_0, p_1)

---

[7] Note that a traditional 'breach of contract' damage remedy, whereby M2 compensates M1 for any loss in profits caused by her not supplying, is not feasible, since M1's losses are not verifiable.

[8] For an analysis that exploits this timing to solve the hold-up problem more generally, see Hart and Moore (1988).

[9] The reader may wonder whether M2's refusal to supply under the original contract is credible; that is, might M1 not take the point of view that M2 will back down and supply M1 at the last moment anyway (particularly if p_1 is slightly above $p_0 + C^*$)? One way M2 might make her refusal credible is by sending M1 a letter saying that, if she does supply under the existing contract, she will refund all of the money that she is paid. (This obviously makes supply unprofitable.) Or she could agree with a third party to pay over money received under the existing contract, and brandish this agreement in front of M1.

are stated in contract (A), the actual (expected) price, $\hat{p}_1$, paid by M1 will be given by (4.6). To establish this, one further assumption is required: in addition to the S 'regular' widgets described above, suppose that there are some 'gold-plated' widgets that cost M2 much more to produce (or that M2 cannot produce at all); moreover, a court cannot distinguish between regular and gold-plated widgets. The proof that (4.6) holds is as follows. The price paid $\hat{p}_1$ cannot be less than $p_0 + \frac{1}{2}R(i) + \frac{1}{2}C^*$ since in this case M2 will prefer to reject M1's offer and renegotiate (assuming a 50 : 50 split of the surplus in bargaining). However, the price paid $\hat{p}_1$ also cannot be greater than $p_0 + \frac{1}{2}R(i) + \frac{1}{2}C^*$, since in this case M1 will prefer to ask for a gold-plated widget, and then renegotiate when M2 declines to supply it.[10]

The conclusion is that, if renegotiation is possible, a long-term contract does not solve the hold-up problem. In fact, the equilibrium level of investment under a long-term contract is just the same as it would be under no contract at all.

Since renegotiation causes problems, it is natural to ask whether there is a way for the parties to commit *not* to renegotiate the original contract. (M2 would then have no incentive to decline M1's offer.) Unfortunately, under the current legal system, it is not clear how M1 and M2 can do this. Suppose the parties write in their original contract that if they ever renegotiate M1 must pay M2 £1 billion. Then the renegotiated contract can always include a clause that waives this penalty. (Moreover, under the current legal system the courts will enforce the renegotiated contract rather than the original contract.) The same is true if M1 and M2 agree to pay a third party £1 billion if they renegotiate: the third party can agree to waive the penalty in the renegotiated contract. (She will never receive the billion pounds anyway.)[11]

Another possibility is that M2 could agree in the original contract that she will never make offers to M1 but will only respond to offers made by M1; in effect, she grants M1 100 per cent of the bargaining power in any contract renegotiation. This would

[10] Segal (1995) also uses the idea of a gold-plated widget in his formalization of contractual incompleteness.

[11] For further discussions of renegotiation, see Tirole (1994). Maskin and Tirole (1995) show that, if renegotiation can be prevented in an incomplete contracting world, then the optimal comprehensive contracting outcome can be achieved under very general conditions.

clearly solve the hold-up problem in the one-sided investment case, but again it is hard to see how it could be enforced. Whatever the formal contract says, there is little to stop M2 from arranging an informal meeting with M1, and proposing a new contract that includes a clause waiving M2's promise not to speak. In this way M2 can recapture some of her bargaining power.

I now briefly consider some other solutions to the hold-up problem, and some related ideas and literature.

Revenue- or cost-sharing

So far I have supposed $R(i)$ and C^* to be observable, but not verifiable. In fact, this assumption is not critical. Suppose $R(i)$ and C^* are verifiable. Then the parties can write a contract that makes M1's payment to M2 depend on her costs or on M1's revenue. (That is, revenue- or cost-sharing becomes feasible.) However, such contracts do not solve the hold-up problem. To see why, let p_0 be the price that M1 must pay if no trade occurs (that is, if revenues and costs both equal zero). Call no trade at price p_0 the 'no-trade outcome'. Then either party can trigger the no-trade outcome, with the intention of renegotiating. M2 can do this by turning down M1's request; M1 can do this by asking for a 'gold-plated' widget which M2 cannot supply. Since either party can trigger the no-trade outcome, the logic used to derive (4.6) still holds. Hence the hold-up problem remains.

The point is that revenue-/cost-sharing contracts give M1 and M2 each an *option* to trade under the existing contract but do not force them to trade under this contract.

Third parties

So far I have focused on two-party contracts. Under certain assumptions, the presence of a third party can help. Suppose M1 and M2 agree that M1 will specify the kind of widget he wants at date 1, and M1 and M2 will then simultaneously send messages to the third party, T, about whether M1's request is appropriate (i.e. whether M1 has asked for a 'regular' widget that costs M2 an amount C^* to produce). If they both say that M1's request is appropriate, M2 must supply M1 with the widget and will receive C^* from M1. If either says it is inappropriate, no trade occurs and M1 and M2 must each pay T a large fine.

It is easy to see that this contract can achieve the first-best. (More precisely, there is one equilibrium of the contracting game ('truth-telling') that achieves the first-best.) However, this relies on T being honest. In particular, there is a great incentive for T to collude with M2 (or M1). M2 can announce that the widget is inappropriate even when it isn't, and M2 and T can share the large fine (perhaps having written a side-contract in advance for this purpose). In fact, it is not difficult to show that, if (perfect) collusion is possible, the introduction of a third party achieves nothing, since T will in effect merge with M1 or M2 and the two-party case again applies.[12]

Investment cost-sharing via messages

It might be thought that, even though M1's investment is not verifiable, investment cost-sharing could be achieved by having M1 and M2 send messages (to each other, say) about how much investment occurred. (I continue to rule out third parties on the grounds that they may collude with M1 or M2.) However, this is not the case. The earlier discussion showed that, as a result of bargaining, the date 1 widget price is given by (4.6):

$$\hat{p}_1 = p_0 + \tfrac{1}{2}R(i) + \tfrac{1}{2}C^*.$$

But this means that the influence of M1 and M2's messages is only through p_0; that is, once p_0 is determined, messages have no further impact on p_1. Since M1 wants a low value of p_0 and M2 wants a high one, M1 and M2 are in effect playing a zero-sum game, the solution of which, p_0^*, will be independent of any sunk investment costs.[13] Thus, a message game about investment is no better than a simple contract with a pre-specified no-trade price p_0^* (which may as well be set equal to zero).

The role of bounded rationality

In formalizing the hold-up problem, I have assumed that the parties are unboundedly rational in the sense that they can calculate

[12] For a preliminary discussion of this, see Hart and Moore (1988); on collusion more generally, see Tirole (1986b, 1992).

[13] For an analysis of this kind of idea in a slightly different context, see Hart and Moore (1988).

the consequences of any action they take. (They know $R(i)$ and C^* and can figure out (4.2).) At the same time, I have supposed that transaction costs cause contractual incompleteness. There is a tension in these positions, but they are not inconsistent. There is no contradiction in assuming on the one hand that the parties cannot write a contract that specifies widget type and investment in a sufficiently unambiguous manner that a court can enforce it, but assuming on the other hand that the parties can figure out the utility consequences of their inability to write an unambiguous contract.

For example, in the house transaction described in the introduction, there are many contingencies that no contract can include. (See n. 3 of the Introduction for one of these.) But it does not follow from this that my wife and I cannot factor these contingencies into our expected utility; for instance, we might discount our utility by some amount to cover outcomes we cannot identify individually.

In reality, a great deal of contractual incompleteness is undoubtedly linked to the inability of parties not only to contract very carefully about the future, but also to *think* very carefully about the utility consequences of their actions. It would therefore be highly desirable to relax the assumption that parties are unboundedly rational.

Apart from making the analysis more realistic, such an approach would have other benefits too. First, it might permit the relaxation of the assumption that the parties cannot commit not to renegotiate their contract. In a world of bounded rationality, parties are unlikely to want to make such a commitment since they will wish to preserve their option to revise their contract as unanticipated events occur. Second, for similar reasons, a bounded rationality approach might allow the relaxation of the assumption that incorruptible third parties cannot be found to improve on two-party contracts. Third parties are useful to sustain message games in which M1 and M2 must pay a large penalty (to the third party) unless they agree on the appropriateness of input. However, such games will be less attractive in a world of bounded rationality where the parties may not agree either *ex ante* or *ex post* on what qualifies as 'appropriate' input.

It is worth noting that one can go only so far in dropping the assumption of rationality. If parties are too irrational, they may not realize that an investment today will be expropriated by an opportunistic trading partner tomorrow. As a result, a party may invest efficiently even when it is suboptimal for him to do so; i.e. the hold-up problem may disappear! In other words, the hold-up problem—as well (probably) as the theory of asset ownership in Chapter 2—seems to rely on a minimal degree of foresight about the future utility consequences of current actions.

The role of asymmetric information (or lack thereof)

Asymmetric information has played a very limited role in the analysis of the hold-up problem (and plays a very limited role in the analysis in this book more generally). Variables such as $R(i)$, C^*, and i were supposed to be observable but not verifiable. I should make it clear that asymmetric information was not de-emphasized because it was judged to be unimportant; rather, this was done because the analysis—particularly the analysis of rene-gotiation—is much more tractable under the assumption of sym-metric information. Also, from a purely economic point of view it is most natural to study the hold-up problem in the context of symmetric information. The hold-up problem is most acute when M2 *observes* M1's investment (or observes the returns from this investment) and can exploit M1's eagerness for the widget to extract a high price. A hold-up problem can also arise if M2 is unsure about whether M1 has invested, but it is less extreme (see Tirole 1986*a*).

There is one place, however, where asymmetric information might be very useful. Suppose that M2's cost C^* is private infor-mation. Consider a contract that states that M1 will specify a wid-get type (and widget price) at date 1, and M2 can either agree to M1's suggestion or decline it. In the case of symmetric informa-tion, this contract achieves the first-best if M1 has all the bargain-ing power. With asymmetric information, however, the first-best is not achieved since M1 may offer a price below M2's costs and M2 may decline it. But this means that M2 may pretend that her costs are high even when they are not in order to force M1 to pay more. As a result, the hold-up problem *may* reappear. (I say 'may' because, as far as I know, this case has not been analysed in the lit-erature.) In other words, asymmetric information may help to jus-tify the analysis of Chapter 2.

Related literature

There are a number of recent articles in the literature showing how the hold-up problem can be solved when contracts are incomplete. Perhaps the most notable contribution is by Aghion *et al.* (1994*c*) (henceforth ADR).[14]

ADR show that under certain conditions the first-best can be achieved even when M2 and M1 both invest. However, they make two assumptions that I do not make. First, they suppose that M1 and M2 trade a standard widget at date 1, whose characteristics are already known at date 0. This means that the parties can write a specific performance contract, whereby M2 agrees to deliver a suitable number of widgets $\bar{q}$ to M1 for a price $\bar{p}$, and this can serve as a starting point for renegotiation. ADR suppose that M1 and M2's benefit and cost functions are uncertain *ex ante* and so the optimal number of widgets to trade varies with the state of the world. This means that the parties will almost always renegotiate to a number of widgets different from $\bar{q}$. However, even though renegotiation will take place, an appropriate choice of $\bar{q}$ will ensure that one of the parties—M2, say—has the right *ex ante* incentive to invest. Thus, one side of the hold-up problem is solved.

In contrast, in our model there are no standard widgets and so in effect $\bar{q} = 0$. This means that neither party's investment pays off in the absence of renegotiation, and hence neither M1 nor M2 can be given the right *ex ante* incentives through a specific performance contract.

Second, ADR show that efficient investment by the *other* party—M1, say—can be achieved by designing the date 1 bargaining game appropriately. ADR consider an alternating offer bargaining game. To understand how their game works in the model of this chapter, imagine that date 1 is divided into two parts, 'the beginning' and 'the end'. Suppose that, at the beginning of date 1, M1 makes an offer to M2. M2 has three choices: to accept M1's offer (in which case the bargaining game is over); to reject M1's offer (in which case the bargaining game continues); or to select an outside option, which corresponds to no trade (in

[14] For other papers on this topic, see Chung (1991), Hart and Moore (1988), Hermalin and Katz (1991), MacLeod and Malcomson (1993), and Noldeke and Schmidt (1995).

which case trade never occurs). If the bargaining game continues, then at the end of date 1 M2 makes an offer, which M1 either accepts or rejects. This ends the bargaining. There is no discounting.

Given the above timing, the following *ex ante* contract provides M1 with all the bargaining power. Set the no-trade price to be zero if no trade is triggered at the beginning of date 1 through M2 exercising her outside option. However, set the no-trade price to be $-D$, where D is a large positive number, if M2 first rejects M1's offer and then has her own offer rejected. D is essentially a large damage payment that M2 must make to M1 if bargaining continues to the end of date 1, and then breaks down.

To see why this gives M1 all the bargaining power, note that M2 will always prefer to exercise her outside option, worth zero, rather than continue with the bargaining, given the large damage payment D. It follows that M1 need only offer M2 an amount $p = C^*$ to persuade her to accept his first offer at the beginning of date 1. But this means that M1 gets all the *ex post* surplus; i.e. M1's payoff is

(4.8) $$R(i) - C^* - i,$$

which leads M1 to choose $i = i^*$. That is, the first-best is achieved.

The ADR solution is ingenious, but it depends on some strong assumptions. In reality, it is hard to find anything corresponding to the outside option of no trade (for ever). Who enforces this outcome, i.e. who ensures that the bargaining game ends at this point and that M2 cannot make any further offers? Another interpretation of the ADR procedure is that, instead of there being an outside option, the damage payment is made to depend on how many offers M2 makes. That is, M2 pays no damages if she turns down M1's offer and makes no further offer, and she pays D if she does make another offer and it is turned down. However, this version supposes that, in the event of a dispute, the courts can determine how many offers M2 has made. This may not be reasonable if M2 can make secret offers. That is, having turned down M1's offer, M2 could come to M1 on the sly and propose that M1 pay her $R(i)$ for the widget and waive the damage payment D. M1 may as well accept this offer since he will not receive D anyway. (There will be no proof that M2 made the second offer if it is rejected.) But this means that M1's net return is

(4.9) $$R(i) - R(i) - i = -i,$$

which is maximized at $i = 0$!

The conclusion is that the ADR procedure is likely to be valid only in particular situations. Under more general conditions, the hold-up problem reappears and the analysis of Chapter 2 becomes relevant.

2. Discussion of the property rights model of Chapter 2

Given a justification for the hold-up problem, it is not difficult to provide some (tentative) support for the model of Chapter 2. Assume as in Chapter 2 that M1 requires an input from M2 and also that each party can make an investment that affects the benefits and costs of this input. (M1 chooses i and M2 chooses e.) Suppose also that the marginal returns from investment depend on how the nonhuman assets a1 and a2 are used. Moreover, there is a huge number of potential, hard-to-describe uses of these assets, only one of which, say, will be relevant in a particular state of the world. (It is supposed that each use is equally likely to be relevant.) Then a contract (of finite length) that attempts to specify particular uses will, with probability close to 1, specify only irrelevant ones, and hence what matters is who has residual rights of control—the right to choose asset uses not specified in the contract.

Given a particular ownership allocation, the parties will bargain over the gains from trade, as in Chapter 2. The logic of the present chapter can be used to show that the parties cannot gain from writing a long-term contract that specifies a no-trade price p_0 and a trade price p_1. The reason is that, if $p_1 - p_0$ lies below the Nash bargaining price (given by (2.6)), then M2 will decline to supply and renegotiate for a higher price; while, if $p_1 - p_0$ lies above the Nash bargaining price, then M1 will make an impossible demand on M2 and renegotiate for a lower price. (p_0 is in effect a lump-sum transfer and has no effect on investment choice.) Thus, the only way to influence investment incentives is by allocating asset ownership.

It remains to analyse the various ownership allocations. In Chapter 2 four were discussed: M1 owns a1, M2 owns a2; M1 owns a1 and a2; M2 owns a1 and a2; and M1 owns a2 and M2 owns a1 (which was dominated by the others). Joint ownership was also considered, but shown to be suboptimal.

Other possibilities are stochastic ownership arrangements and option-to-own contracts, or more generally ownership arrangements that are contingent on messages sent by the parties between dates 0 and 1. Stochastic ownership is helpful because it can act as a smoothing device. Suppose, for example, that, with probability σ, M1 owns a1 and M2 owns a2 (that is, non-integration occurs); and, with probability $(1 - \sigma)$, M1 owns a1 and a2 (type 1 integration occurs). (A coin toss at date 1 determines which of these ownership structures applies.) Then the first-order conditions for Nash equilibrium (see (2.12)–(2.13)) become

$$\tfrac{1}{2}R' \text{ (i)} + \tfrac{1}{2}(\sigma r' \ (i;a1) + (1 - \sigma)r' \ (i;a1,a2)) \qquad = 1,$$
$$\tfrac{1}{2}\,|\,C' \ (e)\,| + \tfrac{1}{2}(\sigma\,|\,c' \ (e;a2)\,| + (1 - \sigma)\,|\,c' \ (e;\varnothing)\,|)= 1,$$

which yields investment levels for M1 and M2 between i_1 and i_0 and e_1 and e_0, respectively. It is easy to show that under some conditions such an outcome will increase total surplus.

In the Appendix to this chapter an example is provided that illustrates the role of option-to-own contracts and/or message schemes.[15]

It is clear from the example—as well as from the discussion of stochastic schemes—that the analysis of ownership structures in Chapter 2 is not complete. In particular, Chapter 2 derives the optimality of non-integration, type 1 integration, and type 2 integration relative to each other, but not relative to all possible arrangements. At the same time, the main ideas behind the analysis—if not all the details—are likely to be robust. First, the more sophisticated schemes that are stochastic or depend on messages are still examples of ownership. In an important sense, the main lesson of Chapter 2 is that the allocation of scarce ownership rights—that is, the allocation of residual rights of control—matters when contracts are incomplete. This continues to be true when stochastic and message-dependent ownership structures are allowed for. Second, it seems probable that Proposition 2 will generalize to the case of stochastic or message-dependent owner-

---

[15] The role of option-to-own contracts has already been noted by Noldeke and Schmidt (1994).

ship structures: that is, it will still be the case that, if only one party's investment matters, or only one party's investment decision is elastic, then that party should own both assets; that if assets are strictly complementary then they should be under common ownership; and that if assets are independent then they should be separately owned. Thus, while more sophisticated ownership arrangements may be an interesting embellishment to the analysis of Chapter 2, they do not undermine the message of that analysis.

3. *More on the role of the hold-up problem*

I have stressed that there are two crucial ingredients of the property rights approach: incomplete contracts, and residual rights of control over nonhuman assets. In the model of Chapter 2, the first ingredient was important because it led to a hold-up problem, given the non-contractibility of relationship-specific investments, while the second was important because it implied that changes in ownership could affect the severity of this hold-up problem.

It is worth pointing out that, although the hold-up problem is a useful vehicle for developing the property rights approach, it is not an essential part of the approach. That is, even in the absence of a hold-up problem, asset ownership would still generally matter. What is required for a theory of asset ownership is that there is some inefficiency in the economic relationship, which the allocation of residual control rights can influence: the inefficiency could be an *ex post* one rather than an *ex ante* one. It is worth briefly mentioning some other ways to generate inefficiency.

1. One obvious approach is to suppose that there is asymmetric information at date 1 (plus incomplete contracts at date 0). (See the discussion in Ch. 1, §3.) For example, M1 may know the value to him of the widget supplied by M2, whereas M2 may not; or M2 may know her production costs, while M1 may not. Under these conditions, ownership matters since it determines the outcome if bargaining breaks down, i.e. the parties' no-trade payoffs. Furthermore, the no-trade payoffs matter, since with positive probability bargaining *will* break down given the asymmetry

of information, and so the no-trade payoffs will be the actual pay-offs.

2. An even simpler—although more controversial—way to generate *ex post* inefficiency is to suppose that there is no (explicit) asymmetric information, but that there is a positive probability that (for unexplained reasons) M1 and M2 will simply 'not get along at date 1'. Assume that in this case the economic relationship breaks down irretrievably. (The parties no longer talk to each other and trade elsewhere.) Under these conditions, ownership again matters since it determines who can take what assets from the relationship if breakdown occurs.

3. A related approach is to suppose that the parties, rather than being opportunistic, simply have different views about the returns from various asset usages and hence disagree about how the assets should be employed; moreover, bargaining does not resolve these differences. Such an approach probably requires a departure from common knowledge, since otherwise the parties would go on talking until agreement was reached (see e.g. Aumann 1976). However, a role is again provided for asset ownership since whoever has the right to determine an asset's use will exercise this right if disagreement persists (which it will some of the time).

All these approaches seem worth exploring in future work. The end result may be a theory of integration that is richer and more realistic than the one described in Chapter 2, even if it may be 'messier' and somewhat less tractable.

APPENDIX

Message-dependent ownership structures

In this appendix I present an example showing how a message-dependent ownership structure can be useful. For much more general discussions of the use of messages in symmetric information environments, see Maskin (1985) and Moore (1992).

To simplify, consider a case where the investment choices for M1 and M2 are discrete (invest or don't invest) and there is only one asset, a*. Treat M1 and M2 symmetrically; in particular, suppose each manager can invest 76, and each investment generates a return of 100. However, the 100 is realized only if that party has access to the asset (otherwise the investment is worthless). So if both parties invest and reach agreement about how to use the asset the gross return is 200 (and the net return is $200 - 152 = 48$); while if M1 or M2 invests and can use the asset alone the gross return is 100 (and the net return is 24). In the language of Chapter 2, $R = r(a^*) = 100$, $r(\varnothing) = 0$ if M1 invests; $C = c(a^*) = -100$, $c(\varnothing) = 0$ if M2 invests. (If M1 does not invest, $R = r = 0$, and, if M2 does not invest, $C = c = 0$.) Note that neither party needs the other party's human capital for their investment to pay off.

Obviously, in the first-best both parties invest. However, under a deterministic ownership structure only one party invests. Suppose M2 owns a*. Then M1 will not invest since

$$\tfrac{1}{2}R + \tfrac{1}{2}r(\varnothing) = 50 < 76.$$

Similarly, if M1 owns a*, M2 will not invest. Stochastic ownership does not work any better. If M1 owns a* with probability σ and M2 with probability $(1 - \sigma)$, then investment by both parties requires

$$\frac{1}{2}R + \frac{1}{2}[\sigma r(a^*) + (1 - \sigma)r(\varnothing)] = 50 + 50\sigma > 76 \Rightarrow \sigma > \frac{26}{50},$$

$$-\frac{1}{2}C - \frac{1}{2}[\sigma c(\varnothing) + (1 - \sigma)c(a^*)] = 50 + (1 - \sigma)50 > 76 \Rightarrow \sigma < \frac{24}{50},$$

which cannot both be satisfied.

I now show that a combination of stochastic ownership and

option-to-own contracts can improve on the above arrangement. In particular, although the first-best is not achieved, one party invests for sure and the other party invests with some probability.

Consider the following ownership structure: M1 owns a* with probability $\sigma = 0.49$ and M2 owns a* with probability 0.51. However, at date 1, before the randomization is made, M2 can buy out M1's ownership right for a price of 23. But, if (and only if) M2 tries to exercise her option, M1 has the right to buy M2's ownership right for 50. (In this case M2 does not pay the 23.)

Under this ownership structure the following is an equilibrium for any $0 \le \mu \le \frac{1}{3}$: M2 invests for sure at date 0, and M1 invests with probability μ.

To understand this, consider the various possible *ex post* situations at date 1.

1. M1 and M2 have both invested

If no buyouts occur, the parties' net payoffs are

(4A.1)　　　　　$\pi_1 = 0.49\,(150) + 0.51\,(50) - 76 = 23,$

(4A.2)　　　　　$\pi_2 = 0.49\,(50) + 0.51\,(150) - 76 = 25.$

Note that, if M1 owns the asset, not only does he receive his own return of 100, but he can also hold up M2 for half of her return, so he gets 150 altogether. Similarly for M2.

If M2 buys out M1, M2 receives $100 + \frac{1}{2}(100) - 76 - 23 = 51$ and M1 receives $23 + \frac{1}{2}(100) - 76 = -3$. However, M1 will pre-empt this by buying M2 out for 50, which makes M2's payoff equal to $50 + \frac{1}{2}(100) - 76 = 24$. Since this is less than π_2 in (4A.2), M2 will not initiate a buyout.

2. M1 has not invested, M2 has invested

If no buyouts occur, the parties' net payoffs are

$$\pi'_1 = 0.49\,(50) = 24.5,$$

$$\pi'_2 = 0.49\,(50) + 0.51\,(100) - 76 = -0.5.$$

In this case M2 can do better by buying M1 out. This yields pay-offs of

(4A.3) $\pi_1 = 23,$

(4A.4) $\pi_2 = 100 - 23 - 76 = 1.$

M1 will not exercise his option, since his payoff would then be $\frac{1}{2}(100) - 50 = 0$.

3. *M1 has invested, M2 has not invested*

If no buyouts occur, the parties' net payoffs are

$$\pi'_1 = 0.49\,(100) + 0.51\,(50) - 76 = -1.5,$$
$$\pi'_2 = 0.51\,(50) = 25.5.$$

In this case M2 can do better by buying M1 out. This yields pay-offs of

(4A.5) $\pi_1 = \frac{1}{2}(100) + 23 - 76 = -3,$

(4A.6) $\pi_2 = \frac{1}{2}(100) - 23 = 27.$

M1 will not exercise his option, since his payoff would then be $100 - 50 - 76 = -26$.

4. *Neither M1 nor M2 has invested*

If neither party invests, each party's net payoff is zero:

(4A.7) $\pi_1 = 0,$

(4A.8) $\pi_2 = 0.$

Comparing (4A.1) and (4A.3), one sees that if M2 invests then M1 is indifferent between investing and not investing. Also, a comparison of (4A.2) and (4A.6), and (4A.4) and (4A.8) shows that if M1 invests then M2 would prefer not to invest, while if M1 does not invest M2 would prefer to invest. This suggests consideration of a mixed-strategy equilibrium, where M2 invests for sure and M1 invests with probability μ. In order to ensure that M2 invests, one requires

$$\mu\,(25) + (1 - \mu)\,(1) \geq \mu\,(27) + (1 - \mu)\,(0),$$

i.e. $\mu \leq \frac{1}{3}$. So there is a continuum of mixed-strategy equilibria. The surplus maximizing one is where $\mu = \frac{1}{3}$. This equilibrium clearly dominates those that can be achieved through deterministic or stochastic ownership.

PART II

Understanding Financial Structure

The first part of the book considered a situation where agents could afford to purchase the assets it was efficient for them to own. Part II relaxes this assumption and provides an analysis of firms' financial decisions. Chapter 5 studies the optimal financial contract written by an entrepreneur who raises funds for an investment project from a rich investor (or a set of investors). The issue is how control should be allocated between the entrepreneur and the investor(s). Chapter 6 discusses the role of capital structure in constraining the behaviour of the managers of a public company that has many small investors who find it difficult to exercise control. Chapter 7 is different in character from the rest of the book. It applies some of the ideas of Chapters 5 and 6 to study an important practical issue, the design of bankruptcy procedure. In contrast to the other chapters, there is no model and the analysis is fairly informal. Finally, Chapter 8 considers how votes should be allocated across shares in a public company, subject to a takeover threat. This chapter, unlike the others in Part II, is not concerned with debt, but shares with Chapters 6 and 7 the idea that automatic mechanisms—in this case take-overs—are an essential tool for controlling the management of a public company.

Since most of the large literature on capital structure does not (at least explicitly) take an incomplete contracting view, it is worth saying a few words about why incomplete contracting ideas provide a natural way to think about financial decisions.

In the absence of contracting costs, the parties to a transaction— entrepreneurs, managers and investors—would write an initial contract that anticipates all future events. Given that all decisions are specified, it is difficult to find a role for financial structure. For example, consider debt. The simplest interpretation of a debt contract is that a sequence of fixed payments is agreed to; if the payments are not made, creditors can foreclose on the debtor's assets and decide what to do with them. In a comprehensive contracting world, however, all the uses of the debtor's assets are specified and so there is nothing left for the creditors to decide. Or take equity. Equity is a claim with votes attached. But in a comprehensive contracting world there is nothing to vote on since there are no residual decisions. (Similarly, there is no role for the take-over mechanism, which relies on the idea that someone acquires enough votes to get control.) Finally, bankruptcy is a situation in which existing claims are inconsistent. Yet in a comprehensive contracting world such an event would be anticipated and the inconsistency removed in the contract. Thus, there would be no need for a formal bankruptcy procedure. These themes are elaborated on in the chapters below.

5

Theories of Financial Contracting and Debt

PREVIOUS chapters have shown that an agent should own an asset if he has important asset-specific investment decisions to make or if he has human capital essential for the asset's use. This chapter considers what happens if the agent is wealth-constrained and cannot buy the asset outright. Under these conditions, the agent will have to raise funds from an outside investor (or from a set of investors) to purchase the asset. This creates a new agency problem. The agent may behave opportunistically, thus depriving the investor of an adequate return on her investment.

The chapter studies how the investor can protect herself against such opportunistic behaviour. (I now depart from the buyer–seller relationship and focus on a single agent and a single investor.) One possibility is for the investor to take a controlling interest in the asset. However, the investor may then abuse her power; for example, she may sell the asset without taking into account the agent's benefit from operating it. It will be shown that in some cases it is better for the investor to enter into a financial contract with the agent of the following form. The agent borrows money from the investor and promises to make certain repayments. If he makes them, he retains control of the asset. If he does not make them, control shifts to the investor. In other words, the theory of incomplete contracts and property rights—when extended to the case of limited wealth—can explain the use of debt financing.

The chapter begins with a description of the leading incomplete contracting theory of debt, which is due to Aghion and Bolton (1992). I argue that the Aghion–Bolton model explains transfers in control but does not explain the use of a standard debt contract. Section 2 discusses a model, based on Hart and Moore (1989), which comes closer to justifying a standard debt contract. (For a related analysis, see Bolton and Scharfstein (1990).) The model in Section 2 extends for two periods and supposes perfect certainty. It turns out to be easy to generalize the analysis to many periods, and this is done in Section 3. (The discussion in Section 3 is based on Hart and Moore (1994*a*).) The dynamic version throws light on the maturity structure of debt repayment paths, and on the role of collateral in determining whether a project is financed. Section 4 introduces uncertainty into the two-period Hart–Moore model, while Section 5 considers the role of multiple investors in hardening the debtor's budget constraint.

The Appendix describes an alternative approach to debt contracting: the costly state verification (CSV) model, introduced by Townsend (1978) and developed by Gale and Hellwig (1985). The CSV model, which is a comprehensive contracting theory, has been an extremely effective workhorse for a wide variety of purposes, but I shall argue that it cannot explain some of the distinguishing features of debt.[1] In this respect the incomplete contracting approach described in the main body of the chapter, even though it is at a much earlier stage of development, may be more fruitful in the long run.

This chapter is concerned with the case of a smallish, entrepreneurial firm, e.g. a closely held company, where there is no separation between ownership and control. Chapter 6 discusses how to extend the analysis to the case of a large public company. In this chapter, and in the remainder of Part II, the role of relationship-specific investments and hold-up problems is de-emphasized, relative to Part I. Instead, the driving force of the analysis is the idea that an agent may receive private benefits from operating or managing an asset, and that he does not have the wealth to pay for these private benefits up front (i.e. to purchase the asset).

1. The Aghion–Bolton model

To introduce the Aghion–Bolton model, it is useful to return to the notation of Chapter 2. Suppose that there is only one asset, a1,

---

[1] Also, the optimal contract in the CSV model can be interpreted as a debt contract only under fairly restrictive conditions. This is a problem with other leading comprehensive contracting models of debt too (e.g. Innes 1990). If the set of feasible contracts is very rich (as it is in a comprehensive contracting world), strong assumptions are required for the optimal contract to have the form of a simple debt contract.

and only one manager, M1, who works with this asset. However, an expenditure of K is required to construct the asset and the manager has no wealth of his own. The manager/entrepreneur approaches a (rich) investor for the funds. (I refer to the manager as an entrepreneur, E, the investor as a capitalist, C, and the asset as a project.) As in Chapters 2–4, suppose that a future action, denoted by $a \in A$, has to be taken with regard to the project, and this action is sufficiently complicated that it cannot be specified in an initial contract. Hence this action will be chosen by the project owner (who may be the entrepreneur or the investor). However, in contrast to Chapter 2, there are no relationship-specific investments. Instead, the project yields two kinds of benefits: a monetary benefit $y(a)$, which is verifiable and can be contracted on, and a private benefit $b(a)$ for the entrepreneur, which is non-verifiable and non-transferable. Both y and b are measured in money terms, even though b is not actually in the form of money (so b represents utility measured in dollars or pounds). Ownership matters because there are conflicts of interest about the choice of action a. Moreover, because the entrepreneur is wealth-constrained, renegotiation does not necessarily resolve these conflicts; that is, the entrepreneur may not be able to bribe the investor to choose a surplus-maximizing choice of a. (This is in contrast to Chapter 2, where negotiation always led to an *ex post* surplus-maximizing outcome.)

Examples of private benefits might be an entrepreneur's desire to keep a family-owned business going, even though it is not very profitable, the entrepreneur's consumption of perks, or the entrepreneur's disutility from dismissing long-standing employees.

In what follows, I simplify matters by supposing that the contract allocates *all* the monetary returns $y(a)$ to C (that is, C is allocated all the 'dividends' from the project). It follows that the payoffs to the parties are

$$U_E = b(a),$$
$$U_C = y(a).$$

This is a natural case to look at since, as will become apparent, the parties wish to devise a contract that gives E maximum freedom to pursue his private goals, but which compensates C for her investment. Other arrangements are however possible; these are discussed later in the chapter. It is also supposed that there is symmetric information and the interest rate is zero.[2]

Start by considering the 'first-best'. By first-best I mean a situation where E is not wealth-constrained and hence arbitrary side-payments can be made *ex post*.[3] Under these conditions, whoever has control, the parties will bargain to the point where total surplus $b + y$ is maximized and will allocate this surplus using side-payments. Let

$$a^* = \underset{a \in A}{\text{argmax}} \; \{b(a) + y(a)\}$$

be the first-best optimal action (assumed unique).

Turn next to the second-best, where E has no wealth. Consider first what happens if E owns and controls the project.

E control

E control corresponds to the case where E has voting equity and C has non-voting equity (and all the dividends). Without renegotiation, E would solve the following problem:

$$\underset{a \in A}{\text{Max}} \; b(a).$$

Denote the solution by a_E (assumed unique). Then C's payoff in the absence of renegotiation is

$$U_C^E = y(a_E).$$

However, renegotiation will take place. To simplify matters, suppose that E has all the bargaining power, both *ex post* and *ex ante* when the contract is written.[4] Then E will offer to choose the first-best action a^* in return for a payment of $y(a^*) - y(a_E)$ from C. Note that this payment is non-negative since, by the definitions of a^* and a_E, $b(a^*) + y(a^*) \geq b(a_E) + y(a_E)$ and $b(a_E) \geq b(a^*)$, from which it follows that $y(a^*) \geq y(a_E)$. The two parties' payoffs will be

---

[2] I make the further technical assumptions that A is a compact, convex subset of Euclidean space and that y and b are continuous and concave in a.

[3] This is not the only possible interpretation of first-best. First-best could also refer to a situation where a is *ex ante* contractible. In the present context, it is more convenient to use the no-wealth-constraint case as a benchmark. Note, of course, that if E is not wealth-constrained he can finance the project himself.

[4] This is a reasonable assumption if there are only a few entrepreneurs with good ideas but many investors with capital for projects.

$$U_C^E = y(a_E),$$

$$U_E^E = b(a^*) + y(a^*) - y(a_E) \geq b(a_E).$$

Clearly, if $y(a_E) \geq K$, E control achieves the first-best since C breaks even and an efficient action is chosen. (Given that E has all the bargaining power, if $y(a_E) > K$, C will make an initial lump-sum payment of $y(a_E) - K$ to E.) The interesting case is where $y(a_E) < K$, that is, where the first-best is not feasible. Under these conditions, it may be necessary to give C control.

C control

C control corresponds to the case where C has all the voting equity. Without renegotiation, C would solve the following problem:

$$\underset{a \in A}{\text{Max}}\, y(a).$$

Denote the solution by a_C (assumed unique). Then C's payoff in the absence of renegotiation is

$$U_C^C = y(a_C),$$

and E's is

$$U_E^C = b(a_C).$$

In fact, no renegotiation will occur. The reason is that any other action by definition yields a lower value of y than does a_C. Hence E cannot compensate C for taking the action, since he has no wealth.

Clearly, the sum of the parties' payoffs will be smaller under C control than under E control since a is chosen to maximize y rather than $(b + y)$. However, C's payoff will be larger. From now on assume

$$(5.1) \qquad\qquad y(a_C) \geq K.$$

If (5.1) were not satisfied, the project would not be undertaken at all.

The interesting case is where (5.1) holds strictly. Under these conditions, it may be optimal to give E and C each control with positive probability. Suppose E and C are risk-neutral. Then E will own the project with probability σ and C will own it with probability $(1 - \sigma)$, where σ is chosen so that C breaks even on average:

$$\sigma\, y(a_E) + (1 - \sigma)\, y(a_C) = K.$$

Stochastic control is hard to interpret, but a slight embellishment of the model leads to something more natural.[5] Suppose that income from the project, y, depends on a verifiable state of the world θ which is realized after the contract is signed but before a is chosen.[6] (The private benefit b is independent of θ.) Assume further that

$$y(a,\theta) = \alpha(\theta)z(a) + \beta(\theta),$$

where $\alpha > 0$, $\alpha' < 0$, $z > 0$. Then it is not difficult to show that the optimal contract has the following form. There is a cut-off θ^* such that E has control when $\theta > \theta^*$. The cut-off is chosen so that C breaks even on average. The intuition behind the cut-off is that, given $\alpha' < 0$, high θ states are those where the choice of action has relatively little effect on y (and so E should control action) and the low θ states are those where the choice of action has a relatively large effect on y (and so C should control action). Note that, if $\alpha'(\theta)z(a) + \beta'(\theta) > 0$ for all $a \in A$, high θ states are high-profit states, i.e. E receives control when profits are high. However, the opposite is true if $\alpha'(\theta)z(a) + \beta'(\theta) \leq 0$ for all $a \in A$. Then E receives control when profits are low.[7]

---

[5] Stochastic control is not always optimal. The analysis has focused on contracts that allocate all the monetary returns to C. There are other possibilities, however, if (5.1) holds strictly. For example, C could retain control but give E a lump-sum transfer by way of compensation, equal to $y(a_C) - K$; E could then use this transfer to bribe C to choose a more efficiently. The advantage of such an agreement is that the action a is deterministic rather than random, which increases total surplus if b or y is strictly concave. One case where stochastic control *can* be shown to be optimal (although not uniquely optimal) is if $b(a) = \lambda a$, $y(a) = Y - a$, $0 \leq a \leq \bar{a}$, and $\lambda > 1$. (Here b and y are not strictly concave and so randomization of action does not reduce surplus.) See also n. 7.

[6] This is the case Aghion and Bolton (1992) consider. See also Berglof (1994).

[7] Throughout the analysis of the Aghion–Bolton model, I have made the simplifying assumption that C is allocated all of the monetary returns $y(a)$. Two new issues arise if this assumption is relaxed. First, if E is entitled to, say, a fraction μ of $y(a)$, then, in the absence of renegotiation, E will maximize $\mu y(a) + b(a)$ if he has control. Perversely, this may *increase* C's pre-renegotiation return (which, recall, is the same as C's post-renegotiation return since E has all the bargaining power). The reason is that, when $\mu > 0$, E puts some weight on monetary returns in his choice of action and this indirect effect of a better choice of action may outweigh the direct effect of a reduction in C's share of the monetary return. However, the importance of this effect is questionable since it is in E's interest to *minimize* C's *ex post* payoff (given that E gets all the gains from renegotiation). If a positive μ increases C's payoff by tilting E's incentives, E could offset this *ex post* by announcing that he will renounce his share of monetary returns, i.e. will give back the fraction μ to C. There is a second effect that may be more important. If E has a share of the monetary returns, he can use these to bribe C to choose a more

Comments on the Aghion–Bolton Model

The Aghion–Bolton model demonstrates that, in a world where one party is wealth-constrained (but there are no relationship-specific investments), it may be optimal to transfer control from that party to another party in certain states of the world. The Aghion–Bolton model captures a key aspect of debt financing: shifts in control. However, in other respects, the model's characterization of debt is not completely convincing.

1. One of the most basic features of a debt contract is the idea that what triggers a shift in control is the non-payment of a debt. In other words, a debt contract has the form: 'I owe you P. If I pay, I keep control of my business. If I don't, you get control (or you can force me into bankruptcy).' However, the Aghion–Bolton contract does not have this property. Shifts in control are stochastic or contingent on the realization of a verifiable state of the world, θ, not on a failure to pay.

2. Related to this, a standard debt contract has the property that control shifts from the debtor to the creditor when the debtor's profits are low. However, it has been observed that this is not a necessary implication of the Aghion–Bolton model.

The next section discusses a model that attempts to deal with some of these problems. Before proceeding, however, I should note that the above features may not really be weaknesses at all. It may be a strength of the Aghion–Bolton model that it can explain financial arrangements that are more general than standard debt contracts since more general arrangements are indeed observed in practice.

2. A diversion model (based on Hart and Moore 1989)

I now consider a model where E's private benefit comes from his ability to divert future cash flows. Suppose there exists an extra date before the action a is chosen. At this date (date 1), the project earns a monetary return, y_1, which is non-verifiable. Assume that

efficiently. In some cases this will increase overall surplus. This has already been noted in n. 5.

E can divert or 'steal' y_1, i.e. that y_1 is a potential private benefit. However, E may be persuaded not to divert y_1, as will be seen shortly.

Identify the action a with the choice about whether to continue the project past date 1. More precisely, suppose that a decision must be made about what fraction of the project assets, $(1 - f)$, to liquidate (see Figure 5.1). Liquidation of a fraction $(1 - f)$ of the project yields a verifiable income $(1 - f)L$ at date 1 and a non-verifiable income fy_2 at date 2.[8] Suppose that E can divert fy_2 also, and so the continuation value of the project is another potential private benefit.

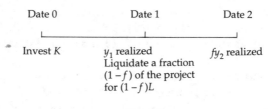

FIG. 5.1

The assumption that E can divert y_1 and fy_2 is of course extreme. It is meant to capture the idea that E has discretion over cash flows, e.g. that he can use them for perks rather than pay them out. With reference to the Aghion–Bolton model, $(1 - f)L$ corresponds to the verifiable income $y(a)$ and fy_2 to the private benefit $b(a)$.

Suppose that the project terminates at date 2 (the assets are

[8] Partial liquidation is permitted for reasons of analytical convenience. If liquidation is a 0 or 1 decision, then the model exhibits discontinuities that are both mathematically and economically troublesome. Note that, although partial liquidation is allowed *ex post*, the project is supposed to be indivisible *ex ante*. The analysis could easily be extended to the case of continuous project size, however. Note also that it is assumed that the fraction of the project to be liquidated, $(1 - f)$, is not *ex ante* contractible. One justification for this is that, if the assets are not truly homogeneous, it may not be clear what liquidating '10 per cent' of the assets means. Thus, a contract that specifies $f = \hat{f}$ may not be enforceable because it is not precise. Another possibility is to specify that enough assets should be liquidated to realize a specified monetary amount. However, it may be unclear whether the asset sales will yield the specified monetary amount until the assets have been sold (by which time it is too late to do anything about it if the monetary amount has not been realized).

worthless then), and the interest rate is zero. Allow also now for the possibility that the entrepreneur has some initial wealth w, where $w < K$ (w could be zero).

The analysis of this and the next section will be concerned with the case where y_1, y_2, and L are *perfectly certain*. Assume

(5.2) $\qquad\qquad\qquad y_2 > L,$

(5.3) $\qquad\qquad\qquad y_1 + y_2 > K \geq L.$

Inequality (5.2) says that it is always first-best efficient not to liquidate the project. (So, in the Aghion–Bolton terminology, the first-best optimal action $a^* = f^* = 1$.) Inequality (5.3) says that the project has positive net present value, and that the assets depreciate.

The first point to note is that there is no way to get E to pay out any of the date 2 receipts, fy_2, to C. The reason is that whatever part of fy_2 E has promised to C, E will default, diverting fy_2 to his own account. C has no leverage over E at date 2 since the project is over and the assets are worthless.[9]

In contrast, it *is* possible to get E to pay over part of y_1 to C. At this stage the project is still worth something to E. If the consequence of not making a payment is the loss of control of the project, then E may prefer to make the payment.

This suggests consideration of the following debt contract. E borrows $B \geq K - w$ at date 0 and promises to repay $\hat{P}$ at date 1. If E makes the repayment, he keeps control and has the right to continue the project until date 2. If E doesn't make the repayment, C has the right to terminate the project, in which case it is supposed that she receives all the liquidation receipts.[10] However, C may choose not to exercise her liquidation right; that is, renegotiation may take place.[11] As in the Aghion–Bolton model, it will be

---

[9] I rule out the possibility that C can get E convicted of theft if E does not repay fy_2. One justification is that there may be a small amount of uncertainty in the background, so that E can always claim that $y_2 = 0$.

[10] More complicated contracts could be conceived in which the liquidation receipts are divided in some pre-specified manner. Allowing these would not affect the analysis in the case of perfect certainty.

[11] It is assumed that the investor cannot run the business by herself and thereby realize the returns y_1, y_2. I take the point of view that the investor would have to hire a substitute manager, who could also divert y_1 and y_2. The best the investor can do by herself is to liquidate the assets for L.

supposed that E has all the bargaining power in any *ex post* renegotiation, as well as at date 0.

Analysis of the optimal debt contract

Make the simplifying assumption that E can liquidate assets himself at date 1 (without C's permission) in order to meet the debt payment $\hat{P}$.[12]

Since E has all the bargaining power, C will never receive more than L at date 1.[13] In particular, if $\hat{P} > L$, E will default at date 1 and beat C down to L in the renegotiation. That is, whatever $\hat{P}$ is chosen in the contract, C will receive

$$(5.4) \qquad\qquad P = \text{Min } \{\hat{P}, L\}.$$

Since only P is relevant, rather than $\hat{P}$, in what follows I represent a debt contract by the two numbers B and P (here P is the *actual* repayment), where $P \leq L$.

The next question to ask is: in what form is P received? Given (5.2), E has an incentive to pay as much as possible of P in the form of cash and as little as possible in the form of asset sales, i.e. liquidation. E's date 1 cash holding equals $B - (K - w) + y_1$. Thus, if $B - (K - w) + y_1 \geq P$, E can pay all of P in the form of cash and there will be no liquidation at date 1. (The fraction of assets, f, remaining in E's hands equals 1.) On the other hand, if $B - (K - w) + y_1 < P$, E pays over $B - (K - w) + y_1$ in the form of cash and the remainder of P is generated by asset sales; i.e. f satisfies

$$(5.5) \qquad\qquad B - (K - w) + y_1 + (1 - f)L = P.$$

The two cases can be summarized as follows:

$$(5.6) \qquad f = \text{Min } \left\{ 1, 1 - \frac{1}{L}(P - B + K - w - y_1) \right\}.$$

Since C must break even, B and P will be chosen so that

$$(5.7) \qquad\qquad L \geq P = B \geq K - w.$$

Substituting $P = B$ into (5.6) yields

---

[12] E cannot 'steal' the proceeds from such liquidation, however. I also suppose that any debt payment made by E to C is verifiable.

[13] I rule out the possibility that C can seize E's savings. (E will have savings if $B > K - w$.)

(5.8) $$f = \text{Min}\left\{1, 1 - \frac{1}{L}(K - w - y_1)\right\}.$$

The project will go ahead as long as two conditions are satisfied. First, there must be a solution to (5.7); that is,

(5.9) $$L \geq K - w.$$

Second, E's participation constraint must be satisfied; that is, E's payoff must exceed w, his initial wealth. This last condition can be written as $B - (K - w) + y_1 - \text{Min}[B - (K - w) + y_1, P] + fy_2 > w$, which, given $P = B$ and (5.5), can be simplified to

(5.10) $$y_1 + fy_2 + (1 - f)L > K;$$

i.e., the project has positive net present value, when account is taken of the fact that some liquidation occurs at date 1. Note that (5.3) implies that (5.10) is automatically satisfied if $f = 1$ in (5.8), i.e. if the first-best is achieved.[14]

Even though the two-period model with perfect certainty is very simple, it already exhibits some interesting properties. First, although the project may go ahead, there can be liquidation on the equilibrium path: this will happen if $f < 1$ in (5.8), i.e. if $K - w > y_1$. Second, some good projects will not be financed. (This will happen whenever (5.9) or (5.10) is not satisfied.) Third, if $L > K - w$, there is a continuum of solutions to (5.7), and hence a continuum of optimal debt contracts. In particular, although E requires only $(K - w)$ to finance the project, he can borrow anything up to L. (I will have more to say about this multiplicity in the next section.)

Examples 1 and 2 illustrate the two kinds of inefficiency: *ex post* inefficiency at date 1 and *ex ante* inefficiency at date 0.[15]

Example 1. Suppose $K = 90$, $w = 30$, $y_1 = 50$, $y_2 = 100$, $L = 60$.

Set $B = P = K - w$; that is, E borrows 60 and promises to repay 60 at date 1. Then E pays 50 of the 60 in the form of cash and the remaining 10 in the form of asset sales. (He liquidates ⅙ of the assets.) The first-best is not achieved.

---

[14] I have made the simplifying assumption that E has all the bargaining power in the debt renegotiation. The main features of the analysis generalize to the case where C has some bargaining power, but the details change. Among other things, C's *ex post* payoff now depends on y_2 as well as on L since C can use her bargaining power to capture some of y_2. On this, see Hart and Moore (1989, 1994a).

[15] Both types of inefficiency also arise in the Aghion–Bolton model.

It is worth going over the source of inefficiency in example 1. The assets are worth 100 in place and only 60 liquidated. Thus, in a first-best world there would be no liquidation: E would persuade C to postpone her debt and pay her 10 out of the 100 received at date 2. The trouble with such an arrangement in a second-best world is that E's promise is not credible. Whatever E may say in advance, C knows that at date 2 E will default and direct the 100 to himself. Hence C will liquidate inefficiently since it is the only way she can be repaid.

Example 2.   Suppose $K = 90$, $w = 30$, $y_1 = 100$, $y_2 = 50$, $L = 30$.

The project is obviously a profitable one (it yields 150 for an investment cost of 90) and in a first-best world it would be financed. However, in a second-best world it will not be. The reason is that a contribution of 60 is required from C. But the most that C can recover at date 1 is 30. Moreover, *even if C has all the bargaining power*, E will never pay more than 50 at date 1 since the assets are worth only 50 to him at this stage. Given this, C will refuse to participate.

In example 1 inefficiency occurs because E cannot commit to hand over the second-period payoff y_2 to C (in return for C agreeing not to liquidate any assets at date 1). In example 2, inefficiency occurs because E cannot commit to hand over the first-period payoff y_1 to C.

3. A multi-period model

There is no role for long-term debt in the above model since, given that the date 2 return, fy_2, is always diverted, the date 2 debt repayment is zero. However, long-term debt becomes possible in multi-period versions of the model. This section sketches a multi-period extension; a much more detailed exposition (albeit for a slightly different model) can be found in Hart and Moore (1994*a*).[16]

[16] Hart and Moore (1994*a*) develop a dynamic theory of debt under the assumption that, rather than being able to steal the project returns, E can quit, that is, withdraw his labour from the project. E can use this threat to force C to make concessions, so that E receives a significant fraction of future cash flows from the project. (There is a close parallel between Hart and Moore (1994*a*) and the model

Date 0	Date 1	Date 2	Date T–1	Date T
Invest K	y_1 realized Liquidate for L_1?	y_2 realized Liquidate for L_2?	y_{T-1} realized Liquidate for L_{T-1}?	y_T realized Liquidate for L_T=0?

Fig. 5.2

Continue to assume perfect certainty and a zero interest rate. Consider a project that costs K and yields a return stream $y_1, y_2, \ldots, y_T$, as in Figure 5.2. The project can be liquidated at date t for L_t, $t = 1, 2, \ldots, T - 1$, and it is worthless at date T. Write $L_0 \equiv K$ and suppose $L_0 \geq L_1 \geq L_2 \geq \ldots \geq L_{T-1}$ (i.e. the assets depreciate). Assume also the following generalizations of (5.2)–(5.3):

$$(5.11) \qquad \sum_{\tau=t+1}^{T} y_\tau > L_t \qquad \text{for all } t = 0, \ldots, T - 1.$$

Condition (5.11) says that the project's going concern value exceeds its liquidation value at every date (including the beginning of the project).

Since there is perfect certainty, one can, without loss of generality, confine attention to contracts that are never renegotiated; i.e. default never occurs.[17] For simplicity, the analysis also focuses on the case where the first-best is achieved, i.e. where no liquidation occurs in equilibrium. Consider a contract that specifies the repayment path $(P_1, P_2, \ldots, P_{T-1}, 0)$. (Without loss of generality, P_T can be set equal to zero, since E will divert the date T return.) Then, since E has all the bargaining power, the conditions for E not to default at dates $1, \ldots, T - 1$ are:

used in Part I of this book, where it was also supposed that an agent could withdraw his human capital in the absence of an agreement at date 1.) The Hart–Moore (1994a) model has some advantages over the one used here. First, in many ways, the quitting assumption is more appealing than the diversion assumption. Second, the model lends itself to a continuous-time formulation and it is easy to incorporate the idea that C has some bargaining power. However, it is more difficult to include uncertainty in the model. Since I wanted to deal with the uncertainty case, at least briefly, I have chosen to work with the diversion model.

[17] For a proof, see Hart and Moore (1994a). The idea is as follows. Suppose renegotiation does occur in equilibrium, at date t, say. Then at date 0 one can replace that part of the contract from date t onwards by the renegotiated contract; this yields a renegotiation-proof (or default-free) contract.

(5.12) $\sum_{\tau=t}^{T} P_{\tau} \leq L_t$ for all $t = 1, \ldots, T$.

That is, the total debt outstanding at any time cannot exceed the liquidation value of the project.[18]

It must also be the case that E can *afford* to make the repayments $P_1, \ldots, P_{T-1}$. The condition for this is

(5.13) $B - (K - w) + \sum_{\tau=0}^{t-1} y_{\tau} - \sum_{\tau=0}^{t-1} P_{\tau} \geq 0$ for all $t = 1, \ldots, T$,

where $y_0 \equiv P_0 \equiv 0$. That is, the amount borrowed, net of the sum allocated towards the project, plus the total cash flows that come in from the project, must be at least as great as the cumulative debt repayments. Given $B = \sum_{\tau=0}^{T} P_{\tau}$ (this is the break-even constraint for C), (5.13) can be rewritten as

(5.14) $\sum_{\tau=t}^{T} P_{\tau} \geq (K - w) - \sum_{\tau=0}^{t-1} y_{\tau}$ for all $t = 1, \ldots, T$.

Combining (5.12) and (5.14) yields necessary and sufficient conditions for the first-best to be achieved,

(5.15) $K - w - \sum_{\tau=0}^{t-1} y_{\tau} \leq L_t$ for all $t = 1, \ldots, T$,

which can be rewritten as

(5.16) $w \geq K - \underset{t=1,\ldots,T}{\text{Min}} \ (L_t + \sum_{\tau=0}^{t-1} y_{\tau})$.

In general, there will be a continuum of repayment paths satisfying (5.12) and (5.14) (just as in the two-period model). (There is an even larger class of debt contracts sustaining these repayment paths since feasible debt contracts include those that are renegotiated on the equilibrium path, e.g. contracts consisting of large amounts of short-term debt that is rolled over.) In particular, there is a *fastest* repayment path, where E's outstanding indebtedness at each date (including date 0) is minimal; a *slowest* repayment path, where E's outstanding indebtedness at each date is

---

[18] If (5.12) does not hold, E will default and renegotiate the debt down to L_t. The formal proof of this is subtle and uses an induction argument. See Hart and Moore (1994a).

maximal; and everything in between. The fastest repayment path is given by $\underline{B} = K - w$, and, for all t,

(5.17) $$\underline{P}_t = \begin{cases} y_\tau & \text{if } \displaystyle\sum_{\tau=1}^{t} y_\tau \leq K - w, \\[2em] K - w - \displaystyle\sum_{\tau=1}^{t-1} \underline{P}_t & \text{if } \displaystyle\sum_{\tau=1}^{t} y_\tau > K - w. \end{cases}$$

That is, E borrows as little as possible and pays back as fast as possible.[19] The slowest repayment path is given by $\bar{B} = L_1$, and

(5.18) $$\bar{P}_t = L_t - L_{t+1} \equiv l_t, \quad t = 1, \ldots, T - 1.$$

Here l_t is the amount by which the project assets depreciate between date t and date $(t + 1)$. That is, E borrows as much as possible and pays back as slowly as possible. (E's total indebtedness is L_t at every date; recall that indebtedness cannot exceed L_t since otherwise E will default.)

The repayment paths can be used to obtain some intuition for (5.16). For simplicity, assume that, although the project returns y_t can initially be less than the depreciation flows l_t, once they exceed them (which they eventually must by (5.11)), they exceed them in all subsequent periods; in other words,

(5.19)   there exists t^* such that $y_t \leq l_t$ for $t \leq t^*$,

and $y_t \geq l_t$ for $t > t^*$.

Then it is easy to see that $L_t + \sum_{\tau=0}^{t-1} y_\tau$ is decreasing for $t \leq t^* + 1$, increasing for $t \geq t^* + 1$, and reaches a minimum, M say, at $t = t^* + 1$. To understand (5.16) in this case, note that along the slowest repayment path E borrows L_1 and repays at the rate of l_t. Prior to date t^*, E's cash flow y_t falls short of l_t. How does E cover the repayments? The answer is that E needs to put aside part of the initial sum borrowed in a (private) savings account, out of which he makes the shortfall $l_t - y_t$. The size of the necessary savings account is

$$\sum_{\tau=1}^{t^*} (l_t - y_t),$$

---

[19] In Hart and Moore (1994a), the fastest path is defined slightly differently. It is supposed that E continues to pay y_t to C *after* he has repaid his debt and then receives a lump-sum transfer from C at date T. I ignore this possibility here.

implying that the amount left of L_1 (the initial loan) which can be used to buy project assets—the *debt capacity*—is

$$L_1 - \sum_{\tau=1}^{t^*} (l_t - y_t) = L_{t^*+1} + y_1 + \cdots + y_{t^*}$$

$$= \underset{t=1, \cdots, T}{\text{Min}} \left(L_t + \sum_{\tau=0}^{t-1} y_\tau \right)$$

$$\equiv M.$$

In other words, E must finance the difference, $K - M$, out of his initial wealth w. But this is precisely what (5.16) tells us.

As noted, there is a continuum of feasible repayment paths. Once (a reasonable amount of) uncertainty is introduced, the multiplicity will typically disappear (see §4). Another way to break the multiplicity is to suppose that E and C have reinvestment opportunities over and above those represented by the project. For example, suppose E can reinvest any extra money he has (including cash flows from the project) at a positive interest rate, whereas reinvestment by C occurs at the market interest rate of zero. Then it is not difficult to show that the unique optimal repayment path is the slowest one. The reason is that this gives E the maximum ability to make additional reinvestments, which contribute to total surplus. On the other hand, if C can reinvest at a positive interest rate, whereas E faces a zero interest rate, then the unique optimal repayment path is the *fastest* one, since this gives C the maximum ability to make additional reinvestments. (For details, see Hart and Moore (1994*a*).)

In the case of no reinvestments, (5.16)–(5.18) can be used to obtain further insight into the kinds of project that will be financed, and the determinants of the repayment paths.

DEFINITION 1. The assets become *longer lived*, or *more durable*, if L_t increases for all $1 \le t \le T - 1$.

DEFINITION 2. The project returns become more *front-loaded* if $\sum_{\tau=1}^{t} y_\tau$ increases for all $1 \le t \le T$.

Note that the second definition is consistent with $\sum_{\tau=1}^{T} y_\tau$ staying the same; that is, although the returns arrive more quickly, the total value of the project may be constant.

It is now easy to use (5.16)–(5.18) to establish the following:

A If the project assets become more durable, then the project is more likely to be undertaken (the right-hand side of (5.15) increases for all t and so the right-hand side of (5.16) decreases) and the slowest repayment path becomes slower ($\sum_{\tau=t}^{T} \bar{P}_\tau$ increases for all $t = 1, \ldots, T$).

B If the project returns become more front-loaded, then the project is more likely to be undertaken (the left-hand side of (5.15) decreases for all t and so the right-hand side of (5.16) decreases) and the fastest repayment path become faster ($\sum_{\tau=t}^{T} \underline{P}_\tau$ decreases for all $t = 1, \ldots, T$).

As a conclusion to this section, it is useful to consider some of the empirical evidence about the determinants of debt contracts and maturity structure.[20] The evidence suggests that long-term loans are used for property, leasehold improvements, machinery, and the like. Also, debt with the longest term is typically on property: real estate mortgages. Short-term loans, on the other hand, tend to be used for working capital purposes—e.g. payroll needs, the financing of inventory, and the smoothing of seasonal imbalances. Moreover, the collateral is usually made up of assets such as the inventories or the accounts receivable.[21]

The analysis is consistent with the evidence. The analysis has shown that, if assets are long-lived, they will support long-term debt. Property and machinery are obvious examples of highly durable assets. Conversely, if the assets are short-lived, as in the case of inventories (which may not retain their value, or which can be disposed of relatively easily) or accounts receivable, then the debt is likely to be short-term.

The evidence on short-term financing is also consistent with result B, i.e. that the faster the returns arrive, the shorter will be the maturity of debt (in the fastest path). A firm that is raising money for payroll needs, for purchasing inventory, or for smoothing seasonal imbalances, is typically the kind of firm whose returns will be coming in soon.

There is also evidence suggesting that the amount of 'equity' an entrepreneur has to put into the project himself, and the value of

---

[20] For a more detailed exposition of what follows, see Hart and Moore (1994a).
[21] See Dunkelberg and Scott (1985: tables 6, 7, 10, 12, and 13) and Dennis *et al.* (1988: table 3.11).

the collateralized assets, are important factors in determining whether a project is financed.[22] This finding is hardly surprising, but it fits in well with the model, in light of result (A) and the fact that w is a crucial variable in determining whether (5.16) is satisfied.

Finally, the model can explain the conventional wisdom among practitioners that 'assets should be matched with liabilities'. To be precise, it has been shown that liabilities (namely the debt repayments $P_1, P_2, \ldots, P_T$) should be matched either with the return stream $(y_1, y_2, \ldots, y_T)$ (in the case of the fastest repayment path), or with the rate of depreciation $(l_1, l_2, \ldots, l_{T-1})$ (in the case of the slowest repayment path).[23]

I am not suggesting that the above evidence is hard to explain or that other theories cannot explain it. However, it is perhaps a selling point of the model that, as well as being simple and tractable, it can be used to understand the basic facts about maturity structure.

4. The case of uncertainty

Sections 2 and 3 showed that in the case of perfect certainty (without reinvestment opportunities) there is a continuum of feasible repayment paths, and an even larger class of optimal debt contracts. One way to reduce or eliminate the indeterminacy is to introduce uncertainty. Unfortunately, the uncertainty case is not yet very well understood, and so I will provide only a brief discussion. (This section is based on Hart and Moore (1989).)

[22] See the regularly featured articles 'Lending to . . .' in the *Journal of Commercial Bank Lending*. Also see Dunkelberg and Scott (1985: tables 1, 2, 12, 13), Dennis *et al.* (1988: table 3.7), and Smollen *et al.* (1977: 21). For more formal empirical work on the determinants of debt levels, see Long and Malitz (1985) and Titman and Wessels (1988).

[23] There is an important caveat. The analysis has concentrated on equilibrium repayment paths. As noted, in a deterministic model one can, without loss of generality, focus on debt contracts that are never renegotiated. However, other contracts, which are renegotiated, could have yielded the same intertemporal allocation, e.g. a contract consisting of a large amount of short-term debt that is rolled over. Thus, in terms of the empirical evidence, the analysis has actually explained the maturity of repayment paths rather than the maturity of the debt contracts themselves.

Return to the two-period model (Section 2). Suppose now that the variables y_1, y_2, L are uncertain at date 0, but that their realizations are learned by both parties at date 1. (There is symmetric information throughout.) However, although y_1, y_2, and L are observable, they are not verifiable, and so state-contingent debt contracts cannot be written. In addition, both parties are risk-neutral. Make the following generalizations of (5.2)–(5.3):

(5.20) $\qquad\qquad y_2 \geq L$ with probability 1,

(5.21) $\qquad\qquad E\,(y_1 + y_2) > K.$

(Here E denotes the expectations operator.)

Denote a debt contract by $(B,\hat{P})$, where $B \geq K - w$ is the amount borrowed and $\hat{P}$ is the amount owed at date 1. Since all uncertainty is resolved at date 1, equations (5.4) and (5.6) still apply. The condition for C to break even is now

(5.22) $\qquad\qquad E[\text{Min}\{\hat{P}, L\}] = B,$

where the expectation is taken with respect to L. The condition for E to participate is $E\,[B - (K - w) + y_1 - \text{Min}\,(B - (K - w) + y_1, P) + fy_2] > w$, where $P = \text{Min}\,\{\hat{P},L\}$. Given (5.16) and (5.22), this can be simplified to

(5.23) $\qquad\qquad E\,(y_1 + fy_2 + (1 - f)\,L) > K;$

i.e., the project has positive expected net present value, when account is taken of the fact that some liquidation occurs at date 1. Another way to understand (5.23) is to note that E's payoff (net of his initial wealth w) plus C's net payoff equals the expected net present value of the project; since C breaks even, it follows that E's (net) payoff is $E[y_1 + fy_2 + (1 - f)\,L] - K$.

I now present two examples. In the first it is optimal to set $B = K - w$. In the second it is optimal to set $B > K - w$. The examples stand in contrast to the case of certainty where $B = K - w$ and $B > K - w$ are typically both optimal (if $L > K - w$).

Example 3. Suppose $K = 90$, $w = 50$ and there are two equally likely states:

State 1: $y_1 = 50$, $\quad y_2 = 100$, $\quad L = 80$.
State 2: $y_1 = 40$, $\quad y_2 = 100$, $\quad L = 30$.

Consider the contract $B = K - w = 40$ and $\hat{P} = 50$. In state 1, E repays 50. In state 2, E renegotiates the payment down to 30. C's average return is 40, and hence C breaks even. In both states $f = 1$, i.e. the first-best is achieved and there is no inefficiency.

Now consider a contract where $B = 40 + \alpha$, and $\alpha > 0$. Then C will be fully repaid in state 1 (as long as $\hat{P} \leq 80$), but will receive only 30 in state 2. Hence, in order for C to break even, $\hat{P}$ must equal $50 + 2\alpha$. (C then receives $\frac{1}{2}(50 + 2\alpha) + \frac{1}{2}30 = 40 + \alpha$.) But E's wealth in state 1 is only $50 + \alpha$ (50 from the project return plus α held over from date 0). Thus, there will be liquidation in state 1 and the first-best is not achieved.

The next example shows that $B > K - w$ may be optimal.

Example 4. Suppose $K = 20$, $w = 10$, and there are two equally likely states:

State 1: $y_1 = 0$, $y_2 = 20$, $L = 20$.
State 2: $y_1 = 0$, $y_2 = 40$, $L = 10$.

Consider the contract $B = K - w = 10$ and $\hat{P} = 10$. C receives 10 in both states from liquidation sales. (E has no cash.) In state 1, $f = 0.5$. In state 2, $f = 0$. E's expected return $= E\,(fy_2) = 0.5(0.5)\,20 = 5$.

Now consider a contract $(B, \hat{P})$, where $B > 10$ and $\hat{P} \leq 20$. C will receive $\hat{P}$ in state 1 and 10 in state 2, and so for C to break even $\hat{P} = 2B - 10$. In state 1 E pays over $B - 10$ (his remaining wealth) and $f = 1 - B/20$ (so B is generated in asset sales). In state 2 E pays over $B - 10$ and $f = (B{-}10)/10$ (so $20 - B$ is generated in asset sales). C breaks even and E's expected return $= E\,(fy_2) = (1/2)\,(1 - B/20)\,20 + (1/2)\,[(B{-}10)/10]\,40 = 3B/2 - 10$, which achieves a maximum at $B = 15$. (At this B, $\hat{P} = 20$.) Thus, the optimal contract is $B = 15$, $\hat{P} = 20$. E's expected return $= 12.5$.

Basically, what's going on here is that it helps when E has some wealth left over from date 0 since this allows him to 'buy back' the assets at date 1, with a considerable reduction in inefficiency in state 2. (Liquidation does not matter in state 1 since, given that $y_2 = L$, it has no social cost.)

In future work, it would be desirable to obtain some general results about the nature of the optimal debt contract for the case of uncertainty. One difficulty is that it is not clear that attention should be confined to contracts of the form (B,P). For example, it might be optimal to arrange that in default states E should receive some part of the liquidation receipts, in order to encourage E and

C to renegotiate in a 'more efficient manner'.[24] Another idea is to make E the owner of the project, but give C an option to buy E out at a specified price.[25] Figuring out the class of feasible contracts when there is uncertainty is an important, but difficult, topic for future research.

5. *Multiple investors and hard budget constraints*

The analysis has so far considered the case of one investor. In reality, of course, there will often be more than one. This might be because no investor is rich enough to finance the project alone, or because no investor wishes to bear the risk of financing the project alone (if investors are risk-averse). There is another reason for multiple investors, however: to harden E's budget constraint.[26]

To understand this idea, return to the two-period model of Sections 2 and 4. In the one-investor case the entrepreneur may default even when he can pay his debts, in order to renegotiate the debt payment down to L. Unfortunately, such a strategic default can have undesirable *ex ante* consequences. In particular, it puts a ceiling on the investor's return from the project and may deter the investor from financing certain projects.[27]

It has been pointed out in the literature that multiple investors may make strategic default less attractive (see e.g. Bolton and Scharfstein 1994).[28] The basic idea is that renegotiation is more likely to break down with multiple investors—because of

---

[24] This idea is explored by Harris and Raviv (1995).

[25] For example, suppose $K = 300$, $w = 260$, and there are three states. In state 1 (probability $1/10$), $y_1 = 10$, $y_2 = 200$, $L = 105$. In state 2 (probability $2/5$), $y_1 = 10$, $y_2 = 20$, $L = 80$. In state 3 (probability $1/2$), $y_1 = 50$, $y_2 = 200$, $L = 200$. Then a (B,P) contract does not achieve the first-best. However, the following 'option-to-own' contract does: E puts 260 into the project and is the owner in all states of the world. However, C has the option to buy the project assets for 120. With such a contract, C will exercise her option only in state 3, where there are no social costs of liquidation. In addition, C breaks even under the contract.

[26] The notion of a hard budget constraint is due to Kornai (1980).

[27] For instance, take example 2 but suppose that $y_2 = 70$. Then in the absence of renegotiation a debt contract with repayment $P = 60$ achieves the first-best: E can afford the repayment and prefers to pay rather than face liquidation, and C breaks even. In contrast, in the presence of renegotiation, E will default and beat C down to 30. Anticipating this, C refuses to finance the project.

[28] A related idea is explored in Dewatripont and Maskin (1990).

free-rider and hold-out problems combined with asymmetric information—and so the entrepreneur may simply choose to pay P even when $P > L$.

A simple way to understand this is to consider the case where there are N investors, each owed P/N. Suppose E defaults and makes the following (take-it-or-leave-it) offer to the investors: 'I propose that at least M of you agree to forgive your debt down to (slightly above) L/N. Otherwise bankruptcy and liquidation will ensue.' Then each investor should reason as follows: 'My decision to forgive my debt is very unlikely to be pivotal in determining whether the critical number M agrees to forgive. (With a small amount of noise, the probability that any investor is pivotal can be shown to tend to zero as $N \to \infty$ if M/N is bounded away from zero and from one.) If I think that at least M investors will forgive, I am better off not forgiving since E will then have to pay me the full amount P/N. If I think the critical number M will not forgive, then there is certainly no advantage to my forgiving and there may be a disadvantage if I have a claim in bankruptcy to L/N rather than P/N.'

Given this logic, no creditor will accept E's offer, and E's attempt to reduce the debt will fail. Moreover, anticipating this, E will pay the full amount owed, P.[29]

Unfortunately, the inflexibility exhibited by a large number of creditors deters not only strategic default, but also productive renegotiation. Consider example 3. In state 2, E cannot pay his debt of 50. In the absence of renegotiation, liquidation would occur at a social cost of $y_2 - L = 70$. With renegotiation, the debt is reduced to 30 and a more efficient outcome is achieved. However, it may be difficult to persuade a large number of creditors to reduce the debt from 50 to 30. The reason is similar to that given above. Each creditor will argue that her decision to forgive is unlikely to be pivotal in determining whether the renegotiation succeeds. If the creditor expects enough other people to forgive, it

---

[29] For formalizations of this idea, see Aggarwal (1994), Gertner and Scharfstein (1991), Holmstrom and Nalebuff (1992), Mailath and Postlewaite (1990), and Rob (1989). One strategy the entrepreneur might adopt is to require unanimous acceptance of his offer, i.e. to set $M = N$, thus making each creditor pivotal. However, when there are many creditors unanimity is hard to achieve: it takes only one ('crazy') creditor with a different belief from the others (e.g. the creditor might think the liquidation value of the project is substantially above L), or a different agenda, to defeat a unanimity offer.

is better for her not to forgive (i.e. to hold-out or free-ride) since that way she gets her full $50/N$. On the other hand, there is certainly no reason to forgive in the event that the renegotiation fails. Since each creditor thinks the same way, a socially desirable renegotiation fails.[30]

So there are costs and benefits from having multiple investors. Multiple investors are good at deterring strategic default but bad at preventing productive renegotiation.[31] It may be possible to develop a theory of the optimal number of creditors along these lines.[32]

So far I have considered the case of multiple investors with the same claim. Another interesting line of research—due to Dewatripont and Tirole (1994) and Berglof and von Thadden (1994)—looks at multiple investors with different types of claims. This is discussed briefly below.

---

[30] It is not being suggested that debt renegotiations always fail in practice. However, Gilson *et al.* (1990), in a study of the companies listed on the New York and American Stock Exchanges that were in severe financial distress during 1978–87, found that workouts fail more than 50 per cent of the time and are more likely to fail the larger the number of creditors. See also Gilson (1991) and Asquith *et al.* (1994), and, for a survey of financial distress, John (1993). One way to make debt renegotiation easier is to include a provision in the initial debt contract that the aggregate debt level can be reduced as long as a majority of creditors approve (i.e. the majority's views are binding on the minority). (It turns out that the Trust Indenture Act of 1939 makes such a provision illegal in the USA for public debt.) The problem with such an arrangement is that, when there are large numbers of creditors, no individual creditor has a strong incentive to vote 'intelligently' (i.e. to incur the cost of collecting information about the firm's financial position), or even to vote at all, since her vote is unlikely to affect the outcome. Thus, one cannot be confident that creditors will be able to distinguish between situations of involuntary default, where debt forgiveness should be encouraged, and situations of strategic default, where it should be resisted.

[31] In arguing that multiple creditors will deter strategic default, I have supposed that E loses control of the project if it is liquidated. However, it is not uncommon for a delinquent debtor to buy back project assets in a liquidation sale (for something close to L). If this strategy is open to E, then he faces a soft budget constraint however many creditors there are.

[32] Leveraged buy-out transactions may be cases where the benefits of a hard budget constraint are large relative to the costs. In these transactions a company is purchased, often by incumbent management, through the issuance of debt to a large number of investors. A desirable feature of such transactions is that managers have a strong incentive to work hard since, if they do not, they risk bankruptcy. Leveraged buy-out transactions were particularly popular in the USA in the 1980s (see Jensen 1989).

6. Related work

There is a considerable literature on financial contracting that is related directly or indirectly to the work described above. Unfortunately, I have space to mention only a few contributions and themes. The Bolton–Scharfstein (1990) paper has already been noted. This paper develops a model that is similar in many ways to the Hart–Moore (1989) model; the main difference is that the penalty for nonpayment of debt is that the creditor withholds future finance rather than liquidating existing assets.[33] I have also mentioned the costly state verification model of Townsend and Gale-Hellwig—a detailed analysis of which is provided in the Appendix. The CSV model is based on comprehensive contracting ideas but it shares the feature of both the Hart–Moore and Bolton–Scharfstein models that a debtor pays his debts only because he will be penalized otherwise. In the CSV model, however, the penalty is that the debtor is *inspected*.

Although most of the analysis of this chapter has been concerned with debt levels rather than with debt maturity, the structure of repayment paths for the special case where returns and liquidation values are perfectly certain was also studied. A rather different approach to debt maturity is contained in some interesting work by Diamond (1991). Diamond analyses the trade-off between short-term and long-term debt in a two-period model which combines asymmetric information and incomplete contracts. He argues that an entrepreneur who knows that his project is profitable will finance it with short-term debt—with the intention of refinancing later on when new information arrives—while an entrepreneur who knows that his project is unprofitable will use long-term debt. The reason is that the 'high-quality' entrepreneur is prepared to bear the risk that the new information about the project's profitability will be adverse, and that the project will therefore not be refinanced, while the low-quality entrepreneur is not prepared to bear this risk.[34]

---

[33] Neher (1994) explores the idea that creditors can threaten to withhold future finance in a dynamic model of a start-up venture.

[34] The idea that an agent may use the contract he writes to signal something about his type may also be found in Aghion and Bolton (1987) and Hermalin (1988).

One benefit of the Diamond approach is that it pins down the optimal contract as well as the optimal repayment path. (In contrast in the perfect certainty model analysed in Section 3, there were many optimal contracts, most of which were renegotiated along the equilibrium path.) However, it is not clear how easy it is to generalize the model to many periods.

The chapter briefly considered the role of multiple investors in hardening the entrepreneur's budget constraint. The analysis focused on the case of identical creditors. Another possibility is to have investors with *different* claims. Two interesting papers that explore this theme are Dewatripont and Tirole (1994) and Berglof and von Thadden (1994). Dewatripont and Tirole consider a model in which the firm's profit is verifiable but the entrepreneur has an unverifiable effort choice. They show that it is optimal to have two outside investors holding debt and equity in different proportions. (Debt-holders and equity-holders are distinguished partly by the fact that they have different claims on verifiable profit.) The basic idea is that, if both investors hold debt and equity in the same proportions, the investors will be too soft on the entrepreneur, i.e. they won't intervene enough. In particular, they won't liquidate the firm if first-period profits are low because the value of continuation may exceed the value of liquidation (as shareholders, they see the upside gains as well as the downside losses). In contrast, if one of the investors holds debt and the firm defaults in the first period, this investor—to whom control now shifts—will be eager to liquidate (since she doesn't see the upside gains from continuation). As a result, the entrepreneur will be forced to make concessions and will also have a strong incentive to avoid default.

Berglof and von Thadden, in independent but related research, show that similar considerations explain why a firm's short-term and long-term debt should be allocated to different investors. In their analysis, the short-term creditor plays the role of the aggressive creditor in the Dewatripont–Tirole model, while the long-term creditor plays the role of the passive shareholder.

I close this chapter by mentioning two directions for future research. First, the models discussed in this chapter portray equity in a rather rudimentary manner. Either a firm's profit is unverifiable—in which case an equity-holder receives a return only because of her ability to hold up the entrepreneur. (For example, in the Hart–Moore (1989) model, if $\hat{P} = \infty$, the investor, who in effect owns the assets, negotiates for an explicit payment at date 1 in return for not liquidating the project.) Or the firm's profit is, at least partly, verifiable (as in the Aghion–Bolton model)—in which case an investor's return can be in the form of a contractually specified payment. In practice, equity-holders often get substantial returns in the form of dividends that are neither explicitly negotiated for, nor contractually specified. (A dividend is a discretionary payment made by management.) It would be very desirable to extend the analysis of this chapter to explain dividend payments of this sort, and thereby provide a more interesting role for equity finance. (Chapter 6 provides a further discussion of equity finance.)

Second, the models of this chapter have been partial equilibrium in nature. Among other things, they have taken the liquidation value of the project assets to be exogenous. In reality, however, liquidation values—the resale value of the project assets—will depend on the financial position of other entrepreneurs and investors, since such parties are the potential purchasers of these assets. The resulting interaction and feedback effects have been studied in two very interesting recent papers by Shleifer and Vishny (1992) and Kiyotaki and Moore (1995). Shleifer and Vishny show that, because of these interactions, firms in cyclical industries will rely less on debt finance, because, when they are financially distressed, potential purchasers—other firms in the same industry—will also be financially distressed and so liquidation values will be low. Kiyotaki and Moore show that feedback effects may cause fluctuations in demand to be amplified: a reduction in the demand for and price of capital goods may lead to further reductions in demand as firms whose collateral has diminished in value find it difficult to borrow for further investment.

The Shleifer–Vishny and Kiyotaki–Moore papers are significant first steps in the general equilibrium analysis of financial contracting. Much remains to be done on this topic.

APPENDIX

The costly state verification approach

In this appendix, a simple version of the CSV approach is described. Consider a risk-neutral entrepreneur, E, who has no initial wealth and wants to invest in a project costing K. The entrepreneur approaches a rich risk-neutral investor, C, to provide the funds. If the investment is undertaken, it yields a return $\tilde{y}$ at date 1. The realization of $\tilde{y}$ is learned by E at date 1, but not by C. That is, there is asymmetric information at date 1. However, this asymmetry of information can be removed if C 'inspects' E at cost c. For simplicity, take the interest rate to be zero. Also suppose that there is symmetric information at date 0 and that the probability distribution F of $\tilde{y}$ has a density function f with support $[\underline{y},\bar{y}]$. The question is: will the investment be undertaken? (See Figure 5A.1 for a time-line.)

The well-known revelation principle tells us that attention can be restricted to contracts (or mechanisms) in which E makes a truthful announcement about y at date 1 (see Fudenberg and Tirole 1991: ch. 7). Depending on what E announces, the contract then specifies whether inspection or non-inspection should occur and how much E must hand over to C.

CONTRACT (A1)   A (deterministic) contract specifies an inspection function $B : \mathbb{R}_+ \to \{0,1\}$ and sharing rules $s : \mathbb{R}_+ \to \mathbb{R}$, $\bar{s} : \mathbb{R}_+ \times \mathbb{R}_+ \to \mathbb{R}$. The interpretation is as follows. E announces y^a at date 1. If $B(y^a) = 0$, no inspection takes place and E hands over $s(y^a)$ to C, keeping the remainder $y - s(y^a)$ for himself. If $B(y^a) = 1$, C inspects E (at a cost of c, paid by C)

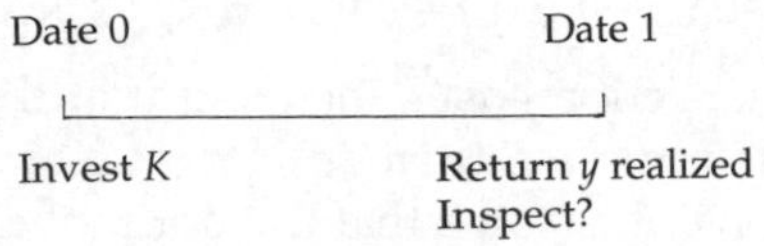

Date 0   Date 1

Invest K Return y realized
                          Inspect?

FIG. 5A.1

and C receives $\bar{s}(y^a,y)$, where y is the inspected value. In this case, E keeps $y - \bar{s}(y^a,y)$ for himself.

Simplify contract (A1) as follows. Since the goal is to encourage truth-telling, it is always optimal to set $\bar{s}(y^a,y) = y$ if $y^a \neq y$. That is, E should receive nothing if an inspection reveals that he has lied. It follows that E will lie only if his false announcement y^a satisfies $B(y^a) = 0$. Define

(5A.1) $\hat{B} = \{y \mid B(y) = 0\}$ to be the non-inspection region,

$\bar{B} = \{y \mid B(y) = 1\}$ to be the inspection region.

The relevant truth-telling (or incentive compatibility) constraints are then that (i) E should not announce $y^a \in \hat{B}$ different from the true $y \in \hat{B}$; (ii) E should not announce $y^a \in \hat{B}$ different from the true $y \in \bar{B}$.

(i) implies that $s(y)$ is a constant, $\hat{s}$ say, on $\hat{B}$. Otherwise, whenever $y \in \hat{B}$ E would announce the y^a that minimizes $s(y)$ on $\hat{B}$ (since E receives $y - s(y^a)$ and is not inspected). (ii) implies that $\hat{s} \geq \bar{s}(y,y)$ for $y \in \bar{B}$, since otherwise E would announce $y \in \hat{B}$ rather than $y \in \bar{B}$.

Finally, $s(y) \leq y$ for all $y \in \hat{B}$ and $\bar{s}(y,y) \leq y$ for all $y \in \bar{B}$, since otherwise it is not feasible for E to tell the truth.

The above observations can be summarized as follows, where $\bar{s}(y,y) \equiv s(y)$:

(5A.2a) $s(y) \equiv \hat{s}$ on $\hat{B}$,

(5A.2b) $\hat{s} \geq \bar{s}(y,y) \equiv s(y)$ on $\bar{B}$,

(5A.2c) $s(y) \leq y$ for all y.

An optimal contract is a mechanism $(s(y), B(y))$ satisfying (5A.2a)–(c) that maximizes E's return,

(5A.3) $\int (y - s(y)) \, dF(y)$,

subject to C's breaking even:

(5A.4) $\int (s(y) - cB(y)) \, dF(y) \geq K$.

Note that the inspection cost—incurred if and only if $B(y) = 1$—has been included in C's return.

The next proposition states that the optimal contract has a very simple form. It is characterized by an amount that E owes C, s^*. If $y \geq s^*$, E pays this amount and is not inspected. If $y < s^*$, E is inspected and C receives the whole of y. If 'inspection' is interpreted as 'bankruptcy', then the optimal contract has the character of a standard debt contract with repayment s^*. The proposition is proved in Gale and Hellwig (1985).

PROPOSITION A1. Assume that the project goes ahead, i.e. that there is a mechanism satisfying (5A.2) and (5A.4). Then the optimal contract has the following form (ignoring sets of measure zero): For some s^*, $\hat{B} = \{y \mid y \geq s^*\}$, $\bar{B} = \{y \mid y < s^*\}$, $s(y) = s^*$ for $y \in \hat{B}$, $s(y) = y$ for $y \in \bar{B}$.

Proposition A1 is the main result of the CSV theory and explains the use of debt financing. However, both the proposition and the CSV approach itself are subject to various qualifications.

1. Proposition A1 is derived under the assumption that only deterministic contracts are feasible. It is easy to see, however, that a stochastic scheme may improve matters. Consider the simple case where y takes on two values, $\bar{y}$ with probability σ and $\underline{y}$ with probability $(1 - \sigma)$ and suppose $\bar{y} < K$ and $\sigma\bar{y} + (1 - \sigma) \, \underline{y} > K$. (The argument generalizes to the case of continuous y.) An optimal deterministic contract will specify a payment s^* where $\bar{y} > s^* > \underline{y}$. As a result, inspection takes place with probability 1 when $y = \bar{y}$.

Now consider the following stochastic contract:

CONTRACT (A2). E announces $\bar{y}$ or $\underline{y}$. If he announces $\bar{y}$, he pays s^* to C. If he announces $\underline{y}$, then with probability $(1 - \rho)$ he is not inspected and pays $\underline{y}$ to C; and with probability ρ he is inspected and pays everything to C. Here ρ is chosen so that

(5A.5) $$\bar{y} - s^* = (1 - \rho)(\bar{y} - \underline{y}).$$

(5A.5) ensures that the stochastic contract satisfies the truth-telling constraints. In state $\bar{y}$, E is prepared to announce $\bar{y}$ since he is indifferent between telling the truth and announcing that the state is $\underline{y}$. On the other hand, in state $\underline{y}$ E must tell the truth since he cannot afford the payment s^*.

This stochastic contract is Pareto-superior to the deterministic debt contract. E receives the same payoffs in both states (($\bar{y} - s^*$) in state $\bar{y}$, zero in state $\underline{y}$), while C receives the same gross payoffs (s^* in state $\bar{y}$, $\underline{y}$ in state $\underline{y}$), but with probability $(1 - \rho)$ avoids inspection costs in state $\underline{y}$. Obviously, s^* could be adjusted so that both E and C are better off than in the deterministic contract.

The main problem with stochastic contracts is that they cannot easily be interpreted as debt. (For a general analysis of stochastic contracts, see Mookherjee and Png (1989).) The contract in (5A.5) seems closer to a (stochastic) auditing scheme than to a debt contract. I return to this theme in point 5 below.

2. The CSV model described above supposes that C can commit to a particular inspection rule and that there is no possibility of *ex post* renegotiation. To see why this is important, consider the following example. Suppose the entrepreneur's return $\tilde{y} = 100$ with probability 1 and the verification cost $c = 20$. According to the CSV model, a debt contract in which the entrepreneur promises to pay 90 can be enforced. The reason is that, *ex post*, the entrepreneur prefers to pay 90 and be left with 10 than default and get nothing. However, this assumes that the investor's threat to incur the verification cost and confiscate the entrepreneur's funds is credible. Suppose the entrepreneur hands over just above 80 instead of the promised 90. Then the investor (unless she has a reputation to uphold) will choose not to inspect the firm since the gain is less than the verification cost of 20. Thus, in the absence of a commitment not to revise or renegotiate the verification decision, the most that the investor can force the entrepreneur to pay is 80.

In the above example, the analysis of renegotiation is relatively straightforward. However, matters become a great deal more complicated when the entrepreneur's payoff $\tilde{y}$ is uncertain. The reason is that the amount handed over by the entrepreneur is a signal of his total return. As in many signalling models, there can be multiple *ex post* equilibria, with the signal being interpreted in various ways. While refinements can eliminate some of these equilibria, the analysis of optimal *ex ante* contracts quickly becomes complicated (see Gale and Hellwig 1989).

3. In reality, debt typically coexists with equity as a financial claim on a firm. Yet the CSV model does not seem able to explain the existence of dividends and (outside) equity. The point is that in non-bankruptcy states E always makes a payment that is just enough to satisfy creditors; there is never anything left over for other claimants (except of course E himself—in this respect E is the 100 per cent equity holder). And, of course, in bankruptcy states outside shareholders receive nothing because there is not enough even to satisfy creditors. (As noted, the incomplete contracting models of debt described in the text also have a hard time

explaining dividends. However, they are consistent with a positive value of equity since equity-holders can use their power to liquidate the firm to extract a payment from the entrepreneur.)

4. The cost c of verifying the state of the world plays a crucial role in the CSV model. But what is c? Is it an auditing cost, the legal cost of bankruptcy proceedings, or what? The reason this matters is that for the model's results to be interesting c must be reasonably large. Otherwise one could approximate the first-best by inspecting E all the time. However, auditing costs do not seem that large and empirical work has not identified large (direct) bankruptcy costs (see e.g. Warner 1977).

5. Perhaps most important of all, the model is based on a comprehensive contracting/mechanism design view of the world. According to such a view, the contracting parties sit down at date 0 and write a renegotiation-proof contract that specifies each party's obligations in every future contingency. This appendix has shown that under a simple set of assumptions the optimal contract can be interpreted as a debt contract. However, this is unlikely to be a very general result. With more periods, one would expect the contract to specify that inspection should take place at several dates—as a (possibly stochastic) function of past events. Moreover, in a multi-period setting there is no reason to think that inspection should be associated with a termination of the firm's operations, in the way that bankruptcy often is. Rather, inspection is simply a normal event in a firm's life.

In other words, the CSV model—when extended—seems to be closer to a theory of optimal inspection or auditing than to a theory of debt or bankruptcy.

6

Capital Structure Decisions of a Public Company

In the last chapter, I discussed the optimal contract written by an entrepreneur who raises capital from an investor (or set of investors). I assumed that the entrepreneur obtained significant (private) benefits from running a firm, and analysed how control rights could be allocated between the entrepreneur and investor, so as to give the entrepreneur maximum freedom to pursue his own goals, subject to the investor breaking even.

In this chapter I extend the analysis to the case of a large, public company. Although there is no sharp economic distinction between the private and public cases, I take the point of view that in the case of a public company the issue of allocating control rights to managers in order to give them a chance to enjoy private benefits may not be of primary importance. Also, it may not be necessary to give managers control rights in order to motivate them to undertake relationship-specific investments, or to be innovative or inventive, given that many of the actions of the managers of a large company are relatively routine.[1] Rather, the crucial issue may be how the company's investors can design financial structure so as to *limit* management's ability to pursue its own goals at the expense of investors. For example, managers may overpay themselves and give themselves extravagant perks; they may carry out unprofitable but power-enhancing investments; or they may refuse to give up their jobs to others who can run the company better. (In contrast, it is supposed that investors are interested only in profit or net market value.)[2]

In the case of a single investor, it is clear how to deal with this problem: give the investor all the control rights; i.e., make her the 100 per cent owner. (See the Aghion–Bolton model in the case

---

[1] This is in contrast to the case of an entrepreneur, where innovation and inventiveness may be extremely important.

[2] On managerial goals, see e.g. Baumol (1959), Marris (1964), Jensen (1986), and Williamson (1964).

where the entrepreneur's utility does not matter, or where the investor has all the bargaining power.) However, this chapter supposes that investors are wealth-constrained and so the company has many small investors.[3] This creates two new issues that were not relevant in the case of the private company considered in Chapter 5. First, those who own the company, the shareholders, are too small and numerous to exercise control on a day-to-day basis. Given this, they delegate day-to-day (residual rights of) control to a board of directors who in turn delegate it to management. In other words, to use the phrase made famous by Berle and Means (1932), there is a separation of ownership and control.[4]

Second, dispersed shareholders have little or no incentive to monitor management. The reason is that monitoring is a public good: if one shareholder's monitoring leads to improved company performance, all shareholders benefit. Given that monitoring is costly, each shareholder will free-ride in the hope that *other* shareholders will do the monitoring. Unfortunately, all shareholders think the same way and the net result is that no—or almost no—monitoring will take place.

Sometimes this free-rider problem can be overcome by someone who acquires a large stake in the company and takes it over (or exerts control in some other way). However, the take-over mechanism does not always work well.[5] The conclusion is that in many cases the managers or board of directors of a public

[3] Investors may also be small because they are risk-averse and want to hold diversified portfolios.

[4] A more accurate description might be that there is a separation of ownership and *effective* control or management. The point is that the shareholders do retain ultimate control in the form of votes.

[5] One reason is that a bidder may have to share a large fraction of the take-over gains with shareholders of the target company, because (i) minority shareholders can earn a capital gain by holding on to their shares (see Grossman and Hart 1980); or (ii) the bid may alert others to the fact that the company is undervalued and a bidding war may ensue. Thus, the bidder may fail to cover the *ex ante* costs of making a bid. Further factors deterring a bidder are management's ability to engage in various defensive measures (lawsuits, poison pills, the introduction of employee stock ownership plans); to invite 'white knights' to make bids and favour these bidders by giving them non-public information; or, at the last moment, to carry out the actions the bidder was planning to undertake. The evidence does indeed show that most of the gains from a successful take-over accrue to shareholders of the target firm rather than to the acquiring firm; see Bradley *et al.* (1988) and Jarrell *et al.* (1988). For a further discussion of takeovers, see Chapter 8.

company can pursue their own goals, possibly at the expense of those of shareholders, with little or no outside interference.[6]

This chapter studies how the owners of a company can constrain the behaviour of management when there is a separation between ownership and control. One possibility is to put managers on an incentive scheme. However, while an incentive scheme may work well in motivating managers to exert effort, it is likely to be less effective in getting managers to cut back on empire-building or to relinquish control. The reason is that, if managers have a strong interest in power, empire, and perks, a very large bribe may be required to persuade managers to give up these things. It may be better for investors to *force* managers to curb their empire-building tendencies. Placing debt in the capital structure is one way to do this. Moreover, debt is more flexible than an incentive scheme in that it makes the set of choices available to the manager sensitive to the market's assessment of company prospects.

This chapter illustrates the constraining role of debt using two simple models. In both there is a conflict of interest over the assets that should be under management control. In the first model the focus is on whether management should shrink its empire over time. The second model considers the closely related question of how much management should expand its empire. The reason for considering two models is that the situations of asset liquidation and expansion are analytically distinct. In the first short-term debt is critically important, while in the second long-term debt plays a more significant role. However, there is a short discussion in the text, and a longer discussion in the Appendix, of a special case in which the two models can be merged.

The chapter is organized as follows. Section 1 introduces some of the assumptions behind the models, while the models are developed in Sections 2–4. Section 5 argues that, even though the

---

[6] In this book no distinction is made between management and the board of directors; that is, the role of the board in ensuring that managers act on behalf of shareholders is ignored. This is a reasonable assumption in many cases. Board members are often picked by incumbent managers, and are likely to feel loyal to them. Also, board members are typically not major shareholders in the company, and therefore have little incentive to play an active role. On the other hand, there are undoubtedly occasions—some of which generate a great deal of publicity—when the board does intervene and constrain management. On these issues, see Mace (1971), Vancil (1987), and Weisbach (1988).

models are very simple and stylized, they can explain some of the empirical evidence about capital structure. Section 6 compares the 'incentive' or 'agency' approach described here with other theories of capital structure in the literature.[7] Much of the literature has either ignored agency problems altogether, stressing the tax or market completion benefits of debt, or has focused on the conflict of interest between shareholders and creditors, rather on that between investors and management.[8] I shall argue that only by considering the conflict between investors and management can one explain why companies issue senior debt, and why a failure to make a debt payment leads to a penalty in the form of bankruptcy, i.e. why debt is associated with a *hard* budget constraint.

1. Introduction to the models

The models used in this chapter differ from those in Chapter 5 in several respects. It is worth spelling out some of the key assumptions made before the formal analysis begins.

1. It is now supposed that the company has a large number of small investors; that is, its equity and debt are dispersed.
2. It is assumed that capital structure decisions are made to maximize the expected return to investors, rather than to maximize management's utility subject to investors breaking even. It is also supposed that management's utility is at least as high as what it can get elsewhere, i.e. that management's participation constraint is not binding.
3. The analysis considers the (admittedly) extreme case where the manager's utility is strictly increasing in the assets under his control, and is completely independent of his monetary compensation (his salary).
4. It is supposed that management cannot divert all of the firm's profit for its own use. As a result, (outside) equity will have a positive market value in equilibrium.

[7] For a survey of the literature on capital structure, see Harris and Raviv (1991).
[8] On the conflict between shareholders and creditors, see Jensen and Meckling (1976). Papers that do deal with the conflict between investors and management include Grossman and Hart (1982), Jensen (1986), and Stulz (1990). The analysis in this chapter is based closely on Hart (1993) and Hart and Moore (1995).

The above four assumptions, although strong, seem to be reasonable starting points for a study of a public company. The first captures the idea that investors are wealth-constrained. Note that this assumption effectively rules out renegotiation with creditors (because of free-rider problems; see Ch. 5, §5, for a discussion). Thus, if a company defaults on its debts then it automatically goes into bankruptcy. Assumption 2 formalizes the idea that managers' preferences are unimportant relative to those of investors. Assumption 3 is made for simplicity; it implies that incentive schemes have essentially no role to play in motivating management. It allows the analysis to focus on debt as a way of constraining managers' behaviour. The final assumption makes the models of this chapter in some ways richer than the Hart–Moore model of Chapter 5, since (outside) equity has a positive market value.

Readers will be in a better position to understand the role of these assumptions, and to judge how restrictive they are (or are not), as the analysis proceeds.

2. Model 1

The first model is concerned with the circumstances under which a firm should be liquidated. Like the other models used in this chapter, it is based on Myers (1977).

Consider a firm consisting of assets in place, and suppose that it exists at three given dates (see Figure 6.1).

At date 0 the firm's financial structure is chosen. At date 1 the assets in place yield a return of y_1. At this time the firm can be liquidated, yielding L (in addition to the y_1 already realized). L stands for the value of the firm's assets in some alternative use. The model allows for the possibility that, in some cases, the firm's assets may be more valuable elsewhere.[9]

If the firm is not liquidated, at date 2 the assets in place yield a

---

[9] In the Hart–Moore model of Ch. 5, it was assumed that liquidation was never efficient. However, in the current analysis the manager's private benefit is being excluded from the efficiency calculation. If this private benefit is taken into account, it is never efficient to liquidate in the present model either.

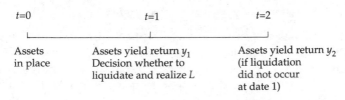

FIG. 6.1

further return y_2. At this date the firm is wound up, and receipts are allocated to investors.

Note that, in contrast to the last chapter, liquidation is a zero–one decision. A more general treatment would allow for continuous asset sales.

Suppose that the firm is run by a single manager. Recall the assumption that the manager's goal is to maximize the extent of the assets under his control. In model 1 it is assumed that there are no possibilities for the manager to expand his enterprise, and hence the manager's only goal is to avoid liquidation; moreover, once he has achieved this goal, he has no further use for company funds.[10]

Assume that all uncertainty about y_1, y_2 and L is resolved at date 1 and there is symmetric information throughout. Assume also a zero interest rate and that investors are risk-neutral.

In a first-best world where contracting is costless, the investors would write the following contract with the manager:

CONTRACT 1. Liquidate if and only if $y_2 < L$.

In other words, liquidate if and only if the firm is more valuable (for the investors) liquidated than as a going concern. Such a contract yields the first-best date 0 present value of the firm,[11]

---

[10] This distinguishes model 1 from a 'pure free cash flow model' of the Jensen (1986) variety. (A Jensen-type analysis is provided in model 3.) In a pure free cash flow model, the manager always has further uses of company funds and so will squander each dollar of investor returns that is not mortgaged to creditors. Thus, in a free cash flow model the value of equity is zero. In contrast, in model 1, as readers will shortly see, the value of equity can be positive. Note that this is not a critical difference between the two analyses since the main results would still hold under the more extreme Jensen assumptions.

[11] Given the simplifying assumption that the manager is interested only in power and not in money (see §1), wages paid to the manager can be ignored. It is also supposed that the manager has no initial wealth and so cannot be charged up front for non-pecuniary benefits.

(6.1) $V = E[y_1 + \text{Max} \{y_2, L\}]$.

The analysis will focus on a second-best situation where y_1, y_2, L, although observable, are not verifiable and hence cannot be made part of an enforceable contract. In particular, contract 1 cannot be enforced since the courts do not know whether or not $y_2 < L$.[12]

I consider the role of financial structure in substituting for an enforceable contract. Suppose that, although y_1, y_2, L are not verifiable, the amount paid out to investors *is* verifiable. (Any payment made to investors is a public event.) Thus, securities can be issued at date 0 with claims conditional on the amount that is paid out. For the time being, confine attention to the case where the firm issues short-term debt due at date 1, long-term debt due at date 2, and equity; and suppose also that both kinds of debt are senior, in the sense that any new claims issued by the firm at date 1 are entitled to payment only if date 0 debt-holders have been fully paid off. The role of more sophisticated securities is considered below.

As mentioned above, I also assume that, if the firm defaults on its short-term debt at date 1, then this triggers bankruptcy, which in turn leads to liquidation, i.e. L is earned.[13]

Consider the situation faced by the manager at date 1 once the uncertainty about y_1, y_2, and L is resolved. Define P_1 to be the amount owed at date 1 and P_2 to be the amount owed at date 2; i.e., P_1 and P_2 are the face values of short-term and long-term debt respectively. (Of course, at date 0 these debt claims will typically trade for less than their face value because of the risk of default.) Given that default leads to bankruptcy and to the loss of control benefits, the manager never defaults voluntarily. If $y_1 \geq P_1$, the manager will pay P_1 to creditors at date 1 and hold $y_1 - P_1$ inside the firm for distribution at date 2. Thus the total return to initial shareholders and creditors will be $y_1 + y_2$, with creditors receiving $P_1 + \text{Min}\{P_2, y_1 - P_1 + y_2\}$ and shareholders the rest.

Suppose next that $y_1 < P_1$. If $y_1 + y_2 \geq P_1 + P_2$, the manager can still avoid default at date 1 by issuing an amount $(P_1 - y_1)$ of junior debt due at date 2 and repaying this together with the senior debt

---

[12] It is one thing to verify L if liquidation occurs at date 1, but it is quite another to verify it in the absence of liquidation. See Ch. 5, n. 8.

[13] I ignore more sophisticated bankruptcy systems that try to preserve the firm's going-concern value. Such mechanisms are the subject of Ch. 7.

P_2 out of date 2 income y_2. Thus, the total return to shareholders and creditors is again $y_1 + y_2$, of which senior creditors receive $P_1 + P_2$ and shareholders the rest. (Junior creditors put in $P_1 - y_1$ and get $P_1 - y_1$ back.) However, if $y_1 < P_1$ and $y_1 + y_2 < P_1 + P_2$, then the manager cannot avoid default, and liquidation will occur. In this case, the return to creditors is $\text{Min}\{P_1 + P_2, y_1 + L\}$ and shareholders receive the rest.

Denote the total return to initial shareholders and creditors by R. Then the above discussion can be summarized as follows:

$$(6.2) \qquad R = \begin{cases} y_1 + y_2 & \text{if } y_1 \geq P_1, \\ & \text{or } y_1 < P_1 \text{ and } y_1 + y_2 \geq P_1 + P_2, \\ y_1 + L & \text{otherwise.} \end{cases}$$

Notice for future reference the two sources of inefficiency here. Sometimes the manager will liquidate even though $y_2 > L$, because P_1 and P_2 are large relative to y_1 and y_2. Other times he will maintain the firm as a going concern even though $y_2 < L$, because P_1 and P_2 are small relative to y_1 and y_2.

I can now discuss optimal capital structure. Suppose that the firm's capital structure—that is, P_1 and P_2—is chosen at date 0 to maximize the firm's date 0 market value, that is, the aggregate expected return to all initial security holders: $E[R]$. This may seem counter-intuitive, given that capital structure decisions are typically made by management (or the board of directors), and I have supposed management to be interested in preserving its empire rather than in market value. The assumption can be justified in two ways. First, the capital structure choice may be made, prior to a public offering at date 0, by an original owner who wishes to maximize his total receipts in the subsequent offering of debt and equity. (He is about to retire.) Second, one can imagine that the firm is all equity prior to date 0, and the threat of a hostile takeover at date 0 forces management to choose a new capital structure which maximizes date 0 market value. (The hostile bidder is present now, but may not be around at date 1, so management must 'bond' itself now to act well in the future since otherwise shareholders will sell to the bidder.)[14]

---

[14] Both of these scenarios are of course special. I believe that the thrust of the analysis applies also to the case where management chooses financial structure to maximize its *own* welfare. In the present three-date model, this leads to the trivial outcome of no debt. (Management clearly prefers not to be under pressure from

In the case where there is no *ex ante* uncertainty about y_2 and L, the choice of capital structure is simple. If $y_2 > L$, it is optimal to set $P_1 = 0$.[15] If $y_2 < L$, it is optimal to set P_1 very large. (P_2 is irrelevant in both cases.) The return to shareholders is $V_0 = \max\{y_1 + y_2, y_1 + L\}$ and so the first-best is achieved.

Matters become more interesting if y_2 and L are uncertain. (Whether y_1 is uncertain or not is less important.) To simplify, focus on the special case in which the vector (y_1, y_2, L) can take on just two values, (y_1^A, y_2^A, L^A) and (y_1^B, y_2^B, L^B), with probabilities π^A and $\pi^B = 1 - \pi^A$, respectively.

Obviously, if $y_2^A \geq L^A$, $y_2^B \geq L^B$, the first-best outcome can again be achieved with no date 1 debt; if $y_2^A \leq L^A$, $y_2^B \leq L^B$, the first-best can be achieved with a high level of date 1 debt. The interesting case is $y_2^A > L^A$, $y_2^B < L^B$ (or vice versa). It is useful to divide this case into three subcases.

1. $y_1^A + y_2^A > y_1^B + y_2^B$. Here the first-best can again be achieved, for example by setting $P_1 = y_1^A + y_2^A$, $P_2 = 0$. That is, short-term debt is set equal to the total value of the firm in state A. The reason is that in subcase 1 the state in which total return is low is also the state in which the firm should be closed down. Hence the firm can avoid default in state A (by borrowing y_2^A) but not in state B. This is the efficient outcome.

2. $y_1^A + y_2^A \leq y_1^B + y_2^B$, $y_1^A > y_1^B$. Now the first-best can be achieved by setting $P_1 = y_1^A$, P_2 very large. The reason is that in subcase 2 the state in which date 1 return is low is also the state in which the firm should be closed down. Hence the firm can avoid default in state A (by paying y_1^A) but not in state B (since it can't borrow any more). Again, this is efficient.

3. $y_1^A + y_2^A \leq y_1^B + y_2^B$, $y_1^A \leq y_1^B$. Now the first-best cannot be achieved. Given any values of P_1, P_2, default in state B occurs if and only if $y_1^B < P_1$ and $y_1^B + y_2^B < P_1 + P_2$ (see (6.2)). But these

creditors.) However, in a model with more periods management may issue debt voluntarily, since this may be the only way to raise funds from investors concerned that their claims may be diluted if management undertakes bad actions in the future.

It would also be interesting to extend the analysis to show that debt has a bonding role when there is a constant probability of a hostile take-over bid (rather than a probability 1 of a bid now and a probability 0 of a bid at date 1). For a model suggesting that debt does have a bonding role under these conditions, see Zwiebel (1994).

[15] Recall the assumption that the manager has no use for company funds if liquidation is avoided. Hence, conditional on the fact that liquidation is undesirable, there is no cost to setting P_1 very low (zero).

inequalities imply that $y_1^A < P_1$ and $y_1^A + y_2^A < P_1 + P_2$, and hence default also occurs in state A. It is impossible to have liquidation in state B, where liquidation is efficient, without also having it in state A, where it is inefficient. Thus, the choice is between having liquidation in both states or neither. The first, which can be achieved by setting P_1 very large, is preferable to the second, which can be achieved by setting $P_1 = 0$, if and only if

(6.3) $$\pi^A L^A + \pi^B L^B > \pi^A y_1^A + \pi^B y_2^B,$$

i.e. if and only if the expected liquidation value exceeds the expected continuation value.

This completes the analysis of optimal capital structure in the two-state case. The main difference relative to the case of perfect certainty is that interior solutions occur: it may be optimal to choose debt levels to take intermediate values (subcases 1 and 2) rather than zero or infinity. Also, high debt sometimes leads to inefficient liquidation and low debt sometimes prevents efficient liquidation (see subcase 3).[16]

It is worth considering how financial structure differs from an incentive scheme as a way of controlling management. As noted earlier, since y_1, y_2, L are not verifiable, state-contingent incentive schemes are not feasible. Also, an incentive scheme that rewards the manager for liquidating will not be effective given the assumption that the manager puts power before money. However, the following incentive scheme could be useful: the firm's capital structure consists of equity and no debt, the manager is not allowed to raise new capital, and the manager is dismissed at date 1 unless he pays a dividend to shareholders of at least P^*.

Note, however, that such a scheme yields a liquidation rule

$$\text{Liquidate} \Leftrightarrow y_1 < P^*,$$

which is equivalent to that obtained by choosing debt levels

---

[16] At this stage, it is worth reviewing the assumption that renegotiation with creditors is impossible. If one were to take the opposite point of view—that renegotiation is costless, as in Ch. 5—one would find that $P_1 = \infty$ is optimal (assuming that one retained the assumption that capital structure is chosen to maximize investor return). The reason is that, with $P_1 = \infty$, investors have the right to insist on liquidation in those states where liquidation is efficient; and at the same time, they can always renegotiate P_1 downwards in those states where liquidation is inefficient. Thus, the assumption that renegotiation is costly plays a very important role in model 1.

$P_1 = P^*$, $P_2 = \infty$. In general, however, one can do better with a more flexible capital structure—in particular, by setting $P_2 < \infty$ (see subcase 1). The reason is that when $P_2 < \infty$ the liquidation rule

$$\text{Liquidate} \Leftrightarrow y_1 < P_1 \text{ and } y_1 + y_2 < P_1 + P_2$$

depends on y_2 as well as y_1. That is, debt, coupled with the manager's ability to refinance at date 1, yields an outcome that is sensitive to y_2 in a way that is not possible with the simple incentive scheme considered above.[17]

3. Model 2

Model 1 is concerned with a situation where the only issue is whether the firm should shrink. Under these conditions, short-term debt is of primary importance (to trigger liquidation), while long-term debt is somewhat less important. Model 2 allows for the possibility of expansion. This provides a more interesting role for long-term debt as a means of regulating the inflow of new capital.[18] Unfortunately, it is difficult to combine liquidation and new investment, and so model 2 makes a simplifying assumption (see Assumption 1 below). This assumption implies that it is optimal to set short-term debt equal to zero, so that no liquidation occurs in equilibrium. The analysis can therefore focus on long-term debt.

The timing is as before, except that at date 1 the firm may undertake an investment project (see Figure 6.2). The project costs i and yields r at date 2. The variables i and r are uncertain as of date 0, but the uncertainty is resolved at date 1.

The manager's empire-building tendencies are such that he always wants to invest if he can. That is, just as the manager wants to avoid liquidation at all cost, so he wants to invest at all cost. The only thing that can stop him is an inability to raise the capital. However, as in model 1, once the investment is financed, the manager has no further use for company funds.

It is assumed that claims cannot be issued on the return from

[17] I have not allowed investors to send messages about the commonly observed values of y_1, y_2, and L. Messages would be an alternative way of making the liquidation rule sensitive to y_2. See e.g. Moore (1992).

[18] Model 2 is based on Hart and Moore (1995).

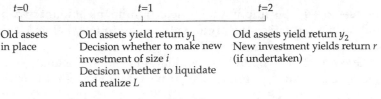

FIG. 6.2

the investment, r, separately from the return from the assets in place, y_2; that is, project financing is ruled out.[19] I also make an assumption that implies that it is optimal to set $P_1 = 0$, so that no liquidation occurs in equilibrium.

ASSUMPTION 1. $y_1 < i$ and $y_2 \geq L$ with probability 1.

Assumption 1 says that the manager can never finance the investment out of date 1 earnings and that it is never efficient to liquidate the firm. The assumption may be plausible for a growth company that, at least initially, requires an injection of new capital to prosper.

PROPOSITION 1. Given Assumption 1, the date 0 market value of the firm is maximized by setting $P_1 = 0$.

The following is a sketch of the proof (for details, see Hart and Moore 1995). Given any choice of $(P_1 + P_2)$, it is better to replace P_1 by zero and P_2 by $(P_1 + P_2)$. The reason is that a zero value of P_1 makes liquidation (which is inefficient) less likely. Also, a zero value of P_1 does not make it easier for the manager to invest in a bad project, since, given that $y_1 < i$, the manager has to go to the market, in which case only the total amount of senior debt in

---

[19] If project financing were possible, the new investment could be financed as a stand-alone entity, whose merit could be assessed by the market at date 1; and debt levels could be set very high to prevent the manager using funds from the existing assets to subsidize investment. There are several justifications for ruling out project financing. First, it may be that i represents an *incremental* investment—e.g. maintaining or improving the existing assets—and the final return $y_2 + r$ is simply the overall return from the (single) project. Second, it may be that the same management team looks after both the old assets and the new project, and can use transfer pricing to reallocate profits between them; hence the market can keep track only of total profits. Finally, even if project-specific financing *is* feasible, it is not at all clear that management will *want* to finance a project that is not part of its empire since it will not enjoy the private benefits of control (on this, see Li 1993).

place—$P_1 + P_2$—is important for determining the amount of capital he can raise. (See the argument leading to (6.4) below.) This establishes the proposition.

Given that $P_1 = 0$, and no liquidation occurs, the analysis of model 2 is relatively simple. The firm's total revenue if the manager invests is $y_1 + y_2 + r$, of which P_2 is mortgaged to the old (senior) creditors. Hence, the most the firm can borrow at date 1 is $y_1 + y_2 + r - P_2$. It follows that the manager will invest if and only if

(6.4) $y_1 + y_2 + r - P_2 \geq i.$

If (6.4) is satisfied, the total return to date 0 investors, R, is

(6.5) $R = y_1 + y_2 + r - i,$

of which date 0 creditors receive P_2 and shareholders receive the rest. (New creditors are paid back in full.)

If (6.4) is not satisfied, the total return to date 0 investors is

(6.6) $R = y_1 + y_2.$

Notice the two sources of inefficiency in model 2. Sometimes the manager will invest even though $r < i$, because $y_1 + y_2$ is big relative to P_2. At other times he will be unable to invest even though $r > i$, because $y_1 + y_2$ is small relative to P_2. (The latter is known as the debt overhang problem; see Myers (1977).)

It is now straightforward to analyse optimal capital structure in model 2. If there is no *ex ante* uncertainty about i and r, it is easy to achieve the first-best outcome. If $r > i$, set $P_2 = 0$; (6.4) is always satisfied and investment takes place, which is efficient. In contrast, if $r < i$, set P_2 very large; (6.4) is never satisfied and investment never takes place, which is again efficient.

Matters become more interesting if r and i are uncertain. To simplify, again suppose that (y_1, y_2, r, i) takes on just two values, (y_1^A, y_2^A, r^A, i^A) and (y_1^B, y_2^B, r^B, i^B), with probabilities π^A and $\pi^B = 1 - \pi^A$, respectively.[20]

It is again trivial to achieve the first-best outcome with no debt if $r^A \geq i^A$ and $r^B \geq i^B$, or with very large debt if $r^A \leq i^A$ and $r^B \leq i^B$. The interesting case is where $r^A > i^A$ and $r^B < i^B$. Divide this into two subcases.

---

[20] For an analysis of the case with more than two states, see Hart and Moore (1995).

1. $y_1^A + y_2^A + r^A - i^A > y_1^B + y_2^B + r^B - i^B$. That is, the firm's net market value and the profitability of the new project are perfectly (positively) correlated. Here the first-best can be achieved by setting P_2 somewhere between $y_1^B + y_2^B + r^B - i^B$ and $y_1^A + y_2^A + r^A - i^A$; (6.4) is satisfied in state A but not in state B, and investment occurs only in state A, which is efficient.

In other words, setting the debt level somewhere between the maximized net value of the firm in state A and the maximized net value in state B gives management enough leeway to finance a profitable new investment in state A, but prevents the financing of an unprofitable one in state B.

2. $y_1^A + y_2^A + r^A - i^A \leq y_1^B + y_2^B + r^B - i^B$. That is, the firm's net market value and the profitability of the new project are perfectly (negatively) correlated. The first-best is no longer achievable for any choice of P_2. The reason is that

$$y_1^A + y_2^A + r^A - P_2 \geq i^A \Rightarrow y_1^B + y_2^B + r^B - P_2 \geq i^B,$$

and so it is impossible to have investment in state A without also having it in state B. Thus, the choice is between having investment in neither state (set P_2 very large) or in both (set $P_2 = 0$). The first is preferable if and only if

$$\pi^A(r^A - i^A) + \pi^B(r^B - i^B) < 0,$$

i.e. if and only if the expected net return from new investment is negative.

The lesson from this second model complements that from the first. If management is interested in empire-building, the danger for investors is that management will try to raise capital for unprofitable investment projects by issuing claims against earnings from existing assets. Senior long-term debt, by mortgaging part of long-term earnings, reduces management's ability to do this. However, too much long-term debt prevents managers from carrying out even those projects that are profitable.

This chapter has restricted attention to 'simple' capital structures consisting of fixed amounts of senior debt. It is not difficult to show, however, that in some cases more sophisticated securities can be useful. Consider model 2 and suppose that $y_1 \equiv 0$ and $y_2 \equiv r$. (That is, the return from assets in place and the return from new investment are always the same.) Then the first-best can be achieved in the following way. The firm issues a large class of senior debt due at date 2 in the amount of K, say, with a covenant attached saying that the firm can issue new debt of the same seniority up to a further amount K (so that the total debt outstanding becomes $2K$). Any debt beyond this is junior to this class of senior debt.

Given such a capital structure, the most that the firm can raise at date 1 is $\frac{1}{2}(y_2 + r)$. The firm does this by issuing the full amount K of new debt and dividing total date 2 income ($y_2 + r$) between the old and new creditors. (Recall that K is very large, so that the firm is bankrupt at date 2.) Thus, the condition for the firm to invest is now

$$\text{Invest} \iff \tfrac{1}{2}(y_2 + r) \geq i$$
$$\iff r \geq i,$$

since $y_2 = r$. But this yields precisely the first-best outcome. Moreover, it is easy to check that the first-best cannot be achieved with a simple capital structure consisting solely of (a fixed amount of) senior debt.

Not only are more sophisticated securities of theoretical interest, but also they are observed in practice (see Ragulin 1994). Unfortunately, a general analysis of sophisticated securities is beyond the scope of this book; for some progress in this direction, readers are referred to Hart and Moore (1995). Note also that the existence of sophisticated securities does not detract from the main theme of this chapter: that debt has an important role in constraining the behaviour of self-interested management.

4. Model 3

Assumption 1 was useful in simplifying model 2, but it ruled out an interesting economic case, stressed particularly by Jensen (1986). If $y_1 > i$, the firm has free cash flow and it may use this to make unprofitable investments (i.e. it may invest when $r < i$). Short-term debt then has a role in forcing the manager to pay out this free cash flow.

Note that this role of short-term debt differs from that in model 1, where short-term debt was used to trigger liquidation, rather than to prevent expansion.

I analyse this new role of short-term debt in the Appendix. To do so I combine models 1 and 2. However, merging the models in general is difficult and so two simplifying assumptions are made. First, it is supposed that the manager has an unlimited number of new investment projects (rather than just one) and that they are unprofitable; i.e., $r < i$ for each of them. (In fact, for simplicity, r is taken to be zero.) Second, it is supposed that $y_2 > L$; i.e. liquidation is always inefficient (as in Assumption 1). The choice of debt is then determined by the following considerations. To minimize the resources the manager has for unprofitable reinvestment, P_1 and P_2 should be set high: as close to y_1 and y_2 as possible. However, to minimize the chances that inefficient liquidation is triggered because of an adverse y_1 or y_2 shock, P_1 and P_2 should be set low. The solution to this trade-off is derived in the Appendix.

One point that is worth noting for future reference is that, if y_1 and y_2 are certain, then the first-best can be achieved in model 3 by setting $P_1 = y_1$ and $P_2 = y_2$.

5. *Observed patterns of capital structure*

Having developed some simple models of debt–equity choice, I consider next what light these models can throw on actual capital structure choices. A great deal of empirical work has been done on capital structure. Although not all the findings agree, some stylized facts have emerged. I shall take these facts as given in what follows.

The stylized facts are that profitable firms have low debt; that firms with a large proportion of tangible assets have high debt; that firms with stable cash flows have high debt; that debt-for-equity swaps raise share prices; that equity-for-debt swaps lower share prices; and that pure equity issues lower share prices.[21]

I shall argue that all of these facts can be explained by the models described above. However, not all are inevitable consequences of these models. In some cases the models predict that reversals

[21] For discussions of these, see Harris and Raviv (1991), Masulis (1988), Myers (1990), Asquith and Mullins (1986), Kester (1986), Long and Malitz (1985), Masulis (1980), and Titman and Wessels (1988).

could also be observed. Some may regard this ambiguity as a weakness of the agency approach to debt. I suspect, however, that this feature is shared by other theories of capital structure. That is, if 'suitable' assumptions are made about parameter values and the structure of information, other theories can also predict reversals. I shall argue below that one advantage of the agency approach over other theories is that the agency approach can explain something that other theories cannot explain: why firms issue 'hard' debt, i.e. debt that is senior and that triggers bankruptcy in the event of default.

Consider the relationship between profitability and debt. Model 1 can explain why profitable firms (in particular, those with high y_2) have low debt. Suppose there are two categories of firms, category 1 firms with $y_2 > L$ and category 2 firms with $y_2 < L$, and it is known which category any firm is in. Suppose also that category 1 firms are more profitable than category 2 firms, say, because L doesn't vary very much across the categories while y_2 does. Then for profitable category 1 firms it is optimal to set $P_1 = P_2 = 0$ since liquidation is inefficient. On the other hand, for unprofitable category 2 firms it is optimal to set P_1 large since liquidation is efficient. Thus, there is a negative relationship between profitability and the debt level.

However, a small change in the assumptions could generate a positive relationship between profitability and the debt level. Suppose that category 1 firms are less profitable than category 2 firms because L varies a lot across the categories while y_2 does not. In other words, suppose profitable firms are profitable because they have high liquidation values, rather than because they have high going concern values. In such cases, high debt levels will be required to force managers of profitable firms to relinquish control by liquidating them (more generally, by selling off assets).

Model 2 does not predict a clear relationship between profitability and debt either. If a firm's profitability refers to the value of new investment, it is optimal for profitable firms to have low debt. (If $r > i$ with certainty, the optimal $P_1 = P_2 = 0$.) However, if profitability refers to the value of old investments, then it is optimal for profitable firms to have high debt. In subcase 1 of the two-state case, i.e. when $r^A > i^A$, $r^B < i^B$, $y_1^A + y_2^A + r^A - i^A > y_1^B + y_2^B + r^B - i^B$, the optimal P_2 lies between $y_1^B + y_2^B + r^B - i^B$ and $y_1^A + y_2^A + r^A$

$- i^A$, and is thus increasing in $y_1^B + y_2^B$, $y_1^A + y_2^A$. (For more on this, see Hart and Moore (1995).)

Model 3 gives a fairly clear prediction that profitability and debt should be negatively related (where debt is measured by the debt–equity ratio). Suppose y_1, y_2 double. If L doubles as well, then the optimal amount of debt doubles by homogeneity (see the Appendix for details). However, if L less than doubles, then, since the cost of inefficient liquidation has effectively risen, the optimal level of debt less than doubles. Thus, the debt–equity ratio falls as going concern value rises relative to liquidation value.

Consider next the fact that firms with a large fraction of assets that are tangible have high debt. If tangibility is associated with high liquidation value, then model 1 explains this fact rather clearly. Other things equal, a high L makes liquidation more attractive and so raises the optimal P_1, P_2. (It is more likely that $y_2 < L$ or that (6.3) will be satisfied.)

Model 2 seems to have little to say about the relationship between debt and asset tangibility because there is no obvious proxy for asset tangibility in this model.

Model 3, like model 1, supports the existence of a positive relationship between debt and asset tangibility. If the liquidation value of the assets goes up, then the cost of high debt—that inefficient liquidation sometimes occurs—falls. However, the benefit of high debt—that unprofitable reinvestment is prevented—stays the same. Thus, the optimal debt level rises. See the Appendix for details.

Consider next the relationship between debt and the stability of cash flows. The best way to understand this is to consider model 3. Start off with the case where y_1 and y_2 are certain. It is then optimal to set $P_1 = y_1$, $P_2 = y_2$. Now introduce uncertainty in date 1 cash flows. There are two effects. On the one hand, in order to reduce the manager's ability to make wasteful investments when y_1 is high, debt must rise. On the other hand, in order to reduce the likelihood that inefficient liquidation occurs when y_1 is low, debt must fall. It is shown in the Appendix that, depending on the parameters, either effect may dominate, and so the optimal level of debt may rise or fall.

So the theory can explain why firms with stable cash flows have more debt, but it can also explain the opposite.

Turn next to the event studies. I will focus on the first of these—

that debt-for-equity swaps typically raise share prices. (A very similar analysis can be applied to the other event studies.) I will also base the discussion on model 1, although similar results could be obtained for the other models. In much of what follows, the driving force behind a recapitalization or swap is the threat of a hostile take-over.

Debt-for-equity swaps typically raise share prices

To see that model 1 can explain this, suppose that management obtains private information just after date 0 that a hostile take-over is imminent. (It will occur at date $\frac{1}{2}$, say.) Assume for simplicity that as far as the market is concerned this is a very unlikely event. However, if management signals the event through a recapitalization, then the market of course reacts.

Assume also that for unspecified (e.g. historical) reasons the firm initially consists of 100 per cent equity, and that the hostile bid will succeed unless management can convince the market that it will run the firm approximately efficiently. (The idea is that management is safe if it is close to efficient, because there are some costs in making a bid.)

Suppose it is known that for this firm $y_1 = y_2 = 100$ and $L = 150$, as in Figure 6.3. In the absence of any action by management before a bid is made at date $\frac{1}{2}$, market participants will reason that, if the bid fails, management will *not* liquidate at date 1 because, given that the firm has no outstanding debt, it will be under no pressure to do so.[22] Anticipating this, shareholders tender to the bidder and the bid succeeds.

To prevent this outcome, management must bond itself just after date 0 to take an efficient action at date 1. An obvious way to do this is to make a debt-for-equity swap.[23] For example, suppose management issues new short-term debt promising 250 (that is, it sets $P_1 = 250$ and $P_2 = 0$) and uses the proceeds to buy back equity. Because $y_1 < P_1$ and $y_1 + y_2 < P_1 + P_2$, the new debt guarantees that the firm will default at date 1 and be liquidated then, which is the efficient outcome. Thus, the hostile take-over is thwarted, and management retains control, if only until date 1.

---

[22] Assume that the chances of another bidder appearing later are negligible.

[23] I assume that it is too late to make such a swap after the take-over bid is announced.

Date 0	Date $\frac{1}{2}$	Date 1	Date 2
Manager learns of existence of hostile bidder	Hostile bid?	$y_1 = 100$ $L = 150$	$y_2 = 100$ (if no liquidation)

FIG. 6.3

What is the effect of the recapitalization on the value of equity? Before the recapitalization the equity was worth (approximately) $y_1 + y_2 = 200$ (given that the take-over was regarded as a very unlikely event). Afterward the total value of the firm is $y_1 + L = 250$. Given that all the capital raised by the new debt is used to buy back shares, all of this 250 accrues to initial shareholders. Thus, the effect of the recapitalization is to raise the value of equity by 50.[24]

Model 1 is thus consistent with the apparent fact that debt-for-equity swaps raise the value of equity. However, I now show that, under a different information structure, model 1 predicts that such swaps can reduce the value of equity.

Debt-for-equity swaps can lower share prices

Suppose that $y_1 = 100$, $L = 80$, and y_2 is known to take on two possible values, $y_2^A = 100$, $y_2^B = 60$, with probabilities π^A and $\pi^B = 1 - \pi^A$, respectively. Assume that, *ex ante*, π^A is very close to 1 and π^B is very close to zero. However, imagine that management receives private information just after date 0 that in fact state B is sure to occur. (The receipt of this information is very unlikely *ex ante*.) This information will very shortly become available to the market—at date $\frac{1}{4}$, say. In addition, in contrast to the previous example, everyone already knows that a hostile bidder is ready to make a bid at date $\frac{1}{2}$. Again, assume that the firm is initially all equity. The information structure is shown in Figure 6.4.

[24] In the above example, the firm was all equity before the debt–equity swap. It is easy to show that the main ideas generalize to the case where the firm has some riskless debt initially outstanding; in this case the threat of a hostile take-over leads the firm to take on more debt. However, matters become more complicated if there is uncertainty and the firm has risky debt. The reason is that the take-over bidder may be deterred from making a bid because he must share some of the gains with creditors. On this, see Israel (1991) and Novaes and Zingales (1994).

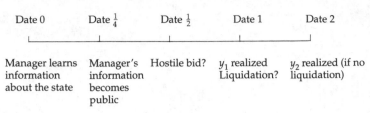

Fig. 6.4

Given that, in *ex ante* terms, state A is very likely, management would have no incentive to deviate from the all-equity structure in the absence of the information that state B is going to occur. (In that case it would adjust its estimate of π^A even closer to 1.) The point is that an all-equity firm is under no pressure to liquidate at date 1. But, since π^A is close to 1, this outcome is approximately efficient, so management is safe from a take-over at date ½. The market's *ex ante* valuation of the initial equity is therefore approximately $y_1^A + y_2^A = 200$.

Management, however, knows that the market will soon learn to its surprise that the bad state B is the true state. Given this, management's job will be in jeopardy unless it can bond itself to liquidate at date 1, since in state B liquidation is efficient.[25] One thing management can do is to make a debt-for-equity swap. For example, it might set $P_1 = 180$. This commits it to liquidation at date 1 in state B and thus thwarts the hostile take-over at date ½.

Of course, given this information structure, management's recapitalization signals that it has learned unfavourable information about the state, in particular that state B will occur. The new debt, however, is riskless (because $y_1^B + L^B = 180$) and so sells for 180. Since all of this accrues to initial shareholders, the value of equity when the recapitalization is announced is also 180. This represents a drop in equity value from 200 even though the recapitalization is in the interest of investors. The point is that the bad news about the state signalled by the recapitalization offsets the increased bonding.[26]

[25] I assume that bonding must occur before the market learns the true state at date ¼ and *a fortiori* before a bid occurs at date ½. (Dates ¼ and ½ might be very close together.)

[26] The idea that a managerial action that serves shareholders can cause a decline in share price because the action reveals bad news about the company is far from new; see e.g. Shleifer and Vishny (1986*b*).

Thus, model 1 can explain not only the apparent fact that debt-for-equity swaps raise the price of equity but also the reverse.

6. *Other theories of capital structure*

As I have noted previously, much of the literature on capital structure does not take an agency perspective. In fact, since Modigliani and Miller's famous irrelevance theorem (Modigliani and Miller 1958), the literature has tended to focus on the role of taxes, asymmetric information, or incomplete markets as explanations of capital structure decisions, rather than on agency problems. In the last part of this chapter, I want to discuss briefly why I think an agency perspective is important, and in particular why the conflict of interest between a company's managers and its investors is crucial for an understanding of capital structure. I shall argue that a great advantage of the agency approach over other theories in the literature is that the agency approach can explain why firms issue senior debt and why a failure to make debt payments leads to a penalty in the form of bankruptcy. A considerably more detailed account of the ideas presented here can be found in Hart (1993).

It is helpful to use model 1 as a vehicle for this discussion. Maintain all the assumptions of model 1, except the assumption that the manager is self-interested. In other words, suppose now that the manager obtains no control benefits and therefore is completely indifferent about whether the firm is liquidated at date 1. (It is supposed that the manager is reliable and honest, but has a 'normal' interest in money.) It is then a simple matter to achieve the first-best with an all-equity capital structure, by putting the manager on the following incentive scheme:

$$(6.7) \qquad I = \theta(d_1 + d_2),$$

where d_1, d_2 are dividend payments made to shareholders at dates 1 and 2, respectively, and θ is a small positive number. The point is that this motivates the manager to maximize the firm's value (and, since θ is small, is almost costless for the shareholders). If the manager keeps the firm going at date 1, he receives

$$(6.8) \qquad \theta(y_1 + y_2),$$

while if he liquidates it he receives

(6.9) $\theta(y_1 + L)$.

Obviously, the manager will liquidate if and only if $y_2 < L$, which is the first-best outcome.

Not only can the efficient outcome be achieved through an all-equity capital structure with a suitable compensation package for management, but any other capital structure will typically lead to inefficiency. This is clear from the earlier discussion of model 1. It was observed there that the manager cannot avoid liquidation if

(6.10) $y_1 < P_1$ and $y_1 + y_2 < P_1 + P_2$.

However, if $P_1, P_2 > 0$, (6.10) may be satisfied when $y_2 > L$, i.e., under weak assumptions, there will be some states where liquidation will occur even when it is inefficient.

A similar argument applied to model 2 shows that debt is also costly because it prevents the (selfless) manager from carrying out some profitable investment projects (the 'debt-overhang problem').

The conclusion so far is that, if managers are not self-interested, firms should not issue debt at all. However, up to now I have ignored taxes. In most advanced capitalist economies, interest income on debt is tax-advantaged relative to dividend income. It is often argued that this explains why firms issue debt. In fact, many papers in the literature develop a theory of optimal capital structure based on this idea: debt is good because it reduces corporate taxes, but bad because it may cause inefficient liquidation (when (6.10) is satisfied).

However, taxes by themselves cannot explain why firms issue debt claims of the type analysed in this chapter.[27] If managers are not self-interested, the first-best can be achieved if the firm issues only *postponable* debt in the form of payment-in-kind (PIK) bonds.[28] In other words, the firm would owe a large amount of money P_1 at date 1 and a large amount of money P_2 at date 2, but the manager would be given the discretion to postpone part of P_1 (in the event that $y_1 < P_1$). The advantage of such an arrangement is that, if P_1 is chosen to be high, the firm can get all the tax advan-

[27] In the following discussion I ignore personal taxes. This means that the issues raised in Miller (1977) do not arise.

[28] PIK bonds give management the option of paying interest in cash or in additional securities. They were used extensively in LBOs in the USA during the 1980s. See Tufano (1993) and Bulow *et al.* (1990).

tages of paying income out as interest rather than dividends; but at the same time the manager can avoid inefficient liquidation by postponing $(P_1 - y_1)$ of the current debt owed when $P_1 > y_1$. Moreover, the selfless manager will never postpone if liquidation really is efficient, given that he is on the incentive scheme (6.7). (d_1, d_2 should now be interpreted as combined payments to creditors and shareholders.)[29]

A similar argument applied to model 2 shows that tax considerations cannot explain why firms issue *senior* (long-term) debt. In particular, if managers initially issue only junior debt (that is, debt with a covenant allowing the firm to issue debt senior to it in the future), then the firm can get all the tax advantages of debt, but at the same time always be able to finance good investment projects later by issuing new, senior debt (i.e. the firm avoids the debt-overhang problem).

In reality, firms issue significant amounts of senior, non-postponable, debt.[30] It may be concluded that other forces than simply taxes are at work.

Next, consider the role of asymmetric information in explaining debt. Myers and Majluf (1984) have argued that a manager who has private information about a firm's profitability may prefer to issue debt rather than equity. To understand their argument in the context of model 1, suppose that the manager learns y_2 at date 1, whereas the market learns this only at date 2. Suppose also that for some (unexplained) historical reason the firm has short-term debt $P_1 > y_1$. Under these conditions, a manager who is a significant shareholder, or who acts on behalf of initial shareholders, will issue debt rather than equity to repay P_1 if he learns that y_2 is high. The reason is that, given that the market undervalues the firm's going concern value, the manager would prefer to raise capital by borrowing than by issuing equity since in the latter case initial shareholders' equity (including his own) is diluted.

---

[29] Before 1989 US corporations apparently faced few restrictions on their ability to use PIK bonds to wipe out taxable income. Since 1989 the Revenue Reconciliation Act has constrained them. See Bulow *et al.* (1990).

[30] Smith and Warner (1979) found that, in a random sample of 87 public issues of debt registered with the Securities and Exchange Commission between January 1974 and December 1975, more than 90% of the bonds contained restrictions on the issuing of additional debt. Although the strength of such debt covenants declined during the 1980s, it is still very common for new public debt issues to contain some restrictions on new debt. See Lehn and Poulsen (1992).

Note, however, that this effect disappears if the manager is on an incentive scheme such as (6.7) (and he is forbidden from holding additional shares). Under these conditions his total reward depends only on the firm's *ex post* total value—$y_1 + y_2$ or $y_1 + L$—and not on the split between shareholders and creditors. Thus, the manager no longer has any incentive to issue debt rather than equity.[31]

Finally, consider the view that firms issue debt in order to 'complete' the market (see e.g. Stiglitz 1974, and Allen and Gale 1994). The idea behind this is that risk-averse investors may be interested in holding claims conditional on a firm's profit, other than just shares, in the absence of a full set of Arrow–Debreu securities. The firm can cater to such investors by issuing risky debt as well as equity and can thereby raise its market value.

There are two difficulties with this as a theory of capital structure, however. First, it is not clear why the firm has to issue these more complicated claims itself; other traders in the market can and do issue such 'derivative' claims. Second, if the purpose of these claims is solely to enrich the available investment opportunities, why does a failure to make a payment to creditors trigger the firm's default and bankruptcy; i.e., why doesn't the firm issue preferred shares that specify that claim-holders are owed a fixed amount, but that the firm can pay out less in the absence of a dividend to shareholders? Preferred shares offer the same return stream as risky debt if the manager is selfless; however, they have the great advantage that they avoid the inefficiency costs of bankruptcy.

This section—and the chapter as a whole—can be summed up as follows. Taxes, asymmetric information, and incomplete markets are all undoubtedly important influences on the choice of a firm's capital structure. However, these factors alone cannot explain why debt has the feature that it is senior and that a failure to pay leads to a penalty in the form of bankruptcy, i.e. why debt is associated with a 'hard' budget constraint.[32] At the risk of belabour-

[31] This observation has also been made by Dybvig and Zender (1991). The above discussion does not do full justice to the Myers–Majluf model (or to other asymmetric information theories of debt). For a fuller account, see Hart (1993).

[32] A qualification should be made. Some writers have argued that, even if the management is selfless, senior debt may be useful as a way of bonding the firm if it engages in strategic behaviour in product markets or in bargaining with unions;

ing the obvious, note that the theory developed in this chapter *does* explain these facts. If debt were postponable, the manager would never be forced to liquidate in model 1 or to pay out free cash flow in model 3. If debt were junior, the manager could finance an unprofitable investment in models 2 and 3 by issuing debt at date 1 that was senior to existing debt.

The conclusion is that, although the agency approach may not be the whole story, it would seem to be an essential part of any fully developed theory of capital structure.[33]

see Baldwin (1983), Brander and Lewis (1986), and Perotti and Spier (1993). Although strategic effects may well be important, however, it would be surprising if they alone could explain the widespread use of (senior) debt or the variations in debt across industries, countries, or over time. On the latter, see Rajan and Zingales (1994).

[33] One weakness of the models I have presented in this chapter is that they do not explain why firms issue dividends. In these models, the managers always (weakly) prefer to retain profits and use them to build a bigger empire. (Shareholders receive a 'liquidating' dividend at date 2, but only because by assumption the firm is wound up.) One way to explain dividends is to drop the assumption that shareholders are completely passive. The manager may then pay a dividend in order to deter a large shareholder or a take-over bidder from intervening in the company's affairs. In fact, the debt–equity swaps considered in §5 had this character. Developing a convincing model of dividend behaviour is a very important topic for future research.

APPENDIX

Another role of short-term debt: model 3

Model 3 combines models 1 and 2; i.e. investment and liquidation are both allowed. The following assumption is made.

> ASSUMPTION A1. $y_2 > L$ with probability 1. Also, given any number i, the manager has a new investment project costing i and this project yields $r = 0$.

Given this assumption, the role of short-term debt is to force the manager to pay out free cash flow without triggering liquidation.

Consider the manager's situation once the uncertainty has been resolved at date 1. If $y_1 \geq P_1$, the manager can invest $y_1 - P_1$ out of current earnings. However, he may be able to invest more by borrowing. The most he can borrow is $y_1 + y_2 - P_1 - P_2$. It follows that his maximum investment is

$$I = \text{Max } \{y_1 - P_1, y_1 + y_2 - P_1 - P_2\}.$$

Since investment is totally unproductive, it follows that the return to initial security-holders is:

$$R = y_1 + y_2 - I = \text{Min } (y_2 + P_1, P_1 + P_2).$$

Suppose next that $y_1 < P_1$. Then the manager can avoid default at date 1 if $y_1 + y_2 \geq P_1 + P_2$. In this case he will invest $y_1 + y_2 - P_1 - P_2$ and the return to investors will be $P_1 + P_2$. On the other hand, if $y_1 + y_2 < P_1 + P_2$, default will occur and the firm will be liquidated.

Putting all the cases together, one finds that the return to investing is

$$(6A.1) \qquad R = \begin{cases} \text{Min } (y_2 + P_1, P_1 + P_2) & \text{if } y_1 \geq P_1, \\ P_1 + P_2 & \text{if } y_1 < P_1 \text{ and } y_1 + y_2 \geq P_1 + P_2, \\ y_1 + L & \text{if } y_1 < P_1 \text{ and } y_1 + y_2 < P_1 + P_2. \end{cases}$$

The next step is to analyse optimal capital structure in this third model. It is easy to achieve the first-best outcome if there is no *ex ante* uncertainty about y_1, y_2, and L. Simply set $P_1 \geq y_1$, $P_1 + P_2 = y_1 + y_2$. Then the manager can't invest since there is no free cash flow; but also he can avoid liquidation (possibly by borrowing).

When there is uncertainty, matters are more complicated. Again simplify by supposing that (y_1, y_2, L) takes on just two values (y_1^A, y_2^A, L^A) and (y_1^B, y_2^B, L^B), with probabilities π^A and $\pi^B = 1 - \pi^A$, respectively. If $y_1^A + y_2^A = y_1^B + y_2^B$, the first-best can be achieved by setting $P_1 \geq \text{Max}(y_1^A, y_1^B)$, $P_1 + P_2 = y_1^A + y_2^A$. The reason is that, as in the case of certainty, there is no free cash flow, but the manager can avoid liquidation in the lower y_1 state by borrowing. So suppose without loss of generality that

(6A.2) $$y_1^A + y_2^A > y_1^B + y_2^B.$$

Consider two subcases.

1. $y_1^A \leq y_1^B$

Here the first-best can be achieved by setting $P_1 = y_1^B$, $P_2 = y_1^A + y_2^A - y_1^B$. In state A, the manager pays the date 1 debt by borrowing $y_1^B - y_1^A$. In state B the manager can repay P_1 out of current earnings. The manager is able to avoid default in both states but has neither the free cash nor the borrowing capacity to make new investments.

2. $y_1^A > y_1^B$

Now the first-best cannot be achieved. The reason is that for there to be no slack in state A it must be the case that

$$y_1^A + y_2^A \leq P_1 + P_2,$$
$$y_1^A \leq P_1.$$

But then the firm will go bankrupt in state B. There are two basic choices. First, P_1 and P_2 can be set so that bankruptcy is avoided in both states but some investment occurs in state A. Second, P_1 and P_2 can be set so that no investment occurs in state A, but the firm goes bankrupt in state B.

Avoiding bankruptcy. Consider the first choice, where bankruptcy is avoided in both states. Obviously there is no reason to have slack in state B as well as in state A. There are two ways to achieve this. One is to set $P_1 \geq y_1^A$, $P_1 + P_2 = y_1^B + y_2^B$, in which case the manager avoids liquidation in state B by borrowing $y_1^B + y_2^B - P_1$, but is able to invest $(y_1^A + y_2^A - y_1^B - y_2^B)$ in state A. That is,

$$I^A \equiv \text{investment in state } A = y_1^A + y_2^A - y_1^B - y_2^B,$$
$$I^B \equiv \text{investment in state } B = 0,$$

and the expected return to initial security holders is

$$R = \pi^A (y_1^A + y_2^A - I^A) + \pi^B (y_1^B + y_2^B - I^B) = y_1^B + y_2^B.$$

The second option is to set $P_1 + P_2 = y_1^A + y_2^A$ but to choose $P_1 = y_1^B$, so that the manager can repay his debts without borrowing in state B. In this case,

$$I^A = y_1^A - y_1^B,$$
$$I^B = 0,$$
$$R = \pi^A (y_1^A + y_2^A - y_1^A + y_1^B) + \pi^B (y_1^B + y_2^B) = y_1^B + \pi^A y_2^A + \pi^B y_2^B.$$

Option 1 is preferred to option 2 if and only if it generates a lower value of (totally unprofitable) investment, i.e. if and only if

$$y_2^A < y_2^B.$$

Triggering bankruptcy. Consider next the second choice, which is to trigger bankruptcy in state B. Under these conditions, it is optimal to set $P_1 = y_1^A$, $P_2 = y_2^A$ to avoid slack in state A. The return to initial security holders is then

$$R = \pi^A (y_1^A + y_2^A) + \pi^B (y_1^B + L^B).$$

The final step of subcase 2 is to compare the values of R from avoiding bankruptcy and triggering bankruptcy. The results for subcase 2 overall are summarized in (6A.3)–(6A.5). (To obtain the results for model 3 overall, one must combine (6A.3)–(6A.5) with subcase 1, which is concerned with the situation $y_1^A \leq y_1^B$.)

(6A.3)   If $y_1^A > y_1^B$, $y_2^A < y_2^B$, and $y_1^B + y_2^B > \pi^A (y_1^A + y_2^A) + \pi^B (y_1^B + L^B)$,

         it is optimal to set $P_1 \geq y_1^A$, $P_1 + P_2 = y_1^B + y_2^B$.

That is, total debt is set such that the firm just avoids bankruptcy in state B by borrowing, but the firm has enough debt capacity in state A to make an unprofitable investment.

(6A.4) If $y_1^A > y_1^B$, $y_2^A > y_2^B$ and $y_1^B + \pi^A y_2^A + \pi^B y_2^B > \pi^A(y_1^A + y_2^A)$
$+ \pi^B(y_1^B + L^B)$,
it is optimal to set $P_1 = y_1^B$, $P_2 = y_1^A + y_2^A - y_1^B$.

That is, debt levels are set such that the firm can avoid bankruptcy in state B by paying its short-term debt out of current earnings, but the firm has free cash flow in state A which it can use to make unprofitable investments.

(6A.5) If $y_1^A > y_1^B$ and $\pi^A(y_1^A + y_2^A) + \pi^B(y_1^B + L^B) >$
$\text{Max}\{y_1^B + y_2^B, y_1^B + \pi^A y_2^A + \pi^B y_2^B\}$,
it is optimal to set $P_1 = y_1^A$, $P_2 = y_2^A$.

That is, debt levels are set such that the firm just avoids bankruptcy in state A by paying its debts out of current earnings, but goes bankrupt in state B.

This concludes our analysis of model 3.

It remains to establish two results from Section 5. To see that model 3 supports the existence of a positive relationship between debt and asset tangibility, consider subcase 2 of the two-state case ($y_1^A > y_1^B$, $y_1^A + y_2^A > y_1^B + y_2^B$). As L^B rises, it becomes more likely that (6A.5) applies rather than (6A.3) or (6A.4). Since $P_1 + P_2 = y_1^A + y_2^A$ in (6A.5), while it is no greater than $y_1^A + y_2^A$ in (6A.3) and (6A.4), the conclusion is that $P_1 + P_2$ rises (weakly) as L^B rises.

Consider next the relationship between debt and the stability of cash flows. Start off with the case where y_1 and y_2 are certain. Then it is optimal to set $P_1 = y_1$, $P_2 = y_2$. Now set $y_1^A = y_1 + \delta$, $y_1^B = y_1 - \delta$, $y_2^A = y_2^B = y_2$, $\pi^A = \pi^B = \frac{1}{2}$, $L^A = L^B = L$, where $\delta > 0$. Then, according to (6A.3)–(6A.5), if $\frac{1}{2}y_2 - \delta > \frac{1}{2}L$, it is optimal to avoid bankruptcy in both states. One way to do this is to set $P_1 = y_1 + \delta$, $P_2 = y_2 - 2\delta$. In this case it can be said that an increase in uncertainty *reduces* (total) debt. On the other hand, if $\frac{1}{2}y_2 - \delta < \frac{1}{2}L$, it is optimal to trigger bankruptcy in state B by setting $P_1 = y_1 + \delta$, $P_2 = y_2$ (see (6A.5)). In this case, an increase in uncertainty *increases* total debt.

7

Bankruptcy Procedure

THE last two chapters have analysed the financial structure of a closely held company (Chapter 5) and a public company (Chapter 6). It was argued that debt can play an important role in constraining managers or owners of both kinds of company. In the Hart–Moore model of Chapter 5, debt forced an entrepreneur to pay out funds to investors rather than to himself. In the various models of Chapter 6, debt forced the sale of assets and limited a manager's ability to make unprofitable, but power-enhancing, investments.

Of course, given that a company takes on debt, there will be circumstances, arising perhaps from an unexpected shock, in which the company will default on this debt. In such a situation, the company is (in effect) bankrupt. The question is: what should happen in a bankruptcy state? (To put it another way, what lies behind the 'liquidation' value L in Chapters 5 and 6?) This is the topic of the present chapter.

The chapter begins with a discussion of the need for, and goals of, a formal bankruptcy procedure (Sections 1 and 2). Section 3 describes existing procedures in the West, with a particular emphasis on US and (to a lesser extent) UK procedures. The two main US procedures are 'Chapter 7' and 'Chapter 11'. Chapter 7 calls for a bankrupt company to be sold off for cash. In contrast, Chapter 11 is an attempt to allow companies to reorganize. Unfortunately, there is widespread dissatisfaction with both procedures. Chapter 7 is thought to lead to the liquidation of healthy companies. Chapter 11 has been criticized for being cumbersome and biased in favour of reorganization under incumbent management. Chapter 11 is also flawed because it mixes the decision of what should happen to the company with the decision of who gets what. This leads to a great deal of haggling.

Section 4 turns to a procedure—proposed elsewhere by Philippe Aghion, John Moore, and myself—that tries to combine the best features of Chapters 7 and 11.[1] (The procedure uses in a significant way an idea of Lucian Bebchuk; see Bebchuk (1988).) In the Aghion–Hart–Moore (AHM) procedure, debt claims are converted into equity, and the decision about whether to liquidate or reorganize is then put to a vote by the new shareholders. Sections 5–7 discuss some practical difficulties concerning the AHM procedure and how they might be resolved, and provide some concluding remarks.

As mentioned earlier, the style of this chapter is very different from that of the others in the book. There is no model, and the argument is conducted at a fairly informal level. The chapter attempts to apply theoretical ideas to throw light on an important practical issue. It should be judged by whether it is successful in this regard.

1. The need for a formal bankruptcy procedure

It is helpful to begin the discussion with the case studied in Chapter 5 of a single debtor and a single creditor. It was observed there that default is an event where control of the assets shifts from the debtor to the creditor; that is, the creditor becomes the new owner of the assets. In this simple case there is little if any need for a formal bankruptcy procedure. Bankruptcy procedure should do no more than ensure that a transfer of ownership and control does take place in the default state, i.e. that the terms of the debt contract are upheld. After this, the creditor should have the right to decide whether to sell off the assets, or renegotiate her debt contract with the entrepreneur, so as to keep the assets in place.[2]

Matters become more complicated when there are many creditors (the situation studied in Chapter 6). The problem is that in this case it is not really clear what a 'transfer of ownership and

---

[1] See Aghion *et al.* (1992, 1994, 1995). This procedure also appears as Appendix E in 'The Insolvency Service, the Insolvency Act 1986: Company Voluntary Arrangements and Administration Orders, A Consultative Document' (1993), London.

[2] However, Harris and Raviv (1995) argue that there is a role for a state-provided bankruptcy procedure even in the single debtor–single creditor case, whose purpose would be to reallocate bargaining power between the debtor and the creditor.

control to (all the) creditors' means. In the absence of a formal bankruptcy procedure, the law provides a creditor with two main remedies in the event of a default. First, with regard to a secured loan, the creditor can seize the assets that serve as collateral for the loan. Second, with regard to an unsecured loan, the creditor can sue the debtor and call on a sheriff to enforce the court's judgment, possibly by selling the debtor's assets (see Baird and Jackson 1985).

Difficulties arise when the debtor has insufficient assets to cover his liabilities (which is very likely to be the case—otherwise why would the debtor have gone bankrupt?). Creditors may then engage in a socially wasteful race to be first to seize their collateral or to obtain a judgment against the debtor.[3] Also—and perhaps more important—this race may lead to the dismantlement of the debtor's assets and to a loss of value for all creditors if these assets are worth more as a whole than as a collection of pieces.

Given this, it is in the collective interest of creditors that the disposition of the debtor's assets be carried out in an orderly manner. This is the rationale for a formal bankruptcy procedure.

Nothing so far implies that the formal bankruptcy procedure needs to be provided by the state rather than by the parties themselves. In a world of costless contracting, debtors and creditors would anticipate the possibility of default and the consequent collective action problems and specify as part of their initial contract what should happen in a default state—in particular, whether the company should be reorganized or liquidated and how its value should be divided up among various claimants.

In practice, transaction costs may be too large for debtors and creditors to design their own bankruptcy procedure contractually, particularly in situations where debtors acquire new assets and new creditors as time passes. Instead, parties may prefer to rely on a 'standard form' state-provided bankruptcy procedure. It is a long way from this observation, however, to any conclusions about the *nature* of an optimal standard-form procedure. The problem is that a satisfactory analysis of an optimal procedure requires a theory both of why contracts are incomplete, and of how the state can overcome this incompleteness. Chapters 2–4 shed some light on the first of these questions, but not on the sec-

---

[3] See Jackson (1986). The race to be first is a negative-sum game since wins and losses cancel out and everybody spends resources to play the game.

ond. In particular, in Chapters 2–4 contractual incompleteness was the result of the courts' inability to observe variables that the parties could observe. Thus, the courts were the *source* of contractual incompleteness rather than the solution.[4]

In what follows, therefore, optimal bankruptcy procedure is not derived from first principles. Instead, some goals that an efficient bankruptcy procedure should satisfy are suggested, and a procedure is described that does a reasonable job of meeting these goals. It will be argued that the procedure presented is practical and avoids some of the pitfalls of existing procedures. Also, the procedure is sufficiently simple and natural that future work *may* show it to be optimal within a reasonable class of procedures.[5]

2. Goals of a bankruptcy procedure

As mentioned above, the analysis does not proceed from first principles. However, economic theory suggests that the following are desirable goals for a bankruptcy procedure.

1. A good bankruptcy procedure should achieve an *ex post* efficient outcome (that is, an outcome that maximizes the total value of the proceeds—measured in money terms—received by the existing claimants).[6]
2. A good bankruptcy procedure should preserve the (*ex ante*) bonding role of debt by penalizing managers adequately in bankruptcy states. However, bankruptcy should not be so

---

[4] For a further discussion of this, see Hart (1990). Also, for an analysis of the courts' role in filling in the gaps in incomplete contracts, see Ayres and Gertner (1989).

[5] It is not suggested that the procedure, if adopted, should be mandatory. Anybody who wishes to deviate from it and design their own procedure should be allowed to do so.

[6] Note that 'external' considerations are excluded from the definition of efficiency; that is, it is assumed that the important benefits and costs have been incorporated into the valuation of the firm. For example, such items as the external benefit from maintaining employment in the local area are not included. If there are external considerations, government action may indeed be warranted, but bankruptcy law is the wrong instrument for dealing with such considerations. It would be better to have a general employment subsidy to save jobs rather than distort bankruptcy procedure in order to save bad firms.

harsh that managers try to avoid it at any cost, e.g. by 'gambling' with the company's assets.

3. A good bankruptcy procedure should preserve the absolute priority of claims; that is, the most senior creditors should be paid off before anything is given to the next most senior creditors, and so on down the ladder (with ordinary shareholders at the bottom).

A brief justification for these goals follows. Goal 1 simply reflects the fact that, other things equal, more is preferred to less; in particular, if a procedure can be modified to deliver higher total *ex post* value, then, given that absolute priority is preserved (i.e. goal 3), everybody will be better off. The motivation for goal 2 should be clear, given the analysis of Chapter 6 on the disciplinary role of debt. It was observed there that debt may have an important role in constraining or bonding managers to act in the interest of claim-holders. A bankruptcy procedure that lets managers off too lightly if they fail to pay their debts—for example by favouring them in the reorganization process—will interfere with this *ex ante* bonding role of debt.

Goal 3 is desirable for several reasons. First, if a structure of debt priority that was agreed to contractually can always be violated within bankruptcy, then people may be unwilling to lend to the company in the first place, since their claims will be unprotected. Second, a discrepancy between entitlements inside and outside bankruptcy can lead to inefficient rent-seeking, with some people bribing management into deliberately precipitating bankruptcy and other people attempting to forestall bankruptcy (see Jackson 1986). Third, model 2 of Chapter 6 shows that management may issue senior debt in order to commit itself not to finance unprofitable projects. This ability to commit will be weakened if the seniority of claims is not respected.

Although goals 1–3 are appealing, they are not beyond question. Bankruptcy scholars have raised doubts about goal 3 in particular. Critics argue that, if equity-holders get little or nothing in a bankruptcy proceeding, then management—acting on the equity-holders' behalf—will engage in risky, but inefficient, behaviour when a company is close to bankruptcy, because, while the shareholders gain if things go well, it is the creditors that lose if things go badly (see White 1989).

This argument supposes that management acts on behalf of shareholders, an assumption that may be plausible for small owner-managed companies but is questionable for large, public companies. Chapter 6 argued that it is more reasonable to suppose that the management of a public company is self-interested. Under these conditions, there is a case for making bankruptcy procedure less harsh for managers—to prevent them from engaging in highly risky behaviour to save their jobs—but this is already covered under goal 2.

Even in the case of small, owner-managed companies, it is far from clear that departures from absolute priority are the best way to soften the blow of bankruptcy. A better method might be to give managers and/or owners a 'golden handshake' (or 'parachute') in the form of senior debt.[7]

Given the above, goals 1–3 will be assumed to be desirable, *ceteris paribus*. It is worth noting, however, that the procedure proposed below could be modified to allow for departures from absolute priority if this were felt to be a good idea.

A final point to make is that some of the three goals may be in conflict. For example, if incumbent management has special skills, then *ex post* efficiency (goal 1) might call for the incumbent management of a bankrupt company to be retained. However, knowing this, management might have little incentive to avoid bankruptcy; i.e. goal 2 would not be served.[8]

In view of this, the best one can hope for is a reasonable balance between the above goals, particularly goals 1 and 2. The procedure discussed below is constructed with this in mind. Although I will argue that it does a satisfactory job, the procedure could be fine-tuned if the balance were felt to be wrong; this point is considered further below.

---

[7] In addition, in order to prevent managers from delaying a bankruptcy filing for too long, it may be desirable to give creditors greater powers to push a company into involuntary bankruptcy. For a discussion of the incentives of creditors to push a company into bankruptcy, see Mitchell (1993).
[8] The conflict between goals 1 and 2 is analysed in Berkovitch *et al.* (1993).

3. Existing procedures

This section discusses existing procedures. Although there are many different bankruptcy procedures used around the world, they fall into two main categories: cash auctions and structured bargaining. These are discussed in turn, with particular attention being paid to their application in the USA and the UK.

Cash auctions (e.g. 'Chapter 7' in the USA or liquidation in the UK)

In a cash auction, a trustee or receiver supervises the sale of the company's assets. Often the assets are sold piecemeal; in other words, the company is liquidated (having been closed down). Sometimes, however, the company is sold as a going concern. Whichever occurs, the receipts from the sale are distributed among former claimants according to absolute priority (usually secured debt, then various priority claims, then unsecured debt, then subordinated debt, and finally equity).

In a world of perfect capital markets, a cash auction would (presumably) be the ideal bankruptcy procedure (see Baird 1986). Anybody who could make the company profitable would be able to raise cash from some source (a commercial bank, an investment bank, the stock market) and make a bid for the company. Perfect competition among bidders would ensure that the company was sold for its true value, and that the company's assets ended up in their highest value use; that is, the company would be maintained as a going concern if and only if its going concern value exceeded its liquidation value.

In practice, there is widespread scepticism about the efficacy of cash auctions. The feeling is that a combination of transaction costs, asymmetric information, and moral hazard makes it difficult for bidders to raise sufficient cash to maintain a company as a going concern (i.e. capital markets are not perfect). As a consequence, there may be a lack of competition in the auction and few bids to keep the company whole. The result will be that some companies are liquidated piecemeal and/or sold at a low price.

It is worth spelling out a transaction cost reason for imperfect capital markets. Suppose that a huge public company such as General Electric were put on the block. Say the expected present

value of GE's earnings is $100 billion. Would any bidder be pre-
pared to offer this much for the company? The answer to this
question might well be no. Someone making a cash bid for the
company is, in effect, taking GE private. (This is unless the bidder
itself represents a public company.) The bidder's intention may
well be to take GE public again later, but in the meantime the
bidder is bearing the risk of changes in GE's value. The bidder
will, of course, 'charge' for this risk-bearing by offering a lower
price in the original auction. The consequence of this is twofold.
First, the going-concern bid may lose to a collection of piecemeal
bids for GE's assets, since the latter achieve risk-sharing by
spreading risk over a large number of bidders. Second, regardless
of who wins the auction, the amount of cash raised will tend to be
lower.[9]

It should be emphasized that the transaction cost being identified here is not to do with management having private information about the company's value (and being unable to verify it to
the market); rather, it is to do with the difficulty of assembling a
suitable group of investors to be risk-bearers for the new
company.[10] Note, however, that there is a natural group of

[9] The problems of financing a cash bid will be exacerbated to the extent that
other companies in the industry, which may be the natural purchasers of the bankrupt company, are also suffering from financial distress, because the shock hitting
the bankrupt company is industry-wide. See Shleifer and Vishny (1992).

[10] There is some empirical support for the idea that it is costly to find investors
to put up the cash to buy a public company. One piece of evidence comes from the
work on initial public offerings (IPOs). Ritter (1987) investigates two quantifiable
components of the costs of going public: direct expenses and underpricing. From
a sample of firms that were taken public by investment bankers in the USA during 1977–82, he finds that these two costs together averaged between 21% and 32%
of the realized market value of the securities issued, depending on the type of IPO.
The underpricing effect can be attributed to the risk aversion of issuers/invest-
ment bankers, in conjunction with various forms of asymmetric information (see
e.g. Rock 1986). A second, more casual, piece of evidence concerns workouts.
When a company is financially distressed, it often tries to persuade its creditors to
renegotiate their claims by lengthening the maturity of their debt or by swapping
their debt for equity. The question is: why do creditors frequently go along with
this rather than pushing for bankruptcy and liquidation? It would seem that the
latter strategy would be rational if a cash auction could be relied on to generate
maximum value, i.e. if bidders could easily raise cash to buy the company. (Part
of the desire for renegotiation can possibly be traced to the fact that most bankruptcies in the USA are filed under Chapter 11, rather than Chapter 7, and creditors may prefer to avoid Chapter 11. However, this does not explain workouts in
other countries where Chapter 11 does not exist.) A third piece of evidence comes
from another area of corporate finance: take-overs. Companies taking over other
companies sometimes offer shareholders a mixture of cash and securities for their

risk-bearers at hand: the former claimants (who were, after all, the previous risk-bearers). Transaction costs would be reduced if bidders could reach this group directly by offering them securities in the post-bankruptcy company. This is not allowed for in a cash-only auction like 'Chapter 7' but is a key feature of the bankruptcy procedure described below (and also of 'Chapter 11').[11]

Neither the above theoretical argument nor the empirical evidence cited in n. 10 provides much indication of the magnitude of the imperfections in capital markets. Given this, it is desirable to adopt a bankruptcy procedure that works well whether capital markets are imperfect or not. The procedure described later has this flexibility. One version of it consists of an auction in which both cash and noncash bids for the company are allowed. If capital markets are perfect, the company will go to the bidder with the highest willingness to pay—moreover, this bidder can do no better than to offer cash—and thus the outcome will be exactly the same as in a cash-only auction. On the other hand, if capital markets are imperfect, the procedure can deliver an outcome that is superior to that achievable by a cash auction.

Structured bargaining (e.g. US Chapter 11 or UK Administration)

Because of the concern about the effectiveness of cash auctions, a number of countries have developed alternative procedures based on the idea of structured bargaining. The basic idea behind these procedures is that the company's claimants are encouraged

existing shares. In fact, in 1993, 55% of all mergers and acquisitions in the USA with value between $100 million and $1 billion had a noncash component (see Merrill Lynch Business Advisory Services, *Mergerstat Review*). Noncash bids are harder to evaluate than cash bids, so one might expect that, particularly in a contested situation, bidding companies would prefer to offer straight cash. The fact that they do not suggests that it is difficult for them to raise cash. (There may, however, be other reasons why companies make noncash bids, such as the presence of taxes and asymmetric information.)

[11] Note that it is not being suggested that managerial private information cannot also cause financing problems. For example, suppose GE's management knows that the company is worth $100 billion, but the market does not. Then management may be unable to raise $100 billion to make a cash bid, and the company could be sold inefficiently. Unfortunately, it is not clear that this problem lies in the province of bankruptcy law (nor is it clear that the law can help). As argued earlier, the rationale for bankruptcy law is to deal with collective-action problems among creditors, and yet this asymmetric information problem would arise even if there were a single creditor.

to bargain about the future of the company—in particular, whether it should be liquidated or reorganized and how its value should be divided up—according to predetermined rules. The leading example of a structured bargaining procedure in the West is Chapter 11 of the US Bankruptcy Code; however, UK Administration is based on similar ideas, as are procedures in France, Germany, and Japan.

The details of Chapter 11 are complicated, but the basic elements are as follows. A stay is put on creditors' claims (that is, they are frozen; no creditor is allowed to seize, or have a sheriff sell, any of the company's assets during the process); claim-holders are grouped into classes according to the type of claim they have (secured or unsecured, senior or junior); committees or trustees are appointed to represent each class; and a judge supervises a process of bargaining among the committees to determine a plan of action and a division of value for the company. During the process, incumbent management usually runs the company. An important part of the procedure is that a plan can be implemented if it receives approval by a suitable majority of each claimant class; unanimity is not required.[12]

UK Administration was introduced in the 1986 Insolvency Act as 'the British version of Chapter 11'. An important difference between UK Administration and Chapter 11 is that the UK administrator (who is an insolvency practitioner) runs the company during bankruptcy, rather than incumbent management. There are also a number of differences in the voting rules between the two procedures. To date, the costs of UK Administration are such that it has rarely been used.

Chapter 11 has been subject to a great deal of criticism in the last few years. Among other things, practitioners and commentators have claimed that it is time-consuming, that it involves significant legal and administrative costs, that it causes considerable loss in the bankrupt company's value, that it is (relatively) soft on management, and that the judges who run it sometimes abuse their powers.[13]

---

[12] Specifically, for a plan to be agreed to, it must receive approval by a two-thirds majority in value terms, and a simple majority in number terms, of each debt class, and a two-thirds majority of equity—although under certain circumstances a plan can be forced on a class (the cram-down provision).

[13] For some of the literature on these issues, see Cutler and Summers (1988), Gilson (1989, 1990), LoPucki and Whitford (1993), and Weiss (1990, 1991).

It would undoubtedly be possible to modify Chapter 11—and procedures like it—to improve matters, and a number of suggestions along these lines have been made. However, there are two fundamental problems inherent in any structured bargaining procedure that no amount of tinkering can solve. These problems are associated with the fact that a structured bargaining procedure like Chapter 11 attempts to make two decisions at once: what to do with the company, and who should get what in the event of a restructuring of claims.

Problem 1. Restructured companies do not have an objective value. Consequently, it is hard to know what fraction of the post-bankruptcy company's securities each group of creditors is entitled to receive. This is true even if there is no dispute about the amount and seniority of each creditor's claim. As a result, there can be a great deal of haggling.

Problem 2. Perhaps even more serious, there is a danger that the wrong decision will be made concerning the company's future. The voting mechanism is fixed in advance, which means that those people whose payoff ought not to be affected by the outcome (either because they are fully protected anyway, or because they are not entitled to anything) may end up controlling the pivotal votes.

Problem 1 is well understood, having been discussed at some length in the literature.[14] Problem 2 has also been noted but has been subject to less analysis. An example may help to illustrate it.

Example 1. Suppose senior creditors are owed 100 (dollars or pounds) and the liquidation value of the company is 90. Assume that, if the company were maintained as a going concern for six months, it would be worth on average 110 (suppose the interest rate is zero). However, there is uncertainty: if things go well, it will be worth 180; if things go badly, it will be worth only 40, where the outcomes are equally likely. (The average of 180 and 40

---

[14] See e.g. Roe (1983) and Bebchuk (1988). The recent bankruptcy of Macy's provides a clear example of problem 1. Senior creditors claimed that the reorganized company was worth little (implying that they should receive a large fraction of it). Junior creditors and shareholders claimed the opposite. See e.g. Patrick M. Reilly and Laura Jereski, 'Macy Strategy Seems to Sway Senior Creditors', *Wall Street Journal*, 2 May 1994, at A4; Laura Jereski and Patrick M. Reilly, 'Laurence Tisch Leads Dissent on Macy Board', *Wall Street Journal*, 29 March 1994, at B1.

is 110.) Clearly, the value-maximizing choice is to keep the company going, since 110 exceeds the liquidation value of 90. However, it is not in the senior creditors' interest to do this. If things go well and the company is worth 180, the senior creditors get only the 100 they are owed; but if things go badly, they get just 40. The average of these amounts is 70, which is less than the 90 the senior creditors receive from immediate liquidation.

In this example senior creditors may vote to liquidate the company immediately rather than enter into a lengthy negotiation which might lead to the company's being saved. This is in spite of the fact that there is enough value in the efficient outcome for the senior creditors to be paid off in full: 110 exceeds the 100 senior debt. Had the senior creditors been paid off, and the vote left in the hands of the junior creditors and the shareholders (whose money is at stake), then the junior creditors would have made the efficient decision about the company's future.

Things may go the other way, though. Consider a variant on example 1.

Example 2. Make assumptions as in example 1, except that the upside value from continuation is lower—only 120 rather than 180. Thus, the average value from continuation is 80 (the average of 120 and 40).

In this example the junior creditors and shareholders are not entitled to anything, since the best that can happen to the company is that it is liquidated for 90, which is less than the senior debt. So the junior creditors and shareholders ought not to be party to the decision over the company's future. And yet, the rules of Chapter 11 dictate that they do have votes, and as a result they may be in a position to press for continuation (since they can see the upside potential of 120).[15] If the junior creditors and shareholders have enough votes to veto a liquidation plan, then at best the senior creditors may have to bribe them to accept it—which would lead to a violation of absolute priority—and at worst the

[15] This is unless the cram-down procedure is adopted; see Baird and Jackson (1985). Under cram-down, junior claimants' voting rights are removed on the grounds that they would receive nothing in liquidation. The cram-down procedure cannot be relied upon, however; among other things, it requires an accurate judicial evaluation of the company's liquidation value.

company may be inefficiently kept going.[16] Notice that, had the vote been left in the hands of senior creditors, they would have made the correct decision about the company's future.[17]

At this point, it is worth asking why the various claimants cannot bargain around the inefficiencies described in examples 1 and 2. Probably the most important reason is that, in the case of large companies, there are often numerous claimants (bondholders, trade creditors, and shareholders), which can make negotiation around a given (inefficient) procedure very difficult and lengthy (owing to free-rider and hold-out problems, combined with asymmetries of information among claimants).

Consider example 1, where senior creditors might vote to liquidate the company. This outcome could be avoided if junior creditors and shareholders could bribe the senior creditors not to liquidate; for example, they could buy out the senior creditors at a price between 90 and 100. However, the more numerous and heterogeneous the junior creditors and shareholders are, the more difficult it is—and the longer it will take—to co-ordinate such an offer. (Each junior claimant will want the other junior claimants to bribe the senior creditors.) As a result, either an

[16] The empirical work on departures from absolute priority suggests that junior claimants do indeed have enough power to force concessions from senior creditors; i.e. the problem described in example 2 is relevant in practice; see Franks and Torous (1989). There is less formal empirical evidence on the problem described in example 1. However, practitioners frequently mention (and write about) this problem, so it would seem to be a mistake not to take it seriously. Also, the conflict between the desire of senior creditors to terminate a bankruptcy proceeding quickly, and that of junior creditors to drag it out on the off-chance that there will be something of value for them, seems to have been a factor in the recent Macy's bankruptcy; see, e.g., Patrick M. Reilly and Laura Jereski, 'Media and Marketing: Macy May Seek Shorter Period for Extension', *Wall Street Journal*, 18 February 1994, at B2.

[17] It is worth mentioning another bankruptcy procedure used in the UK, called Administrative Receivership. Under Administrative Receivership, a senior creditor with what is known as a 'floating charge'—typically a bank—has the right to appoint a receiver when a company goes bankrupt. The receiver takes charge of the company and decides whether to close it down or maintain it as a going concern with a view to selling it later. The receiver's prime responsibility is to the bank. Receivership increases the chance that a company will be kept going relative to liquidation. However, receivership suffers from the same problem as that described in example 1. In particular, the bank has only a fixed claim, which means that there is a ceiling on how much it can earn. As a result, the bank may decide against keeping a good company going because it does not see the upside potential. Moreover, even when the bank does decide to sell a company as a going concern, it may not have an incentive to push for a high sale price, given the ceiling on its return. As a result, there may be little left over for junior claimants.

agreement will not be reached, or it will require lengthy negotiation (there may be a 'war of attrition').[18]

Similar problems arise in example 2, where senior creditors must collectively decide to make concessions to junior claimants to compensate them for not pursuing reorganization. It may be easier to achieve agreement in example 2, however, to the extent that the number of senior creditors is relatively small and co-ordination problems are therefore reduced.

A structured procedure like Chapter 11 reduces the severity of the above bargaining problems by making the majority's will binding on the minority. (In contrast to an out-of-bankruptcy workout, unanimity is not required, which mitigates free-riding and hold-out behaviour.) However, even in this case an efficient outcome may not be reached, e.g. because of asymmetries of information. Suppose, in example 1, that junior claimants are unsure whether the company's liquidation value is really 90 as opposed to some lower figure, while senior creditors know the true value. Then junior creditors may quite rationally 'low-ball' the senior creditors by offering them less than 90 to compensate them for not liquidating. In this case the senior creditors will turn them down if the true liquidation value is 90, and a valuable going-concern opportunity will be lost.[19]

4. An alternative procedure

The previous discussion can be summarized as follows. Existing bankruptcy procedures are flawed for two reasons: either they assume perfect capital markets (as in US Chapter 7), or they mix the decision of what should happen to the company with the decision of who gets what (as in US Chapter 11). I now describe a procedure (the AHM procedure) that does not suffer from these defects. The key lies in transforming a group of people with different claims (and therefore different objectives) into a homogeneous

---

[18] The factors that make negotiation difficult here are similar to those that cause out-of-bankruptcy workouts to fail when there are many creditors. See the discussion of hold-out and free-rider problems in Ch. 5.

[19] For a general discussion of bargaining under asymmetric information, see e.g. Fudenberg and Tirole (1991: ch. 10).

class of shareholders, and then putting the company's future to a simple vote. The AHM procedure also avoids bargaining over the division of the pie, since it uses a mechanical scheme for distributing shares that preserves absolute priority. (The scheme is due to Lucian Bebchuk; see Bebchuk 1988.)[20]

It turns out that the idea behind the proposal is more important than the details. Thus, there are several versions of the procedure, all of which are consistent with the same basic philosophy. Two versions are presented here. They differ with respect to their treatment of secured debt and with respect to the role played by the judge, or bankruptcy practitioner, in charge of the procedure. Version 1 is closer in spirit to US Chapter 11; version 2 is closer in spirit to UK Administrative Receivership or UK Administration. (It also bears a resemblance to old US Chapter X.) If the proposal were to be adopted, the version appropriate for a particular country would depend on that country's institutional structure and legal traditions. (Mixtures of versions 1 and 2 are also possible.)

Version 1

At the outset, after the company has declared (or been pushed into) bankruptcy, the company's debts are cancelled. The company's creditors do not go away empty-handed, however; as described in task B below, they will typically become significant shareholders. What matters is that the company starts out life in bankruptcy as a 'new', all-equity company.

An individual—a judge, say—is appointed to supervise the process. The judge has two immediate tasks: (A) soliciting cash and noncash bids for the new all-equity company; and (B) allocating rights to the shares in this company. These tasks could be carried out in parallel and completed within a pre-specified period of time: three months might be reasonable.[21]

Task A: Soliciting bids. The judge solicits bids for the company over a three-month period. However, in contrast to a standard

---

[20] However, the AHM procedure does not avoid disputes over the amounts and seniorities of claims. Judges and the courts would have an important role in resolving these disputes under the procedure, just as they currently do.

[21] The procedure does not depend on this particular time horizon, and adjustments might be desirable.

auction, individuals can make cash or noncash bids for the company. In a noncash bid, someone would offer securities in the post-bankruptcy company instead of cash; thus, a noncash bid embraces the possibility of reorganization and/or recapitalization of the company as a going concern. The following are some examples of a noncash bid:

1. The old managers propose to keep their jobs, and offer claimants a share in the post-bankruptcy company.
2. The same financial arrangement might be offered by a new management team.
3. The managers of another company might propose to buy the bankrupt company, offering shares in *their* company as payment.
4. Management (old or new) might induce some debt in the company's capital structure. One way to do this would be to arrange for a bank to lend money to the post-bankruptcy company (the loan is conditional on the bid succeeding), and offer claimants a combination of cash and equity in the (levered) company. Another way would be to offer claimants a combination of shares and bonds in the post-bankruptcy company.

Note that, for the bidding process to work well, it is important that potential bidders have reasonably accurate information about the company's prospects. Part of the bankruptcy judge's job will therefore be to ensure that (serious) bidders have access to the company's books during the three-month bid solicitation process.

Task B: Allocating rights. Before the judge can allocate rights to the shares of the new (all-equity) company, he must first determine who the company's claimants are and what are the amounts and priorities of their claims. This is a difficult job, which must be carried out currently in bankruptcy. The procedure envisages no changes regarding how this job is carried out.

Thus, it is supposed that the judge's deliberations lead to the identification of n classes of creditors who are owed (in total) the amounts $D_1, \ldots, D_n$, respectively, with class 1 having the most senior claim, class 2 the next most senior claim, and so on. The company's shareholders form the $(n + 1)$th class, with a claim junior to all others.

Having identified these classes, the judge can proceed to allocate rights to shares in the new (all-equity) company. If the 'true' value, V, of the company were publicly known (i.e. were verifiable), then it would be easy to figure out the total (monetary) share each class i is entitled to, based on absolute priority. Unfortunately, the value of a noncash bid is not objectively known. (This is why there is so much haggling in Chapter 11.) Therefore in order to allocate shares the procedure adopts an approach due to Bebchuk (1988). The nice feature of Bebchuk's approach is that it achieves absolute priority in spite of the fact that V is not objectively known.

Bebchuk's approach is to allocate equity to senior creditors and options to buy equity to junior creditors. To be precise, the most senior class (class 1) is allocated 100 per cent of the company's equity. (So if an individual creditor in that class is owed d_1, she receives a fraction d_1/D_1 of the company's shares.) However, investors in the next most senior class (class 2) are given the option to buy the equity from the class 1 creditors for D_1 per 100 per cent— that is, for the amount class 1 is owed. (So if an individual creditor in class 2 is owed d_2, she receives an option to buy (up to) a fraction d_2/D_2 of the company's shares for a price of $(d_2/D_2) D_1$.) Similarly, class i investors ($3 \le i \le n$) have the option to buy equity from creditors senior to them at a price of $(D_1 + D_2 + \ldots + D_{i-1})$ per 100 per cent. Finally, shareholders (class $(n + 1)$) are given the option to buy equity at a price of $(D_1 + \ldots + D_n)$ per 100 per cent. (Note that the rules of the procedure require senior claimants to relinquish their shares if they are bought out; they cannot hold on.)

The following example may clarify the allocation process. Suppose that $n = 2$, and that there are five senior creditors each owed 200, ten junior creditors each owed 200, and 100 equal former shareholders, each of whom owned one share. Then in the 'new' company each senior creditor would receive 20 shares. Also, each junior creditor would be given an option to buy up to ten shares at 10 a share. (If all junior creditors exercised their options, the senior creditors would be bought out for 1,000.) And each shareholder would be given the option to buy one share for 30. (If all shareholders exercised their options, the junior and senior creditors would be bought out for 3,000.)[22]

---

[22] Notice that it is not necessary that all option-holders behave in the same way. For instance, suppose that one junior creditor exercises her option to buy ten

This completes the judge's second task, task B.

Once the three months are up, the judge reveals the bids arising from task A, and everyone can make an assessment of their worth (possibly with the help of some outside expert, such as an investment bank; claimants are, however, free to ignore any advice given). At this point, option-holders are given some period of time—a further month, say—to exercise their options. During this period there can be a market in equity and options, although the process does not depend on this.

At the end of this fourth month, some options will have been exercised and other will not. (The ones not exercised lapse.) The final step in the process is that the company's equity-holders (that is, those people who hold equity in the company at the end of month 4) vote on which of the various cash and noncash bids to select. (Voting is on the basis of one share–one vote; see below.) Once the vote is completed, the winning bid is implemented and the company emerges from the bankruptcy process.

The sequence of events is summarized in Figure 7.1. Note that

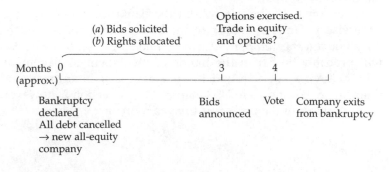

FIG. 7.1

shares for 100 (nobody else exercises an option). Then her 100 is used to buy 10% of each senior creditor's equity. Senior creditors are left with 90% of the equity and the junior creditor now has 10%. To take another example, suppose one share-holder exercises his option to buy a share for 30. (No other shareholder and no junior creditor exercise options.) First, 20 of this 30 is used to buy 1% of the options from each junior creditor, and then 10 is used to buy 1% of the shares from each senior creditor. The senior creditors end up with 99% of the equity and the share-holder has 1%. For more on this, see Bebchuk (1988).

at the time of the vote all claimholders' interests are (roughly) aligned. Whether those voting are former creditors or former shareholders (who have bought out the creditors), they are now all shareholders and have an incentive to vote for the highest-value bid.

It is worth returning to the numerical example to understand the interplay between the bids and the options. Suppose that after month 3 the best bid is perceived to value the company at less than 1,000. Then no one will want to exercise their options (the junior creditors will not want to spend 1,000 to get something worth less, and, *a fortiori*, the former shareholders will not want to spend 3,000), and the senior creditors will end up with all the equity. Suppose next that the best bid is perceived to be worth more than 1,000, but less than 3,000. Then the junior creditors will choose to buy out the senior creditors, but the former shareholders will not want to exercise their options. Finally, if the best bid is perceived to be worth more than 3,000, then the shareholders will buy out both classes of creditors.

It should be clear from this example how options preserve the absolute priority of claims even though there is no objective valuation of the company.

In version 1 the judge's role in the bankruptcy procedure is supervisory. He is in charge of the bankruptcy process, but he does not run the company during bankruptcy—in fact, this job will probably be left in the hands of incumbent management. (The judge may be required to approve major investment and financing decisions, as in US Chapter 11.) In version 2, however, the supervisor of the process is given a more major role.

Version 2

Version 2 differs from version 1 in two principal ways.[23] First, secured debt is left in place. Second, the supervisor of the bankruptcy process takes on the job of running the company for a period of time.

Treatment of secured debt. In version 1, all debt is converted into equity (secured and unsecured). This is attractive because it clears

---

[23] Version 2 is based on Aghion *et al.* (1995).

up the balance sheet. But it has the disadvantage that creditors receive a security that they may not really want to hold. In version 2 only unsecured debt is converted into equity: secured debt is left in place. That is, when bankruptcy commences, an appraisal is made of the collateral underlying each secured claim. If the appraised value is found to be more than the secured creditor's debt, then the debt is left in place. If it is found to be less, then only the secured portion of the debt is left in place; the residual is treated in the same way as unsecured claims; that is, it is converted into equity.[24]

Note that this 'minimal' debt–equity swap has the desirable property that it turns the company into a solvent one. (Of course, a complete debt–equity swap has the same virtue.) The reason is that one can be confident that the value of the company is at least as great as the sum of the appraised values of its physical assets. However, one cannot *a priori* judge the value of the remainder of the company—that is, the more nebulous going-concern value. Accordingly, in version 2, as in version 1, all unsecured debt is converted into equity. (In version 2, the most senior (unsecured) creditors receive equity directly, while subordinated creditors and former shareholders receive options to buy equity.)

Role of the bankruptcy practitioner. In version 2, it is supposed that the bankruptcy practitioner actually runs the company during the four months that the procedure lasts. That is, she replaces incumbent management—or, more precisely, the board of directors. (She can, however, retain certain inside directors/managers, if she wishes.)

---

[24] In contrast, in version 1 secured debt is treated just like any other senior debt; i.e., it is converted into equity. To be more precise, in version 1 a secured creditor's collateral is appraised. If the appraised value is greater than the debt, then the creditor is treated as if all her debt is senior (so she receives shares). If the appraised value is less than the debt, the creditor is treated as if she has a mix of senior and junior debt (so she receives a mixture of shares and options). In both versions 1 and 2, it is envisaged that secured creditors will not have the right to seize collateralized property (unless this property can be shown to be unnecessary to the company's reorganization). The reason is that seizure could lead to an inefficient dismantlement of the company's assets through a 'me-first' grab. (Note that this is also the position taken by current US bankruptcy law; see Baird 1992: §8C.) However, it seems reasonable in version 2 to allow a secured creditor to seize her collateral after the four-month bankruptcy period is over if the company remains in default *vis-à-vis* this creditor.

The bankruptcy practitioner has two main duties. First, she has a general obligation to act in the interest of shareholders and option-holders combined, that is, to maximize the value of the company during her term of office.[25] Second, she is obliged to draw up a plan (or plans) for the future of the company, to be presented to shareholders at the end of month 3 (before the options are exercised).[26] No restrictions are put on the nature of the plan. For example, the plan might be to reorganize the company— maybe with new management and/or a new financial structure (in which case shareholders would receive new securities in the company); to sell it as a going concern; or to close the company down and sell off its assets piecemeal. In fact, a plan is just like a cash or noncash bid. The plan is put to a shareholders' meeting at the end of month 4 (after the options are exercised) and is implemented as long as it receives majority approval. (The bankruptcy practitioner may choose to put more than one plan to shareholders and see which one receives greatest support.)

An important difference from version 1 is that a formal auction is dispensed with. The bankruptcy practitioner may hold one if she believes this would increase value, but she is not obliged to do so.[27] Similarly, the practitioner has discretion about who should have access to the company's books and—if bids are made— which bids should be presented to shareholders. In this respect, the practitioner is in a similar position to the board of directors of a solvent company that is thinking of selling it.

In version 2, the bankruptcy practitioner would also have the authority to take other actions. For example, she could sell some or even all of the company's (unsecured) assets before month 3 if she deemed it necessary to do so. (This might be important in cases where uncertainty about the company's future threatened the customer or supplier base.) In addition, she would have the authority to raise new capital or to release cash from the business.

[25] This could be formalized in two ways. First, a fiduciary duty towards shareholders and option-holders could be imposed on the bankruptcy practitioner. Second, the practitioner could be put on an incentive scheme.

[26] The bankruptcy practitioner would be paid out of company funds in the same way that a receiver or administrator is paid under current UK insolvency law.

[27] In some situations, an open auction might allow rivals to learn sensitive information about the company's operations or plans, which could reduce the company's value in the long run.

For example, she might use profit earned by the business or cash from asset sales to pay off (secured) creditors or to pay out a dividend to the (new) shareholders. (In the latter case, the option exercise price for junior claimants would be reduced accordingly.)[28]

The bankruptcy practitioner's appointment is obviously an important issue in version 2, given the power of the position. In many cases a large (senior) creditor is in the best position to make the appointment. For example, in the UK a senior creditor—usually a bank—often negotiates as part of its debt contract the right to appoint a 'receiver'. (This right is embodied in what is called a 'floating charge'.) It might make sense for such a creditor also to appoint the bankruptcy practitioner in version 2 of our procedure. A similar arrangement might be used in Germany or Japan, where companies often have a 'lead bank' as a significant creditor.[29] In other cases, when there is no natural large creditor the appointment might be made by the court.

Note that, once appointed, the practitioner has a responsibility to *all* shareholders (not just the person making the appointment). This raises the question of who has the authority to remove the practitioner if she is doing a bad job. Prior to month 4, it probably makes most sense to leave this decision in the hands of the court, with action being taken only when a majority of each class of claimants has expressed dissatisfaction. The point is that, until the ownership of shares has been settled, it is not clear whom the practitioner is representing, and so she should have a degree of security and a broad remit to 'maximize the value of the company'. Another possibility, however, is to give shareholders the power to dismiss the practitioner from the beginning. The disadvantage of this is that new shareholders may push the practitioner towards a quick sale of the company: they know that if good news arrives within the four months they will be bought out by the option-holders, whereas if bad new comes in they will be

---

[28] An obvious danger with giving the practitioner so much discretion is that she may abuse her power. For example, the practitioner, hoping to extend her term of office past month 4, might engage in empire-building activities. Note, however, that the practitioner could be required to obtain majority approval from shareholders for an extension, which would reduce the likelihood of this kind of self-interested behaviour.

[29] For a discussion of the possible role of lead banks in bankruptcy procedure, see Aoki (1994).

left holding equity and so they prefer to avoid uncertainty. (This is the same phenomenon as described in example 1 of Section 3.)

5. An assessment

Consider how well the AHM procedure satisfies the three goals of a bankruptcy procedure discussed earlier. Arguably, the AHM procedure does a reasonable job of meeting goal 1: since the new owners decide the future of the company, they have an incentive to vote for an efficient outcome. Also, the procedure preserves the *ex ante* bonding role of debt (goal 2). In particular, since shareholders may accept a bid or plan involving another management team, managers' jobs are at risk. However, managers have the opportunity to convince shareholders that the bankruptcy was not their fault and that they should be retained. In this respect, bankruptcy is arguably not so harsh that managers will avoid it at any cost.

Note also that the procedure could be modified to be softer or harder on incumbent management (at some probable cost in terms of *ex post* inefficiency) if that were thought to be desirable. For example, in version 1 incumbent management could be favoured by handicapping other bidders in the auction; for example, the auction rules could state that an outside bidder has to win more than two-thirds of the votes. (Another way to soften the blow of bankruptcy in both versions 1 and 2 is to give managers a 'golden handshake' (or 'parachute') in the form of senior debt in their company.) Conversely, management could be disfavoured in version 1 by a requirement that *they* must win more than two-thirds of the votes to retain their jobs.

Finally, the option scheme ensures that absolute priority (goal 3) is met (as long as junior claimants have enough cash to exercise their options; this is discussed further below).[30]

---

[30] At the same time that the AHM proposal was being developed, two other proposals for bankruptcy reform appeared in the literature: Adler (1993) and Bradley and Rosenzweig (1992) (see also Adler 1994). These proposals, like the AHM one, envisage that when a company goes bankrupt the company's equity is transferred to creditors. Adler's proposal removes the right of individual creditors to foreclose on a bankrupt company's assets while Bradley and Rosenzweig's does not. In both proposals, the company's debt is not accelerated and no bids are

It is worth returning to examples 1 and 2 to see how the AHM procedure compares with a structured bargaining procedure like US Chapter 11.

In example 1 there are two alternatives: liquidate for 90, or keep the company going for an average value of 110. The big difference between the AHM procedure and structured bargaining is that, if the former creditors as shareholders get to vote, they will choose to keep the company going, since they enjoy all of the potential upside gains from continuation. Of course, in this instance the former shareholders will be eager to exercise their options, since by spending 1 they obtain a share worth 1.1. (Junior creditors are being ignored.) In other words, the former creditors will get paid their 100 in full by the former shareholders, and the former shareholders, as residual claimants, will vote to maintain the company as a going concern. A good company has been saved.

In example 2, the alternatives are to liquidate for 90 or keep the company going for an average value of 80. Here, the former shareholders will not exercise their options, and the former creditors—as the new shareholders—will vote to liquidate and receive 90. A bad company has been shut down.

Notice that problems 1 and 2 have been resolved without eliminating the possibility of reorganization. In example 1, incumbent managers are able to retain their jobs even though they may not have the cash in hand, and any incentive on the part of the creditors to liquidate the company prematurely is avoided. In example 2, managers are rightly unable to keep their jobs. In neither example is there room for haggling. And in both examples the people who end up voting over the future of the company are the residual claimants (i.e. those who bear the consequences of their actions); as a result, the final outcome is the value-maximizing choice.

6. *Further considerations*

This section briefly raises some additional issues and discusses a number of practical problems that might arise under the AHM procedure.

solicited. Also, while both proposals envisage that the transfer of control to creditors will bring about improved management, neither is very explicit about how this will happen.

Treatment of junior creditors and former shareholders

In the AHM procedure, junior creditors, before they receive anything, are required to buy out senior creditors. A concern may be that junior creditors do not have the cash on hand to exercise their options and, therefore, will be unduly disadvantaged . (Also, they may be unable or unwilling to raise the necessary funds by borrowing.)

There is a modification of the procedure which ameliorates this problem. (The following discussion concerns version 1, but similar arguments apply to version 2.) Once the bids are in, the bankruptcy judge will be able to place a lower bound on the value of the company, equal to the size of the best cash bid, V^c (an objective amount). Given this, he could proceed as if the firm were worth V^c, and distribute shares accordingly. If V^c exceeds the amount owed to senior creditors, the junior creditors will receive a fraction of the shares in the initial distribution. For example, if the senior creditors are owed 100 and the best cash bid that comes in is for 150, then the senior creditors would be issued two-thirds of the shares and the junior creditors would be issued one-third. Of course, there may be a noncash bid which the junior creditors perceive to be worth more than 150, in which case the senior creditors would still be getting too much; but in that case the junior creditors could exercise their options to buy them out.

Of course, even with this modification, junior creditors might still be short-changed. The worst case would be that there is no cash bid; here $V^c = 0$, and all the equity is initially allocated to senior creditors. How bad are things for the junior creditors in such a case? Arguably not too bad, for at least three reasons.

First, junior creditors do not collectively have to raise the cash to buy out the senior creditors. Each junior creditor can act as an individual. The pro rata cash injection may be quite small. (Indeed, an individual need not exercise her options in full; she may choose to exercise only a fraction.) Second, a market for options may well develop during the bankruptcy process—especially for large firms. (Indeed, the bankruptcy judge might be obliged to establish such a market.) In this case, junior creditors need not come up with cash; they could simply sell their options. Third, even if some junior creditors are unable to raise the cash, and so are left empty-handed, they will probably fare no worse than they do under current arrangements.[31]

Finally, it is important to realize that the problem facing junior creditors who wish to raise cash in order to exercise their options is quite different from that of a bidder who wishes to make a cash bid for the whole company. Because junior creditors act individually, no junior creditor who exercises her option bears much risk; nor does someone who buys the option and exercises it on her behalf. In contrast, someone who makes a cash bid for the whole company may bear a great deal of risk.[32] Hence, there is no contradiction between supposing on the one hand that capital markets are sufficiently imperfect that noncash bids have a role to play, and supposing on the other hand that junior claimants will be able to obtain a reasonable fraction of the post-bankruptcy pie by exercising or selling their options.

Claims disputes

The discussion has so far paid little attention to the question of how the amounts and seniorities of creditors' claims are established. The adjudication process is complex and forms an important part of any bankruptcy procedure, including the above one. It may be argued that the time scale of three months is too short for the purpose of allocating shares and options.

There is a way of dealing with awkward claims disputes without jeopardizing the procedure, as long as a reasonable proportion of the claims can be established within the three months: take the claims that can be established, allocate shares and options on the basis of these claims alone, carry out the vote, and emerge from bankruptcy with the contentious claims still outstanding.

---

[31] LoPucki and Whitford (1990) examined 43 firms that filed for bankruptcy in the USA after 1 October 1979, had declared assets in excess of $100 million, and had a plan confirmed by 31 March 1988. They found that the mean return to unsecured creditors was 49.5 cents per dollar, and the median return was 38.7 cents per dollar. Fisher and Martel (1994) studied 236 incorporated firms that filed for reorganization in Canada during the period 1978–87. They divided the sample into 16 'large' firms (with liabilities in excess of C$ 5 million) and 220 'small' firms (with liabilities below C$ 5 million). For large firms, the mean return to unsecured creditors was 57.7 cents per dollar and the median return was 30 cents per dollar. For small firms, the mean return was 46.9 cents per dollar and the median return was 35 cents per dollar.

[32] See the discussion in §3 about the transaction costs of making a cash bid.

Once these claims have been decided, there could be an appropriate *ex post* settling up—with the claimants being given securities in the post-bankruptcy company.[33] Notice that the people with contentious claims do not participate in the vote, but this is not too serious, since one may presume that they too would have voted for the value-maximizing bid.[34]

New money

Companies typically need new money during the bankruptcy procedure, for example to pay suppliers and workers. The bankruptcy practitioner or management (with the approval of the judge) can raise such money in the usual way that solvent companies raise money. The point is that, thanks to the debt–equity conversion, this company *is* a solvent company (either it has no debts or its only debts are secured)—and so there is scope to issue new debt, which of course would be junior to any remaining secured debt, but senior to equity.

Voting procedures

Another issue concerns the voting procedure *per se*. If there are only two bids, it seems natural to have a simple vote between them. However, with more than two bids, there are many possibilities. Shareholders could cast their votes for their most preferred plan, with the plan that receives the most votes being the winner; or they could rank the plans, with the plan that receives the highest total ranking being chosen; or there could be two rounds, in which shareholders rank the plans in the first round, with a subsequent run-off between the two highest ranked plans in the second round. One point to note is that thorny issues in voting theory (such as the Condorcet Paradox) are less likely to arise in the present context, given that shareholders have a common objective: value maximization.

---

[33] There are several ways of doing this; one is to give new claimants the same securities that equivalent creditors elected to hold as a result of the bankruptcy process.

[34] This is an oversimplification. Those shareholders who think that a senior claim may materialize later have an incentive to choose a risky reorganization plan since they gain if things turn out well and do not suffer if they turn out badly. (See example 2 of §3 for a similar phenomenon.)

Small companies

The procedure is likely to be most valuable in the case of medium to large companies with multiple creditors, for which bankruptcy raises the thorniest problems. However, most bankruptcies relate to small companies, for which a bank is typically the single main creditor. Under the AHM procedure, the bank would get all the equity (presuming that it is not bought out) and could 'vote' on whether to liquidate or reorganize the company. (It might choose to liquidate if it needs cash and does not feel that it will be able to sell its shares.) In addition, the procedure allows junior creditors—e.g. trade creditors—to buy out the bank; trade creditors might have an incentive to vote to keep the company going because they anticipate profitable trade with the company in the future. In short, the procedure may also have a role to play in the case of small companies.

Workouts. Many of the problems of bankruptcy plague company workouts. (There are free-rider and hold-out problems.) There is no reason why companies could not, of their own accord, choose the AHM procedure as a vehicle for facilitating workouts in the event that the procedure is not adopted by the state.

7. *Concluding remarks*

It is worth summarizing the main point of this chapter. Current reorganization procedures are flawed because they mix the decision of who should get what with the decision of what should happen to a bankrupt company. The chapter has described a procedure that separates these two issues. The key lies in transforming a group of people with different claims (and therefore different objectives) into a homogeneous class of shareholders, who then decide on the company's future by a simple vote.

It may help to say a few more words about the philosophy underlying the procedure. The basic idea is that a bankrupt company is not fundamentally different from a solvent company that is performing badly. In the case of a solvent company, shareholders elect a board of directors, who are entrusted with deciding, on a day-to-day basis, whether to keep the company going, sell it, or close it down. The same menu of options should be available to the claimants of a bankrupt company. In other words, there is no particular reason why bankruptcy should automatically trigger the termination of a company via a cash sale (either as a going concern or in pieces). According to the agency cost theory of debt presented in Chapter 6, bankruptcy is an indication that something is wrong with management rather than with the company itself. (Management has failed to live up to a commitment.) The appropriate response is to allow new management teams the opportunity to replace existing management. The AHM procedure does this through the device of a noncash bid (or a plan). Noncash bids allow for Chapter 11-type reorganization plans. However, in contrast to Chapter 11, the company's future is decided by a simple vote— a procedure that is standard for solvent companies—rather than by a complex bargaining procedure that is never seen outside bankruptcy.

An interesting insight into how the procedure might work is provided by the recent (1994) take-over battle for Paramount in the USA. There were two bidders for Paramount—Viacom and QVC—and each put in a bid with a noncash component as well as a cash component. Paramount shareholders chose between the bids—and the option of keeping Paramount independent—by what was in effect a vote. (Viacom won the vote.) Thus, the choice Paramount shareholders were asked to make is analogous to the choice claimants would make in the AHM procedure in the presence of noncash bids.

In closing, it is worth emphasizing a point made earlier. A good bankruptcy procedure should work well both when capital markets are imperfect and when they are perfect. The AHM procedure has this feature. If capital markets are perfect, the company will go to the bidder willing to pay the highest amount—moreover, this bidder can do no better than offer cash—and thus the outcome will be exactly the same as in US Chapter 7. (Similarly, the bankruptcy practitioner should always propose a cash sale if capital markets are perfect.) For this reason, while believers in perfect capital markets may not see the merit of the AHM procedure relative to US Chapter 7, they should not be strongly opposed to it. In contrast, those with doubts about the adequacy of capital markets should find value in the procedure.

8

The Structure of Voting Rights in a Public Company

CHAPTER 6 discussed some of the agency problems that arise in a public company when there is a separation of ownership and control (or management). It was argued that these agency problems are greater than in the case of a closely held company because of a free-rider problem: individual, small shareholders have little incentive to monitor management, given that monitoring is a public good.[1] A similar free-rider problem affects the corporate voting process: it may not be in the interest of an individual shareholder to incur the often considerable expense of launching a proxy fight to replace an incompetent management team, given that the costs are borne by this one shareholder, while the gains from improved management are enjoyed by all shareholders.[2] In fact, shareholders may not even vote (intelligently) in corporate board elections, in view of the fact that an individual, small shareholder's vote is unlikely to be pivotal.[3]

The above free-rider problems can sometimes be overcome by someone who acquires a large stake in a company and takes it over.[4] In practice, the ease with which a take-over can occur depends on a variety of factors, including the range of defensive measures available to management, the attitudes of the courts,

[1] This chapter continues to ignore the distinction between management and the board of directors.

[2] A proxy fight is a campaign to persuade other shareholders to vote for a particular management team (or board of directors). For a discussion of proxy fights, see Ikenberry and Lakonishok (1993) and Pound (1988).

[3] Both of these free-rider problems are reduced to the extent that a company has one or more large shareholders. A large shareholder has an incentive to monitor or launch a proxy fight, since she receives a sizeable fraction of the gains. Also, a large shareholder has an incentive to vote (intelligently) since she recognizes that her vote may be pivotal. This chapter focuses on the case where all shareholders are (initially) small. For an extensive discussion of voting issues in public companies, see Manne (1964).

[4] Sometimes a large shareholder can exert control on management without launching a formal take-over. This chapter focuses on formal take-overs.

the existence of anti-takeover legislation, the ability of a successful bidder to expropriate minority shareholders, etc. This chapter
argues that, in addition to these institutional, legal, and political
factors, an important influence on the take-over process is a company's security-voting structure—in particular, how the company's votes are allocated across securities. Before a company
goes public, it is in the interest of the company's initial owner to
design the security-voting structure in such a way that future
management is subject to an appropriate amount of pressure
from the market for corporate control, and to ensure that changes
in management occur in the right situations. It will be shown that,
under a reasonable set of assumptions, the optimal security-voting structure is a single class of shares with votes attached ('one
share–one vote'). This result may explain why many companies
in the USA and UK adopt a one share–one vote rule and also why
stock exchanges and regulatory authorities are often suspicious
of companies that try to do otherwise.

The basic idea behind the analysis is simple. Suppose the total
value of a company under a particular management team is
divided into two parts: one part representing the present value of
the dividend stream received by shareholders (call this the company's public value), the other part representing a (monetary) private benefit enjoyed by management (call this the private value).
If a company has several classes of shares with different voting
rights, a bidder can obtain control—that is, 50 per cent of the
votes—by acquiring *less* than 50 per cent of the company's dividend stream if restricted or partial offers are allowed (that is, if the
bidder does not have to offer to buy all the shares in a particular
class); or by acquiring less than 100 per cent of the company's dividend stream if restricted offers are not allowed (that is, if the bidder does have to offer to buy all the shares in a particular class). As
a result, a rival management team, which produces low public
value for shareholders but has large private value, may be able to
seize control from a superior incumbent—i.e. an incumbent with
high public value but low private value—by paying a premium on
shares representing a small fraction of the company's dividend
stream. In the same way, an incumbent with low public value for
shareholders but large private value may be able to maintain control by outbidding a superior rival—i.e. a rival with high public
value but low private value—over shares representing a small

fraction of the company's dividend stream. Thus, deviations from one share–one vote create two kinds of 'error': some control transfers take place that should not, and some control transfers do not take place that should. The risk of both kinds of error is reduced (if restricted offers are allowed) or eliminated (if they are not) by one share–one vote.

Although one share–one vote works well in a wide class of cases, it is not always optimal. The analysis will show that, if both the incumbent and the rival have significant private benefits, a departure from one share–one vote can increase the intensity of competition in the market for corporate control and enable shareholders to extract some of the incumbent's and rival's private benefits. This can raise the total value of the company.

For certain classes of companies there may be another reason why one share–one vote is not optimal. This chapter operates within the framework of Chapter 6, where management's preferences are 'unimportant' relative to those of investors and do not receive any weight in the choice of capital structure. However, in some companies it may be efficient to allocate control rights to managers in order to allow them to enjoy their private benefits, or to motivate them to undertake relationship-specific investments. Alternatively, the company's initial owner may 'sell' the private benefits to a large investor, along with voting control, so that the investor can consume the private benefits without risk of expropriation. If managers and investors are wealth-constrained and cannot afford to purchase a large equity stake (or if they are risk-averse), it may be necessary to depart from one share–one vote to achieve these outcomes.[5] The Aghion–Bolton model of Chapter 5 shows that allocating control to an agent who enjoys private benefits may indeed be optimal under certain conditions. (See the comparison between 'E control' and 'C control'.)

There is a large theoretical literature on corporate control transactions, including Bebchuk (1994), Grossman and Hart (1980), Manne (1965), Scharfstein (1988), Shleifer and Vishny (1986a), Stein (1988), Zingales (1995), and Zwiebel (1995), among others. The recent literature on security-voting structure starts with Easterbrook and Fischel (1983), who give an informal justification for one share–one vote, arguing that 'as residual claimants, the

---

[5] For an analysis of security-voting structures in companies that have a large investor or vote-holder, see Zingales (1993) and Bebchuk and Zingales (1995).

shareholders are the group with the appropriate incentives (collective choice problems to one side) to make discretionary decisions'. The current chapter is based on Grossman and Hart (1988) and Harris and Raviv (1989). These two articles suggest that one share–one vote is optimal not so much because it gives shareholders the right incentives to take decisions, but rather because it forces someone who wants to obtain control of the company to acquire a share of the company's dividend stream commensurate with this control.[6]

The chapter is organized as follows. Section 1 presents an example that illustrates the main ideas behind the one share–one vote result. Section 2 analyses a general model. Section 3 discusses the case of restricted offers, together with some other extensions. Finally, Section 4 contains concluding remarks and a discussion of some of the evidence.

1. Inefficiencies: an example

In this section an example is presented to illustrate how a departure from one share–one vote can create inefficiencies. Throughout the example, and the chapter, it is supposed that the company under consideration has a large number of very small (negligible) shareholders and that each shareholder regards herself (correctly) as too small to affect the outcome of a control contest.

Suppose a company has two classes of shares: class A has a claim to 50 per cent of the dividends and no votes; class B has a claim to 50 per cent of the dividends and all the votes. Suppose that the company's public value under the incumbent management team is 200 (so each class is worth 100), and that there is a

[6] Other contributions on one share–one vote include Blair *et al.* (1989), Harris and Raviv (1988), and Gromb (1993). Blair *et al.* (1989) show that security-voting structure is irrelevant in the absence of taxes. However, they suppose that bidders can make only conditional tender offers (that is, the bidder's offer to buy shares must be conditional on the bidder winning the control contest), whereas this chapter allows unconditional tender offers (where the bidder agrees to buy shares regardless of whether the bid is successful). Harris and Raviv (1988) and Gromb (1993) identify cases where a departure from one share–one vote can increase the market value of the company. However, in contrast to this chapter, they suppose that individual shareholders are large enough for their tender decisions to affect the outcome of a control contest, i.e. shareholders regard themselves as pivotal.

rival management team which is less efficient: the public value under the rival is 180 (so each class is worth 90). However, the rival has a significant private benefit of control, 15 say, whereas the incumbent's private benefit is negligible in comparison.

Clearly, it is undesirable for the rival to obtain control since she reduces total value. However, the rival *can* get control by making an unconditional tender offer for all the class B shares at 101, say. (In an unconditional offer, a bidder offers to buy the shares tendered, regardless of whether the bid is successful.) In the absence of a counter-offer, a class B shareholder faces the choice of not tendering, and thus holding on to a claim worth 100 if the rival loses and 90 if she wins, or of tendering to the rival and receiving 101. Since no shareholder regards herself as pivotal, all shareholders tender and the rival wins.[7]

The rival makes a capital loss of 11 on the shares she purchases. (She pays 101 for them and their public value is only 90.) However, this capital loss is offset by her private benefit of 15. Shareholders lose in aggregate since the two classes combined receive only 191—class B shareholders are bought out for 101 and class A shareholders are left holding shares worth 90. Finally, note that the incumbent cannot successfully resist this offer by making a counter-offer, since the most he is prepared to pay for the class B shares is 100. (He has insignificant private benefits.) But with such a counter-offer, class B shareholders will tender to the rival.

Under one share–one vote, the rival cannot get control. (I am ruling out restricted offers.) If class B has all the votes *and* all the dividends, the rival needs to offer more than 200 to get class B shareholders to tender to her. But this means that she makes a capital loss of 20 (200 – 180), which exceeds her private benefit. Moreover, even if her private benefit is more than 20, so that a bid is profitable, shareholders do not lose from the transaction, since they are bought out at a premium on shares representing 100 per cent of the dividend stream.

In this example, a departure from one share–one vote is bad because it allows an inferior rival (with a high private benefit) to get control. The example can easily be modified to show that a

---

[7] Note that an investor who holds the same number of class *A* and class *B* shares—say, a proportion α of each—would not tender if she regarded herself as pivotal, since the value of her holdings would fall from 200α to 191α (see below).

departure from one share–one vote can also prevent a superior rival from obtaining control.

Suppose that the public value under the incumbent is still 200, but the public value under the rival is now 220. Assume now that the incumbent's private benefit is 15, whereas the rival's is negligible in comparison. Then, under the above dual-class structure, the rival cannot get control, even though the company is worth more under her. The reason is that the most she is prepared to offer for the class B shares is 110, since this is their public value under the rival's management and she has an insignificant private benefit. If the rival makes such an offer, however, the incumbent will make a counter-offer at 111, say. The incumbent will make a capital loss of 11 on the counter-offer, but this capital loss is offset by his private benefit of 15. The conclusion is that the rival will not bother to bid, and the incumbent will retain control.

Again, this problem does not arise under one share–one vote. If class B has all the dividends *and* all the votes, the rival is prepared to offer up to 220 to the class B shareholders. The incumbent cannot resist such a bid since the class B shares are worth only 215 to him.

In the above examples, only one of the management teams had a significant private benefit. It will be seen below that, if both teams have a significant benefit, a departure from one share–one vote may increase the total value of the company.

2. The model

This section presents a general model of the effects of security-voting structure on control transactions. Consider an initial owner who designs the security and voting structure of a company that he will take public. The objective of the owner is to maximize the total value of the securities issued; imagine that he plans to retire.[8] The owner recognizes that the management team of the company cannot be relied on to run the company well. In particular, a situation may arise where an outside management team

---

[8] I assume that the initial owner retains no shares or votes in the company. For analyses of the case where he does, see Zingales (1993), Bebchuk (1994), and Bebchuk and Zingales (1995).

can run the company better, but incumbent management is unwilling to cede control, because of the large private benefits it obtains from running the company.[9] Given this, the initial owner creates a security-voting structure for the public company that allows (hostile) take-overs to occur in certain states of the world.

The total value of the company under a particular management team (the incumbent or the rival) is divided into two parts: the public value (enjoyed by shareholders) and the private value (enjoyed by the management team). Denote the public value under the incumbent and the rival by y^I and y^R, respectively, and the private value under the incumbent and the rival by b^I and b^R, respectively.[10]

Private benefits may be realized in several ways. For example, managers may be able to pay themselves large salaries and obtain large perquisites, thus reducing the amount of profit available for shareholders. Or it may be the case that part of the value of the company is in the form of a synergy which accrues directly to another company that management owns. Another possibility is that managers merge the target company with another they own at a price that is (*ex post*) disadvantageous to minority shareholders (a 'freeze-out merger'). Finally, managers may be able to divert value by buying inputs from other companies they own at inflated prices or selling inputs to other companies they own at deflated prices.[11]

The company goes public at date 0 and at this time the security-voting structure is chosen and the incumbent management team is installed. At date 1, a single rival team appears.[12] At date 0,

[9] This chapter ignores the role of debt as a way of forcing management to give up control.

[10] These private benefits differ from those in the Aghion–Bolton model of Ch. 5, and those in the models of Ch. 6, in that they are in the form of money. However, it is still assumed that the managers have no (or little) initial wealth and so cannot be charged up front for these private benefits.

[11] There is empirical research suggesting that private benefits can be substantial. Barclay and Holderness (1989) estimate that in the USA they are about 4% of the value of equity, while Zingales (1994) finds much higher estimates—of the order of 60%—for Italy. Researchers have also determined that voting shares have high premia relative to non-voting shares in dual class companies (e.g. Levy (1982) finds a premium of 45.5% in Israel; Rydqvist (1992) finds a premium of 6.5% in Sweden; and Zingales (1994) finds a premium of 81% in Italy). The high premia are consistent with large private benefits of control.

[12] This is a simplifying assumption. The main ideas of the model generalize to the case of multiple rivals. However, security-voting structure becomes less

there is uncertainty about the characteristics y,b of both incumbent and rival teams. Suppose that the uncertainty about y and b is resolved at date 1 and there is symmetric information throughout. Also, take y and b to be exogenous for each management team; i.e., they do not depend on managerial actions.[13] At date 1 either the rival launches a take-over or she does not. If the rival does launch a take-over, the incumbent must choose whether to resist. Management is replaced if and only if the rival's bid is successful.[14] At date 2 the company is wound up and dividends are paid to shareholders. All investors are risk-neutral and the interest rate is zero. The time-line is shown in Figure 8.1.

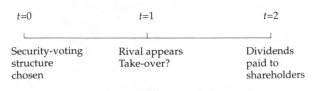

$t=0$	$t=1$	$t=2$
Security-voting structure chosen	Rival appears Take-over?	Dividends paid to shareholders

FIG. 8.1

To simplify matters, focus on the case where there are only two classes of shares, A and B, with dividend and vote entitlements given by s_A, v_A, and s_B, v_B, respectively, where $s_A + s_B = 1$, $v_A + v_B = 1$. (In words, class A is entitled to receive a fraction s_A of the dividends and has a fraction v_A of the votes, and class B is entitled to receive a fraction s_B of the dividends and has a fraction v_B of the

important to the extent that competition among bidders can be relied on to generate maximum value for shareholders.

[13] For an analysis of managerial actions in the presence of take-over bids, see Scharfstein (1988) and Stein (1988).

[14] The possibility of 'friendly' mergers—i.e. a situation where the rival and the incumbent negotiate about a change in management—is not allowed for in this chapter. One justification for ignoring friendly mergers is the following. In order to compensate the incumbent for the loss of his private benefits, the rival might have to make a substantial side-payment to the incumbent. (Although b^I is sometimes supposed to be negligible relative to b^R, it may still be large in absolute terms.) However, such a side-payment may not be feasible because the acceptance of it may be regarded as a breach of fiduciary duty by the incumbent to his shareholders. Thus, if there is a chance that the incumbent can successfully resist a hostile bid, he will prefer to decline a friendly merger and risk a take-over. (There is no uncertainty in the model, but uncertainty could easily be added so that any bid fails with positive probability.)

votes.)[15] Without loss of generality, B is taken to be the superior voting stock, i.e. $v_B > \frac{1}{2}$.[16] Note that one share–one vote is a special case of this dual-class structure where $s_B = v_B = 1$.[17]

The control contest

Suppose that, to get control, the rival must make a public tender offer. If the rival makes a bid, the incumbent will choose whether or not to resist it.[18] Faced with one or two offers, shareholders decide whether to tender to the rival, to tender to the incumbent, or to hold on to their shares.

At the time of the bid, the characteristics of both bidders are known. Assume that there is a large number of very small (negligible) shareholders and that no shareholder can affect the outcome of the control contest.[19] As a result of shareholders' tender decisions, the rival will either accumulate more than 50 per cent of the company's votes necessary for her to win control or she won't.[20] Thus, the outcome of the control contest is deterministic.[21] Assume that shareholders have rational expectations. In the present context, this means that shareholders predict the winner with certainty. The assumption of shareholder negligibility com-

---

[15] All the results extend without difficulty to the case of n classes.

[16] The case $v_B = v_A = \frac{1}{2}$ is uninteresting and is ignored.

[17] It will be seen that in the absence of restricted offers all security-voting structures with $s_B = 1$ are equivalent to one share–one vote (given $v_B > \frac{1}{2}$). If restricted offers are allowed, however, the condition for one share–one vote becomes $s_A/v_A = s_B/v_B = 1$ (see §3).

[18] One can imagine that the incumbent finances the counter-offer out of the private benefit b^I (as in a leveraged buyout); or that he finds a 'friendly' company (i.e. a white knight), to which the private benefit can be transferred, and which will make the counter-offer on the incumbent's behalf.

[19] For formalizations and a discussion, see Bagnoli and Lipman (1988), Bebchuk (1989), Kovenock (1984), and Holmstrom and Nalebuff (1992).

[20] It is supposed for simplicity that, if the rival fails to acquire 50% of the votes, she is unable to get her own slate of candidates elected as directors of the company. That is, the assumption is made that anyone who does not tender to the rival votes for incumbent management in a proxy fight. This is not unreasonable, given that small shareholders have little incentive to think about how they are voting, and may therefore adopt the 'simple' strategy of voting for incumbent management.

[21] Under reasonable assumptions, even if shareholders' tender decisions are stochastic—that is, even if they tender to the rival with some probability between 0 and 1—the (aggregate) outcome of the control contest will be (approximately) deterministic, given that there is a very large number of shareholders. See e.g. Holmstrom and Nalebuff (1992).

bined with the assumption of rational expectations has the important implication that it never pays a bidder to make a losing bid. This is because a bidder cannot make a capital gain on any shares purchased, since if he offers less than $s_i y^w$ for class i ($i = A$ or B), where y^w represents the public value under the winning management team ($w = R$ or I), then individual shareholders in class i can do better by holding on to their shares and receiving their pro rata share of the value $s_i y^w$ in the post-takeover company. Hence the only return a bidder can make is through the private benefit that he receives if he wins.[22]

Form of bid

Confine attention to 'any or all' (that is, unrestricted) tender offers. That is, suppose that, if a bidder offers to buy any shares in a particular class, the bidder must offer to buy all the shares in that class at the same price. (But the bidder does not have to extend the offer to the other class.) One justification for this is the idea that the courts may be unsympathetic to restricted offers, regarding them as coercive. (For an example of a coercive restricted offer, see Section 3.) In any case, this assumption is merely a simplification; in Section 3 it is shown that the main results generalize to the case of restricted offers. (See also Grossman and Hart (1988) and Harris and Raviv (1988, 1989).)

It is also supposed that any tender offer is unconditional—that is, the bidder agrees to buy shares tendered even if the bid fails. The analysis would not change in any way, however, if conditional offers were allowed as well.

Given that bidders must make any or all offers, one can conclude that the competition for control will take place over the class B shares—which have more than 50 per cent of the votes. The point is that, since the rival cannot get control by bidding only for the class A shares, she must bid for (all) the B shares. There is no point bidding for the A shares in addition, since she cannot make a capital gain on these. (If she could, a (negligible)

---

[22] This is the free-rider problem described in Grossman and Hart (1980). In addition, the losing bidder incurs the costs of a bid. It will be supposed that the costs of a bid—although positive—are small in relation to the private benefits of control, b.

class A shareholder would do better not to tender to her and make the same capital gain himself.) Equally, if the incumbent resists, he will do so by making a counteroffer for the B shares, since the A shares do not provide him with enough votes to defeat the rival.[23]

The results

It is now shown that one share–one vote is optimal when either the incumbent's private benefit or the rival's private benefit is insignificant (or both). That is, the example in Section 1 generalizes. However, one share–one vote may not be optimal if the incumbent and rival both have significant private benefits. The analysis is divided into four cases.

Case 1: b^I is insignificant in relation to b^R, y^I, y^R. To see under what conditions control shifts, it is useful to consider how the incumbent would react to a bid from the rival. The incumbent's best response is to:

(*)   offer (just above) $s_B\, y^I$ for class B.

The point is that, if the incumbent offers less than $s_B\, y^I$, class B shareholders will not tender to him if they expect him to win (they do better by holding on to their shares); while the incumbent cannot afford to offer more, given that he does not have a significant private benefit.

The issue for the rival then is whether she can make a bid that (*a*) will deter the response (*) from the incumbent (i.e. if both these offers are made, the rival will win) and (*b*) is profitable for the rival.

Consider first the case in which $y^R \geq y^I$, i.e. where the rival is the superior management team (in terms of public benefits). Then the following bid by the rival satisfies (*a*) and (*b*): offer a price just above $s_B\, y^R$ for class B. To see why, note that with only this bid on the table shareholders from both classes will tender to the rival because, whether they think the rival will win or not, they are being offered more than the post-take-over value of the company. In addition, if the incumbent resists with the counteroffer (*), the

[23] It is assumed that neither the incumbent nor the rival has an initial shareholding in the company.

incumbent will receive no shares since his offer is dominated by the rival's; hence the rival's bid does deter the incumbent. Finally, the rival makes a profit of (almost) b^R on her offer because she (almost) breaks even on the shares tendered to her. (She pays just above what they are worth.)

There is no more profitable bid for the rival that wins her control. This follows immediately from the previous observation that, since no bidder can make a capital gain on shares tendered to her, a bidder's return is bounded above by her private benefit of control.

Consider next the case in which $y^R < y^I$, i.e. where the incumbent is the superior management team. Then, to deter the incumbent, the rival must offer (slightly) more than $s_B y^I$ for the class B shares. The reason is that, if the rival does not make such an offer, the incumbent can pick up the 50 per cent votes necessary to defeat the rival with the counteroffer (*). Now at the price $s_B y^I$, the rival makes a capital loss on the class B shares of $L = s_B(y^I - y^R)$. This loss must be weighed against the rival's private benefit of control b^R. The conclusion is that the rival will win control if and only if $b^R > L$.

Case 1 can be summarized as follows.

1. If $y^R \geq y^I$, the rival wins control with an offer of (just above) $s_B y^R$ for class B shares. All shareholders will tender and the market value of the company will be y^R.[24]
2. Given $y^R < y^I$, the rival will win control if and only if $b^R > L$, where $L = s_B(y^I - y^R)$. In the event $b^R > L$, the rival will offer (just above) $s_B y^I$ for the class B shares (and the class A shares will be worth $s_A y^R$). Given $b^R > L$ (i.e. the rival does take control), the market value of the company will therefore be $V = s_B y^I + s_A y^R = y^R + L$. On the other hand, if $b^R \leq L$ (i.e. if the incumbent retains control), the market value of the company will be y^I.

It is easy to see from the summary how the security-voting structure influences the outcome of the control contest. If $y^R \geq y^I$, it has no effect, since the rival wins regardless of the structure. However, if $y^R < y^I$, the security-voting structure does matter, since it determines the size of L and hence both whether the rival

---

[24] Market value here refers to the value of the company after the uncertainty about the characteristics of the incumbent and rival is resolved.

takes control and the value of the company if the rival does take control. Shareholders never benefit when an inferior rival wins control, since the market value doesn't rise above y^I (its status quo value) and in some cases it falls. Furthermore, the capital loss experienced by shareholders is decreasing in L. Therefore, if $y^I >$ y^R, shareholders want to make L large. This goal is accomplished by setting s_B large. In particular, one share–one vote (or, more generally, any structure with $v_B > \frac{1}{2} \Rightarrow s_B = 1$) will dominate all other structures, since this forces the rival to buy up 100 per cent of the profit stream and so the company's market value never falls below y^I. In contrast with any other structure, there will be values of y^I, y^R, and b^R such that an inferior rival takes control by buying up less than 100 per cent of the profit stream and reducing the value of the company.

Case 2: b^R is insignificant in relation to b^I, y^I, y^R. The analysis of case 1 can be adapted, where the roles of the rival and the incumbent are reversed. However, there is one slight difference: it has been assumed that, in order to win control, the rival must make an offer that deters the incumbent. In contrast, in order to retain control, the incumbent does not have to make an offer at all. Because of this, the formulae in case 2 change slightly.

It is useful to start by considering the most aggressive bid that the rival can make for the company. Given that she will win control, the rival is prepared to

(**)   offer (just above) $s_B y^R$ for the class B shares,

since this will allow her just to break even. The rival cannot offer more because her private benefit is insignificant; on the other hand, she cannot offer less than $s_B y^R$ and receive any shares, since, given that she is expected to win, shareholders will prefer to hold on rather than to tender.

If $y^I \geq y^R$, it is clear that the incumbent can easily defeat this offer by bidding (just above) $s_B y^I$ for class B, since then, whether shareholders think the incumbent or the rival will win, they will tender to the incumbent. Hence in this case the rival will not make an offer at all and the incumbent will retain control.

On the other hand, suppose $y^I < y^R$. Now, to defeat the rival's offer, the incumbent must offer (just above) $s_B y^R$ for the class B shares. This means that the incumbent makes a capital loss of $L' =$

$s_B(y^R - y^I)$. Of course, the incumbent will be prepared to incur this loss only if it is less than his private benefit. We may conclude that, given $y^I < y^R$, the rival will take control if and only if $b^I \leq L'$.

Case 2 can be summarized as follows:

1. If $y^I \geq y^R$, the incumbent retains control and the market value of the company is y^I.
2. Given $y^I < y^R$, the rival wins control if and only if $b^I \leq L'$, where $L' = s_B(y^R - y^I)$. If $b^I \leq L'$, the rival makes the offer (**) and the market value of the company is y^R. If $b^I > L'$, the rival does not make an offer and the market value of the company is y^I.

As noted, there is an asymmetry between cases 1 and 2. In case 1, when $y^R < y^I$, the size of L affects both whether the rival takes control and the value of the company in this event; in contrast, in case 2, when $y^I < y^R$, L' affects whether the incumbent retains control but the value of the company is independent of L' in this event. The difference stems from the assumption that, in order to win control, the rival must make an offer that deters the incumbent and this offer will disgorge some of the rival's private benefits; on the other hand, when the incumbent retains control, the rival does not bid at all and so the incumbent is not forced to make an offer that disgorges some of *his* private benefits.[25]

The effects of the security-voting structure on control contests in case 2 are straightforward. If $y^I \geq y^R$, security-voting structure has no effect since the incumbent retains control regardless. However, if $y^I < y^R$, security-voting structure does have an effect by determining the size of L'. When a superior rival takes control, this is good for shareholders because the value of the company increases from y^I to y^R. Therefore a good security-voting structure is one that maximizes L'. It follows that one share–one vote (or, more generally, $v_B > \frac{1}{2} \Rightarrow s_B = 1$) dominates all other structures. In particular, under such a structure $L' = (y^R - y^I)$, whereas under all other structures $L' < (y^R - y^I)$.

Case 3: b^I, b^R are both insignificant (in relation to y^I, y^R). This situation is very straightforward. If $y^R > y^I$, the rival wins control by

---

[25] To put it another way, the asymmetry arises because the rival moves first and then the incumbent responds; and also because the rival has no incentive to make a losing bid given that there is a (small) cost of making a bid.

making an offer at (just above) $s_B y^R$ for the B shares. The incumbent cannot resist this offer because he would incur a large capital loss by doing so. On the other hand, if $y^R < y^I$, the incumbent retains control, because the rival cannot afford to bid $s_B y^I$ for class B and this would be required to deter the incumbent.

Hence, in case 3 the superior management team always wins control regardless of the security-voting structure, because neither party's private benefit is large enough to offset any disadvantage in public benefit.[26] Although this conclusion is fairly obvious, it confirms the idea that private benefits are a crucial ingredient in determining optimal security-voting structure.

The above analysis can be summarized as follows. One share–one vote (more generally, $v_B > \frac{1}{2} \Rightarrow s_B = 1$) dominates all other security-voting structures if either the incumbent's or the rival's private benefits are insignificant. If both private benefits are insignificant, one share–one vote is neither better nor worse than other structures.

However, there is a fourth case, where one share–one vote is not generally optimal.

Case 4: b^I, b^R are both significant in relation to y^I, y^R. If both b^I and b^R are significant, a departure from one share–one vote may be desirable. Such a departure can increase the intensity of competition between the rival and incumbent and permit the extraction of some of the rival's private benefits.

The example of Section 1 can be used to illustrate this. Suppose $y^I = 200$, $y^R = 300$, $b^I = 51$, $b^R = 3$. Consider the dual-class structure in the example ($s_A = \frac{1}{2}$, $v_A = 0$, $s_B = \frac{1}{2}$, $v_B = 1$). Under this structure, the competition for control takes place over the class B shares. The rival is prepared to pay up to 153 for them ($\frac{1}{2}$ (300) + 3), whereas the incumbent is prepared to pay only 151 ($\frac{1}{2}$ (200) + 51). Thus, the rival will win with an offer of 152, say. The class A shareholders are left holding shares worth 150 (half the public value under the rival). So the total value of the company is 302.

Consider next one share–one vote. Now the rival will win control by making an offer for all the shares at 301, say. Shareholders

---

[26] There is one situation in which this conclusion does not hold and it occurs when class B consists of pure votes ($s_B = 0$). This structure is inferior to all others in case 3, however, and so will be disregarded.

will tender because they are being offered more than the post-takeover value of the company under either the rival or the incumbent. (If the rival offers less than 300, shareholders who expect the bid to succeed will not tender, preferring to remain as minority shareholders.) Moreover, the incumbent cannot resist this offer since the most he can afford to pay for 100 per cent of the shares is 251, comprising the public value under his management plus his private benefit. Hence under one share–one vote the rival will win and the value of the company will be 301.

To put it very simply, shareholders benefit when the rival and incumbent compete over products for which they have a similar willingness to pay. In the example, a class consisting of 50 per cent of the dividends and 100 per cent of the votes qualifies better for this than shares and votes bundled together in the same proportion. Note, however, that the example is quite fragile. If the incumbent's private benefit is 54 rather than 51, the incumbent will be able to outbid the rival for the votes, and the value of the company will be only 200. (The rival will not bid at all.) In contrast, under one share–one vote, the rival would win and the company would be worth 301.

How important is case 4 relative to the other cases? For some kinds of companies, private benefits may be large and case 4 may be significant. Examples might be newspapers (where the ability to influence public opinion yields significant (non-monetary) private benefits) and sports teams and entertainment companies (where being associated with a winning team or mixing with famous people yields high (non-monetary) private benefits). However, for many other companies private benefits are likely to be less important. One reason for this is that corporate law makes it difficult for a controlling party to realize significant (monetary) private benefits. The corporation's directors have a fiduciary duty to all shareholders, and overt diversion of wealth to the controlling party violates this duty.[27] Of course, the courts cannot always be relied on to ensure that the minority is protected, and the level of protection may vary greatly from one country to another or from one legal jurisdiction to another. Hence, the initial owner who is designing the security-voting structure must take into account the possibility that b^R, b^I are large. However, for a

---

[27] For discussions of fiduciary duty, see Clark (1986) and Macey (1992). For an economic analysis, see Barca and Felli (1992).

reasonably wide class of companies, it may be unlikely that both are large at the same time (and that both are in the form of money, i.e. that both can be used to purchase votes). For such companies, cases 1–3 are the relevant ones. (For a further discussion of this point, see Section 4.)[28]

Proposition 1, which follows directly from the analysis above, is stated without proof.

> PROPOSITION 1. Suppose the case where the incumbent's and the rival's private benefits are both significant occurs with (vanishingly) small probability relative to the case where just one private benefit is significant. Then one share–one vote (more generally, a structure with $v_B > \frac{1}{2} \Rightarrow s_B = 1$) maximizes the date 0 market value of the company's securities.[29]

3. Extensions

This section discusses two extensions of the model.

Restricted offers

Proposition 1 on the optimality of one share–one vote generalizes to the case of restricted offers. (With a restricted offer, a bidder offers to buy a fraction of the shares of a class for some price and prorates equally if more shares are tendered.) It is not difficult to see why this is. (The following is a sketch of the argument; for details, see Grossman and Hart (1988) and Harris and Raviv (1988, 1989).)

---

[28] As noted, the level of protection of minority shareholders is not the same in all countries. Hence case 4 may be empirically more relevant in some countries than in others. This fact may explain why departures from one share–one vote are more common in some countries than in others. See Zingales (1994).

[29] It is worth noting that one share–one vote also leads to a *socially* optimal outcome (i.e. an outcome that maximizes public plus private value, $y + b$). Moreover, this is true even if both the incumbent's and rival's private benefits can be significant. The reason is that a management team's willingness to pay for a single class of voting equity is given by $(y + b)$, and therefore under one share–one vote the corporate control contest will be won by the team with the higher total (i.e. public plus private) value.

Suppose there are two classes with dividend and vote entitlements given by s_A, v_A and s_B, v_B, respectively, where $v_B > \frac{1}{2}$, and $s_A + s_B = v_A + v_B = 1$. Continue to assume that only one bidder has a significant private benefit. Consider a rival with a significant private benefit but with a lower public value than the incumbent's: $y^R < y^I$. (A similar argument applies if the incumbent has a significant private benefit and $y^I < y^R$.)[30] Then it is clear from the logic of Section 2 that the rival will obtain control—that is, 50 per cent of the votes—by *minimizing* the fraction of the company's dividend stream she purchases. The reason is that she makes a capital loss of $y^I - y^R$ on this dividend stream. There are two cases. If $s_B / v_B \leq 1 \leq s_A / v_A$, then the class B shares are rich in votes relative to dividends and the cheapest way to obtain control is to make an offer for a fraction λ of the class B shares (at a price of just above $s_B y^I$ per 100 per cent), where $\lambda v_B = \frac{1}{2}$. This way, the rival's capital loss is

$$(8.1) \qquad L = \frac{s_B}{2 v_B} (y^I - y^R) \leq \frac{1}{2} (y^I - y^R)$$

with equality if and only if $s_A / v_A = s_B / v_B = 1$. On the other hand, if $s_B / v_B \geq 1 \geq s_A / v_A$, then the class A shares are rich in votes relative to dividends and the cheapest way for R to get control is to make an offer for all the class A shares (at a price just above $s_A y^I$ per 100 per cent) and a fraction μ of the class B shares (at a price just above $s_B y^I$ per 100 per cent) where $v_A + \mu\, v_B = \frac{1}{2}$. This way the rival's capital loss is

$$(8.2) \qquad L = \left[s_A + \left(\frac{\frac{1}{2} - v_A}{v_B} \right) s_B \right] (y^I - y^R)$$
$$\leq \tfrac{1}{2} (y^I - y^R),$$

with equality if and only if $s_A / v_A = s_B / v_B = 1$.

However, the argument of Section 2 shows that the initial owner who designs the security-voting structure wants to *maximize* the rival's capital loss, L. Combining the inequalities in (8.1) and (8.2) shows that one share–one vote, that is, $s_A / v_A = s_B / v_B = 1$, is the (unique) security-voting structure that does this.[31] That is,

---

[30] If $y^R \geq y^I$ (and $b^R \geq b^I$), security-voting structure is irrelevant, just as in the case of no restricted offers (see §2).

[31] Readers may wish to refer to n. 17 here.

with one share–one vote the rival is forced to buy up 50 per cent of the dividend stream to obtain 50 per cent of the votes, whereas under any other security-voting structure she will buy less.

Although one share–one vote continues to be optimal in the presence of restricted offers, one share–one vote no longer fully protects shareholder property rights. In particular, an inferior rival may be able to get control (or a superior rival may be prevented from obtaining control).

To see this, suppose $y^I = 200$, $b^I \simeq 0$, $y^R = 180$, $b^R = 15$. Then the rival can get control by making an unconditional offer for (just over) 50 per cent of the shares at a price of just over 100. (The bidder prorates equally if more than 50 per cent of the shares are tendered.) In the absence of a counter-offer from the incumbent, it is a dominant strategy for a small shareholder to tender to the rival (since the rival is offering a premium and the shares will be worth only 90 if she wins), and so the rival wins. This is in spite of the fact that in the aggregate the shareholders lose by the take-over: they obtain a slight premium on 50 per cent of their shares, but the rest are worth only 90. The rival makes a profit, since her private benefit exceeds her capital loss of $\frac{1}{2}(200) - \frac{1}{2}(180) = 10$ on the shares she purchases.

Could the incumbent block this bid? The answer is no. Given that the incumbent does not have a significant private benefit, he cannot offer a premium for the shares, and so he may as well offer to buy them all at 200. However, given this offer and the rival's offer, it is not a rational expectations equilibrium for the rival to lose, since, if it is thought that the rival will lose, her offer will not be prorated and so shareholders will obtain a higher return by tendering to her. Thus, the only equilibrium has the rival winning; i.e. the incumbent fails to block.

Similar examples can be constructed showing that restricted offers may prevent a superior rival from getting control.[32]

---

[32] One way to make it more difficult for an inferior rival to get control through a restricted offer is for the company to adopt a super-majority voting rule; that is, a rival is required to obtain a fraction α of the votes to displace incumbent management, where $\alpha > \frac{1}{2}$. In fact, if the only goal were to prevent inferior rivals from obtaining control, it would be optimal to set $\alpha = 1$. However, this would make it very easy for an incumbent with a private benefit to resist a superior rival. For a discussion of optimal plurality levels, see Grossman and Hart (1988) and Harris and Raviv (1988, 1989).

More complex security-voting structures

So far the optimal security-voting structure has been analysed under the assumption that all claims to dividends are proportional, i.e. that each security is characterized by a share s of profit. More general structures are, however, possible. For example, security i could be entitled to some nonlinear share $f_i(y)$ of total profit y. Harris and Raviv (1989) show that, if the functions $f_i(y)$ are restricted to be non-decreasing, then (as long as private benefits are not simultaneously large) an optimal security-voting structure consists of (any amount of non-voting) riskless debt and a single class of shares with votes attached. Since one share–one vote, with no debt, is a special case of this, one may conclude that (monotonic) nonlinear securities do not add anything.

The intuition behind the riskless debt result is as follows. A claimant holding riskless debt is unaffected by a control transaction, and so the winner of the control contest imposes no externality on such a claimant. (It is supposed that the rival creates enough public value so that the debt remains riskless.) Therefore an efficient outcome is achieved by giving all the votes to claimants other than the riskless debt-holders. In fact, if riskless debt-holders are given votes, this can lead to an *inefficient* outcome, since a bidder may be able to obtain control by buying their votes instead of the votes of the variable claim-holders, who are actually affected by the outcome. (Harris and Raviv (1989) call this the 'no cheap votes' principle.)

The result that riskless debt-holders should not have votes accords with observation. However, it is not clear that the analysis can explain why risky debt-holders also typically do not have votes.

Vote selling

It has been assumed throughout that it is illegal or infeasible for a bidder to unbundle a security-voting structure by making an offer for the votes or proxies of shareholders in which the bidder pays only for the votes and gets none of the dividend claims. In particular, I have not allowed a bidder to make an offer to shareholders of the following form: in exchange for each share tendered, a shareholder will receive a small amount of cash together with a share of a new company. The new company, whose assets will consist entirely of the tendered shares and votes of the original company, will pass through all dividends of the original company, but the bidder will maintain voting control of the new company (that is, the bidder will be able to vote the original company's shares). If offers like this were allowed, it is not difficult to show that the outcome of a control contest would be as if the company had a dual-class structure in which one class had all the votes and none of the dividends, and the other class had all the dividends and none of the votes.

Thus, if votes can be unbundled from shares, the security-voting structure does not matter. Note that one share–one vote is neither better nor worse than any other structure under these conditions. In practice, it may be hard to unbundle votes from shares. For example, Easterbrook and Fischel (1983) argue that a public market in votes separated from shares is illegal in the USA.[33] To the extent that this is true, the earlier results apply and one share–one vote dominates all other security-voting structures.

4. Conclusions

This chapter has argued that a company's security-voting structure can have an important influence on whether the company will be taken over. It has been shown that, if a competition between bidders with significant private benefits is unlikely, the optimal choice of security-voting structure is one share–one vote.

There is a link between the material in this chapter and that in earlier chapters. Chapter 3 gave some reasons why residual control rights (in the form of votes) and residual income rights (in the form of dividends) should be bundled together. In that chapter, however, it was supposed that the holder of residual control rights and the holder of residual income rights could bargain costlessly. The analysis of this chapter provides further justification for the linking of voting rights and income rights, but for the case where large numbers make bargaining impossible and

---

[33] However, there may be 'private' ways to separate votes from shares through the use of voting trusts, standstill agreements, stock pyramids, and the like. On this, see DeAngelo and DeAngelo (1985).

where shareholders face free-rider and collective action problems.

It is interesting to relate the results of this chapter to the empirical evidence on departures from one share–one vote. DeAngelo and DeAngelo (1985: 39) identified 78 companies publicly traded on the American Stock Exchange and over the counter that had classes of securities with different voting rights (out of a universe of thousands of companies).[34] They found that, in most of the companies that deviated from one share–one vote, incumbent managers had enough votes so that a change in control was impossible without their approval. That is, the deviation from one share–one vote did not correspond to a situation in which widely held securities had different effective voting rights; instead, it corresponded to a situation in which the incumbent had all the effective votes necessary to maintain control. Moreover, in many of the cases the incumbent represented a family.[35]

The evidence suggests that the forces responsible for a deviation from one share–one vote may not be those discussed in case 4 of the model of this chapter, where the incumbent's and rival's private benefits are both significant, so much as those analysed in the Aghion–Bolton model of Chapter 5. As noted earlier, this chapter has supposed that management's preferences are 'unimportant' relative to those of investors and do not receive any weight in the choice of capital structure. However, if this is not the case—and family-run companies may be a leading example where it is not—then it might be efficient to allocate control rights to managers in order to allow them to enjoy their private benefits, or to motivate them to undertake relationship-specific investments.[36] Alternatively, the initial owner might 'sell' the private benefits to a large investor, along with voting control, so that the investor can consume the private benefits without risk of expropriation. In fact, if private benefits are reliably significant, it would perhaps be surprising if one of the above scenarios did not arise; that is, it would be surprising if the company remained

[34] Note that until recently it has been a requirement for listing on the New York Stock Exchange that a company have a one share–one vote security structure. Thus, the authors had to look to other exchanges to find deviations.

[35] Zingales (1994) finds an even more concentrated pattern of insider ownership in dual-class companies in Italy.

[36] For a similar idea, see Laffont and Tirole (1988).

widely held. But this means that case 4, where there are no large shareholders and yet where there is a high probability of a competition between bidders with significant private benefits at some future date, is not a leading one.

In future work, it would be desirable to incorporate the entrepreneurial incentives and private benefits of Chapter 5 into the model of this chapter. It would be interesting to see whether the optimal security-voting structure consists of a single class of shares that are widely held, together with a class of superior voting stock held by insiders. Such a result would appear to be consistent with the empirical evidence.

Finally, it is useful to relate the results of this chapter to the recent US policy debate on whether a company should be required to adopt one share–one vote as a condition for listing on various stock exchanges. The chapter has argued that an initial owner has an incentive to choose a value-maximizing security-voting structure since he bears the full consequences of his actions through the effect on the prices of the company's securities. It has been shown that one share–one vote is often, but not always, optimal. Given this, there seems little reason to put restrictions on the security-voting structures of a new company; such restrictions will simply raise the cost of capital.

However, deviations from one share–one vote often occur at a later stage in a company's life, when the company's shareholders are dispersed. At this point, management—unlike an initial owner—does not have the right incentive to choose a value-maximizing security-voting structure since the consequences are borne by existing shareholders rather than by management. There is thus a suspicion that *ex post* changes may be carried out by management to entrench itself and may be value-reducing.[37]

Of course, changes in security-voting structure are sometimes justified as new events occur that were not anticipated when the original corporate chapter was written. Thus, some mechanism for change should probably be in place. However, in order to reduce the possibility of abuse, it makes sense to put the burden of proof on those who want to make the change. In particular,

---

[37] In fact, management may even be able to get shareholders to approve a change that makes them worse off by persuading them to accept inferior voting stock in place of superior voting stock through a 'coercive' exchange offer (see Ruback 1988).

there should be protection for shareholders who oppose the transaction. One possibility is to allow a (relatively small) number of shareholders to veto the transaction. Another possibility is to give dissenting shareholders appraisal rights; that is, if the change in security-voting structure goes through, a shareholder could ask to be bought out at the 'appraised' value of the assets, in the absence of the change.

References

Adler, B. E. (1993). 'Financial and Political Theories of American Corporate Bankruptcy'. *Stanford Law Review*, 45:311.

—— (1994). 'A World Without Debt'. *Washington University Law Quarterly*, 72(3):811–27.

Aggarwal, R. (1994). 'Renegotiation, Reorganization, and Liquidation: Corporate Financial Distress and Bankruptcy with Multiple Creditors'. Ph.D. dissertation, Harvard University.

Aghion, P., and Bolton, P. (1987). 'Contracts as a Barrier to Entry'. *American Economic Review*, 77:388–401.

—— —— (1992). 'An "Incomplete Contracts" Approach to Financial Contracting'. *Review of Economic Studies*, 59:473–94.

—— and Tirole, J. (1994). 'The Management of Innovation'. *Quarterly Journal of Economics*, 109:1185–1209.

—— —— (1995). 'Formal and Real Authority in Organizations'. Mimeo, Oxford University.

—— Hart, O., and Moore, J. (1992). 'The Economics of Bankruptcy Reform'. *Journal of Law, Economics and Organization*, 8:523–46.

—— —— —— (1994). 'Improving Bankruptcy Procedure'. *Washington University Law Quarterly*, 72(3):811–27.

—— —— —— (1995). 'Insolvency Reform in the UK: A Revised Proposal'. *Insolvency Law and Practice*; 11(3): 4–11.

—— Dewatripont, M., and Rey, P. (1994c). 'Renegotiation Design with Unverifiable Information'. *Econometrica*, 62:257–82.

Alchian, A., and Demsetz, H. (1972). 'Production, Information Costs, and Economic Organization'. *American Economic Review*, 62(5):777–95.

Allen, F., and Gale, D. (1992). 'Measurement Distortion and Missing Contingencies in Optimal Contracts'. *Economic Theory*, 2:1–26.

—— —— (1994). *Financial Innovation and Risk Sharing*. Cambridge, Mass.: MIT Press.

Anderlini, L., and Felli, L. (1994). 'Incomplete Written Contracts: Undescribable States of Nature'. *Quarterly Journal of Economics*, 109:1085–1124.

Aoki, M. (1994). 'Controlling the Insider Control: Issues of Corporate Governance in the Transition'. Mimeo, Stanford University.

Arrow, K. J. (1975). 'Vertical Integration and Communication'. *Bell Journal of Economics*, 6(1):173–83.

Asquith, P., and Mullins, D., Jr (1986). 'Equity Issues and Offering Dilution'. *Journal of Financial Economics*, 15:61–89.

—— Gertner, R., and Scharfstein, D. (1994). 'Anatomy of Financial

Distress: An Examination of Junk-Bond Issuers'. *Quarterly Journal of Economics*, 109:625–58.

Aumann, R. J. (1976). 'Agreeing to Disagree'. *Annals of Statistics*, 4:1236–9.

Ayres, I., and Gertner, R. (1989). 'Filling Gaps in Incomplete Contracts: An Economic Theory of Default Rules'. *Yale Law Review*, 99:87–130.

Bagnoli, M., and Lipman, B. (1988). 'Successful Takeovers without Exclusion'. *Review of Financial Studies*, 1:89–110.

Baird, D. (1986). 'The Uneasy Case for Corporate Reorganizations'. *Journal of Legal Studies*, 15:127–47.

—— (1992). *The Elements of Bankruptcy*. New York: Foundation.

—— and Jackson, T. (1985). *Cases, Problems, and Materials on Bankruptcy*. Boston: Little, Brown.

Baldwin, C. Y. (1983). 'Productivity and Labor Unions: An Application of the Theory of Self-Enforcing Contracts'. *Journal of Business*, 56:155–85.

Barca, F., and Felli, L. (1992). 'Fiduciary Duties, Ownership and Control'. Mimeo, London School of Economics.

Barclay, M. J., and Holderness, C. G. (1989). 'Private Benefits from Control of Public Corporations'. *Journal of Financial Economics*, 25:371–95.

Barnard, C. I. (1938). *The Functions of the Executive*. Cambridge, Mass.: Harvard University Press.

Baumol, W. (1959). *Business Behavior and Growth*. New York: Macmillan.

Bebchuk, A. L. (1988). 'A New Approach to Corporate Reorganizations'. *Harvard Law Review*, 101:775–804.

—— (1989). 'Takeover Bids below the Expected Value of Minority Shares'. *Journal of Financial and Quantitative Analysis*, 24:171–84.

—— (1994). 'Efficient and Inefficient Sales of Corporate Control'. *Quarterly Journal of Economics*, 109:957–93.

—— and Zingales, L. (1995). 'Corporate Ownership Structures: Private versus Social Optimality'. Mimeo, University of Chicago Graduate School of Business.

Berglöf, E. (1994). 'A Control Theory of Venture Capital Finance'. *Journal of Law, Economics and Organization*, 10(2):247–67.

—— and von Thadden, E. L. (1994). 'Short-Term versus Long-Term Interests: Capital Structure with Multiple Investors'. *Quarterly Journal of Economics*, 109:1055–84.

Berkovitch, E., Israel, R., and Zender, J. (1993). 'The Design of Bankruptcy Law: A Case for Management Bias in Bankruptcy Reorganizations'. Mimeo, University of Michigan.

Berle, A. A., and Means, G. C. (1932). *The Modern Corporation and Private Property*. New York: Macmillan.

Bernheim, D. and Whinston M. D. (1995). 'Incomplete Contracts and Strategic Ambiguity'. Mimeo, Harvard University.

Blair, D. H., Golbe, D. L., and Gerard, J. M. (1989). 'Unbundling the Voting Rights and Profit Claims of Common Shares'. *Journal of Political Economy*, 97:420–43.

Bolton, P., and Scharfstein, D. (1990). 'A Theory of Predation Based on Agency Problems in Financial Contracting'. *American Economic Review*, 80:94–106.

—— —— (1994). 'Optimal Debt Structure and the Number of Creditors'. Mimeo, MIT.

—— and Whinston, M. D. (1993). 'Incomplete Contracts, Vertical Integration and Supply Assurance'. *Review of Economic Studies*, 60(1):121–48.

Boyco, M., Shleifer, A., and Vishny, R. (1995). *Privatizing Russia*, Cambridge, Mass.: MIT Press.

Bradley, M., and Rosenzweig, M. (1992). 'The Untenable Case for Chapter 11'. *Yale Law Review*, 101:1043–95.

—— Desai, A., and Kim, E. H. (1988). 'Synergistic Gains from Corporate Acquisitions and their Division between the Stockholders of Target and Acquiring Firms'. *Journal of Financial Economics*, 21:3–40.

Brander, J. A., and Lewis, T. R. (1986). 'Oligopoly and Financial Structure: The Limited Liability Effect'. *American Economic Review*, 76:956–70.

Brynjolfsson, E. (1994) 'Information Assets, Technology and Organization'. *Management Science*, 40(12):1645–62.

Bulow, J. I., Summers, L. H., and Summers, V. P. (1990). 'Distinguishing Debt from Equity in the Junk Bond Era'. In J. B. Shoven and J. Waldfogel (eds.), *Debt, Taxes, and Corporate Restructuring*. Washington: Brookings Institution, 135–56.

Burkart, M., Gromb, D., and Panunzi, F. (1994). 'Large Shareholders, Monitoring and Fiduciary Duty'. Mimeo, MIT.

Chandler, A. D. (1990). *Scale and Scope: The Dynamics of Industrial Capitalism*. Cambridge, Mass.: Harvard University Press.

Chung, T. Y. (1991). 'Incomplete Contracts, Specific Investments, and Risk Sharing'. *Review of Economic Studies*, 58:1031–42.

Clark, R. C. (1986). *Corporate Law*. Boston: Little, Brown.

Coase, R. H. (1937). 'The Nature of the Firm'. *Economica*, 4:386–405.

—— (1960). 'The Problem of Social Cost'. *Journal of Law and Economics*, 3:1–44.

—— (1988). 'The Nature of the Firm: Influence'. *Journal of Law, Economics and Organization*, 4(1):33–47.

Cremer, J. (1994). 'A Theory of Vertical Integration Based on Monitoring Costs'. Mimeo, IDEI.

Cutler, D., and Summers, L. (1988). 'The Costs of Conflict Resolution and

Financial Distress: Evidence from the Texaco–Pennzoil Litigation'. *Rand Journal of Economics*, 19:157–72.

DeAngelo, H., and DeAngelo, L. (1985). 'Managerial Ownership of Voting Rights'. *Journal of Financial Economics*, 14:33–69.

Dennis, W., Dunkelberg, W., and Van Hulle, J. (1988). *Small Business and Banks: The United States*. Washington: National Federation of Independent Business Research and Education Foundation.

Dewatripont, M. (1989). 'Renegotiation and Information Revelation over Time: The Case of Optimal Labor Contracts'. *Quarterly Journal of Economics*, 104(3), 589–619.

—— and Maskin, E. (1990). 'Credit and Efficiency in Centralized and Decentralized Economies'. Mimeo, Harvard University.

—— and Tirole, J. (1994). 'A Theory of Debt and Equity: Diversity of Securities and Manager–Shareholder Congruence'. *Quarterly Journal of Economics*, 109:1027–54.

Diamond, D. (1991). 'Debt Maturity Structure and Liquidity Risk'. *Quarterly Journal of Economics*, 106:709–37.

Dunkelberg, W., and Scott, J. (1985). *Credit Banks and Small Business: 1980–1984*. Washington: National Federation of Independent Business Research and Education Foundation.

Dybvig, P. H., and Zender, J. F. (1991). 'Capital Structure and Dividend Irrelevance with Asymmetric Information'. *Review of Financial Studies*, 4:201–19.

Easterbrook, F. H., and Fischel, D. R. (1983). 'Voting in Corporate Law'. *Journal of Law and Economics*, 26:395–427.

Fisher, T., and Martel, J. (1994). 'Facts about Financial Reorganization in Canada'. Mimeo, University of Montreal.

Franks, J. R., and Torous, W. N. (1989). 'An Empirical Investigation of US Firms in Reorganization'. *Journal of Finance*, 44:747–69.

Fudenberg, D., and Tirole, J. (1991). *Game Theory*. Cambridge, Mass.: MIT Press.

Gale, D., and Hellwig, M. (1985). 'Incentive-Compatible Debt Contracts: The One-Period Problem'. *Review of Economic Studies*, 52:647–63.

—— —— (1989). 'Reputation and Renegotiation: The Case of Sovereign Debt'. *International Economic Review*, 30:3–31.

Garvey, G. (1991). 'Encouraging Specific Investments in a One Shot and Repeated Partnership: Some Comparisons'. Mimeo, Australian Graduate School of Management.

Gertner, R., and Scharfstein, D. (1991). 'A Theory of Workouts and the Effects of Reorganization Law'. *Journal of Finance*, 46: 1189–1222.

Gilson, S. (1989). 'Management Turnover and Financial Distress'. *Journal of Financial Economics*, 25:241–62.

—— (1990). 'Bankruptcy, Boards, Banks, and Blockholders'. *Journal of Financial Economics*, 27:355–87.

—— (1991). 'Managing Default: Some Evidence on How Firms Choose between Workouts and Chapter 11'. *Journal of Applied Corporate Finance*, 4:62–70.

—— John, K., and Lang, L. (1990). 'Troubled Debt Restructuring: An Empirical Study of Private Reorganization of Firms in Default'. *Journal of Financial Economics*, 26:315–53.

Gromb, D. (1993). 'Is One Share–One Vote Optimal?" Mimeo, Ecole Polytechnique.

Grossman, S., and Hart, O. (1980). 'Takeover Bids, the Free-Rider Problem, and the Theory of the Corporation'. *Bell Journal of Economics*, 11:42–64.

—— —— (1982). 'Corporate Financial Structure and Managerial Incentives'. In J. J. McCall (ed.), *The Economics of Information and Uncertainty*. Chicago: University of Chicago Press, 107–40.

—— —— (1986). 'The Costs and Benefits of Ownership: A Theory of Vertical and Lateral Integration'. *Journal of Political Economy*, 94:691–719.

—— —— (1988). 'One Share–One Vote and the Market for Corporate Control'. *Journal of Financial Economics*, 20:175–202.

Grout, P. A. (1984). 'Investment and Wages in the Absence of Binding Contracts: A Nash Bargaining Approach'. *Econometrica*, 52(2): 449–60.

Halonen, M. (1994) 'Reputation and Allocation of Ownership'. Mimeo, Helsinki School of Economics.

Hansmann, H. (1996). *The Ownership of Enterprise*, Cambridge; Mass.: Harvard University Press.

Harris, M., and Raviv, A. (1988). 'Corporate Governance: Voting Rights and Majority Rules'. *Journal of Financial Economics*, 20:203–35.

—— —— (1989). 'The Design of Securities'. *Journal of Financial Economics*, 24:255–87.

—— —— (1991). 'The Theory of Capital Structure'. *Journal of Finance*, 46:297–355.

—— —— (1995). 'The Role of Games in Security Design'. *Review of Financial Studies*, forthcoming.

Hart, O. (1988). 'Incomplete Contracts and the Theory of the Firm'. *Journal of Law, Economics and Organization*, 4(1):119–39.

—— (1989). 'An Economist's Perspective on the Theory of the Firm'. *Columbia Law Review*, 89:1757–74.

—— (1990). 'Is "Bounded Rationality" an Important Element of a Theory of Institutions?' *Journal of Institutional and Theoretical Economics*, 146:696–702.

Hart, O. (1993). 'Theories of Optimal Capital Structure: A Managerial Discretion Perspective'. In Margaret Blair (ed.), *The Deal Decade: What Takeovers and Leveraged Buyouts Mean for Corporate Governance*. Washington: Brookings Institution.

—— and Holmstrom, B. (1987). 'The Theory of Contracts'. In T. F. Bewley (ed.), *Advances in Economic Theory*. Cambridge: Cambridge University Press, 71–155.

—— and Moore, J. (1988). 'Incomplete Contracts and Renegotiation'. *Econometrica*, 56:755–86.

—— ——. (1989). 'Default and Renegotiation: A Dynamic Model of Debt'. MIT Working Paper no. 520.

—— —— (1990). 'Property Rights and the Nature of the Firm'. *Journal of Political Economy*, 98:1119–58.

—— —— (1994a). 'A Theory of Debt Based on the Inalienability of Human Capital'. *Quarterly Journal of Economics*, 109:841–79.

—— —— (1994b). 'The Governance of Exchanges: Members' Cooperatives Versus Outside Ownership'. Mimeo, Harvard University.

—— —— (1995). 'Debt and Seniority: An Analysis of the Role of Hard Claims in Constraining Management'. *American Economic Review*, 85(3):567–85.

—— and Tirole, J. (1990). 'Vertical Integration and Market Foreclosure'. *Brookings Papers on Economic Activity*, Microeconomics: 205–76.

Hermalin, B. (1988). 'Three Essays on the Theory of Contracts'. Ph.D. dissertation, MIT.

—— and Katz, M. (1991). 'Moral Hazard and Verifiability'. *Econometrica*, 59:1735–54.

Holmes, O. W. (1881). *The Common Law*. Boston: Little Brown (1963 edn.).

Holmstrom, B., and Milgrom, P. (1990). 'Regulating Trade Among Agents'. *Journal of Institutional and Theoretical Economics*, 146(1):85–105.

—— —— (1991). 'Multitask Principal–Agent Analyses: Incentive Contracts, Asset Ownership, and Job Design'. *Journal of Law, Economics and Organization*, 7 (Special Issue):24–52.

—— —— (1994). 'The Firm as an Incentive System'. *American Economic Review*, 84(4):972–91.

—— and Nalebuff, B. (1992). 'To the Raider Goes the Surplus? A Reexamination of the Free-Rider Problem'. *Journal of Economics and Management Strategy*, 1:37–62.

—— and Tirole, J. (1989). 'The Theory of the Firm'. In R. Schmalensee and R. D. Willig (eds.), *Handbook of Industrial Organization*, vol. 1, *Handbooks in Economics*, no. 10, Amsterdam: North-Holland, 61–133.

—— —— (1991). 'Transfer Pricing and Organizational Form'. *Journal of Law, Economics and Organization*, 7(2):201–28.

Ikenberry, D., and Lakonishok, J. (1993). 'Corporate Governance through the Proxy Contest: Evidence and Implications'. *Journal of Business*, 66:405–35.

Innes, R. (1990). 'Limited Liability and Incentive Contracting with Ex-ante Action Choices'. *Journal of Economic Theory*, 52(1):45–67.

Israel, R. (1991). 'Capital Structure and the Market for Corporate Control'. *Journal of Finance*, 46:1391–1409.

Itoh, H. (1991). 'Incentives to Help in Multi Agent Situations'. *Econometrica*, 59(3):611–36.

Jackson, T. (1986). *The Logic and Limits to Bankruptcy*. Boston: Little, Brown.

Jarrell, G. A., Brickley, J. A., and Netter, J. M. (1988). 'The Market for Corporate Control: The Empirical Evidence Since 1980'. *Journal of Economic Perspectives*, 2:49–68.

Jensen, M. (1986). 'Agency Costs of Free Cash Flow, Corporate Finance and Takeovers'. *American Economic Review*. 76:323–29.

—— (1989). 'Active Investors, LBOs and the Privatization of Bankruptcy'. *Journal of Applied Corporate Finance*, 2:35–44.

—— and Meckling, W. (1976). 'Theory of the Firm: Managerial Behavior, Agency Costs and Ownership Structure'. *Journal of Financial Economics*, 3:305–60.

John, K. (1993). 'Managing Financial Distress and Valuing Distressed Securities: A Survey and Research Agenda'. *Financial Management*, 22(3):60–78.

Joskow, P. A. (1985). 'Vertical Integration and Long Term Contracts: The Case of Coal-Burning Electric Generating Plants'. *Journal of Law, Economics and Organization*, 1(1):33–80.

Kester, W. C. (1986). 'Capital and Ownership Structure: A Comparison of United States and Japanese Manufacturing Corporations'. *Financial Management*, 15:5–16.

Kiyotaki, N., and Moore, J. (1995). 'Credit Cycles'. Mimeo, London School of Economics.

Klein, B. (1988). 'Vertical Integration as Organizational Ownership: The Fisher Body–General Motors Relationship Revisited'. *Journal of Law, Economics and Organization*, 4(1):199–213.

—— Crawford, R., and Alchian, A. (1978). 'Vertical Integration, Appropriable Rents, and the Competitive Contracting Process'. *Journal of Law and Economics*, 21(2):297–326.

Kornai, J. (1980). *Economics of Shortage*. Amsterdam: North-Holland.

Kovenock, D. (1984). 'A Note on Takeover Bids'. Mimeo, Krannert Graduate School of Management, Purdue University.

Kreps, D. (1990). 'Corporate Culture and Economic Theory'. In J. Alt and K. Shepsle (eds.), *Perspectives on Positive Political Economy*. Cambridge: Cambridge University Press.

Laffont, J.-J., and Tirole, J. (1988). 'Repeated Auctions of Incentive

Contracts, Investment, and Bidding Parity with an Application to Takeovers'. *Rand Journal of Economics*, 19:516–37.

—— —— (1993). *A Theory of Incentives in Procurement and Regulation*. Cambridge, Mass.: MIT Press.

Lazear, E. P. (1989). 'Pay Equality and Industrial Politics'. *Journal of Political Economy*, 97(3):561–80.

Lehn, K., and Poulsen, A. (1992). 'Contractual Resolution of Bondholder–Shareholder Conflicts in Leveraged Buyouts'. *Journal of Law and Economics*, 34:645–74.

Levy, H. (1982). 'Economic Valuation of Voting Power of Common Stock'. *Journal of Finance*, 38:79–93.

Li, S. (1993). 'Essays on Corporate Governance and Finance'. Ph.D. dissertation, MIT.

Long, M., and Malitz, I. (1985). 'Investment Patterns and Financial Leverage'. In B. M. Friedman (ed.), *Corporate Capital Structures in the United States*. Chicago: University of Chicago Press.

LoPucki, L. M., and Whitford, W. C. (1990). 'Bargaining over Equity's Share in the Bankruptcy Reorganization of Large, Publicly Held Companies'. *University of Pennsylvania Law Review*, 139:125–96.

—— —— (1993). 'Corporate Governance in the Bankruptcy Reorganization of Large, Publicly Held Companies'. *University of Pennsylvania Law Review*, 141: 669–800.

Mace, M. L. (1971). *Directors, Myth and Reality*. Boston: Harvard Business School Press.

Macey, J. R. (1992). 'An Economic Analysis of the Various Rationales for Making Shareholders the Exclusive Beneficiaries of Corporate Fiduciary Duties'. *Stetson Law Review*, 21:23–44.

MacLeod, B. and Malcomson, J. (1993). 'Investments, Holdup and the Form of Market Contracts'. *American Economic Review*, 83:811–37.

Mailath, G., and Postlewaite, A. (1990). 'Asymmetric Information Bargaining Problems with Many Agents'. *Review of Economic Studies*, 57:351–67.

Manne, H. G. (1964). 'Some Theoretical Aspects of Share Voting'. *Columbia Law Review*, 64:1427–45.

—— (1965). 'Mergers and the Market for Corporate Control'. *Journal of Political Economy*, 73:110–20.

Marris, R. (1964). *The Economic Theory of Managerial Capitalism*. Glencoe, Ill.: Free Press of Glencoe.

Marx, K. (1867). *Capital*, vol. 1. New York: International Publishers (1967 edn.).

Mas-Colell, A., Whinston, M. D., and Green, J. (1995). *Microeconomic Theory*. Oxford: Oxford University Press.

Maskin, E. (1985). 'The Theory of Implementation in Nash Equilibrium: A Survey'. In L. Hurwicz, D. Schmeidler, and H. Sonnenschein (eds.),

Social Goals and Social Organization: Essays in Memory of Elisha Pazner. Cambridge University Press.

—— and Tirole, J. (1995). 'Dynamic Programming, Unforseen Contingencies, and Incomplete Contracts'. Mimeo, Harvard University.

Masten, S. E. (1988). 'A Legal Basis for the Firm'. *Journal of Law, Economics and Organization,* 4(1):181–98.

Masulis, R. W. (1980). 'The Effects of Capital Structure Change on Security Prices: A Study of Exchange Offers'. *Journal of Financial Economics,* 8:139–77.

—— (1988). *The Debt/Equity Choice.* Cambridge, Mass.: Ballinger.

Milgrom, P. (1988). 'Employment Contracts, Influence Activities, and Efficient Organization Design'. *Journal of Political Economy,* 96(1):42–60.

—— and Roberts, J. (1992). *Economics, Organization and Management.* Englewood Cliffs, NJ: Prentice-Hall.

Miller, M. H. (1977). 'Debt and Taxes'. *Journal of Finance,* 32:261–75.

Mitchell, J. (1993). 'Creditor Passivity and Bankruptcy: Implications for Economic Reform'. In C. Mayer, and X. Vives (eds.), *Capital Markets and Financial Intermediation.* Cambridge University Press.

Modigliani, F. and Miller, M. H. (1958). 'The Cost of Capital, Corporation Finance, and the Theory of Investment'. *American Economic Review,* 48:261–97.

Mookherjee, D. and Png, I. (1989). 'Optimal Auditing, Insurance, and Redistribution'. *Quarterly Journal of Economics,* 104(2):399–415.

Moore, J. (1992). 'Implementation in Environments with Complete Information'. In J. J. Laffont (ed.), *Advances in Economic Theory.* Cambridge: Cambridge University Press, 182–282.

Myers, S. (1977). 'Determinants of Corporate Borrowing'. *Journal of Financial Economics,* 5:147–75.

—— (1990). 'Still Searching for Optimal Capital Structure'. In R. Kopcke and E. Rosengren (eds.), *Are the Distinctions Between Debt and Equity Disappearing?* Boston: Federal Reserve Bank of Boston Conference Series no. 33.

—— and Majluf, N. (1984). 'Corporate Financing and Investment Decisions when Firms Have Information that Investors Do Not Have'. *Journal of Financial Economics,* 13:187–221.

Myerson, R. and Satterthwaite, M. (1983). 'Efficient Mechanisms for Bilateral Trading'. *Journal of Economic Theory,* 29(2):265–81.

Neher, D. V. (1994). 'Stage Financing: An Agency Perspective'. Mimeo, School of Management, Boston University.

Noldeke, G., and Schmidt, K. (1994). 'Debt as an Option to Own in the Theory of Ownership Rights'. Mimeo, University of Bonn.

—— —— (1995). 'Option Contracts and Renegotiation: A Solution to the Hold-up Problem'. *Rand Journal of Economics,* 26(2): 163–79.

Novaes, W., and Zingales, L. (1994). 'Financial Distress as a Collapse of Incentives'. Mimeo, University of Chicago Graduate School of Business.

Osborne, M. J., and Rubinstein, A. (1990). *Bargaining and Markets*. San Diego: Academic Press.

Perotti, E. C., and Spier, K. E. (1993). 'Capital Structure as a Bargaining Tool: The Role of Leverage in Contract Renegotiation'. *American Economic Review*, 83:1131–41.

Pound, J. (1988). 'Proxy Contests and the Efficiency of Shareholder Oversight'. *Journal of Financial Economics*, 20:237–65.

Radner, R. (1992). 'Hierarchy: The Economics of Managing'. *Journal of Economic Literature*, 30:1382–1415.

Ragulin, V. (1994). 'Why Firms Use Payment-in-kind Debt: A Study of Bridge Financing with Contingent Debt Instruments'. Senior thesis, Harvard University.

Rajan, R. G., and Zingales, L. (1994). 'What Do We Know about Capital Structure? Some Evidence from International Data'. Mimeo, University of Chicago Graduate School of Business.

Riordan, M. H. (1990). 'What is Vertical Integration?" In M. Aoki, B. Gustafsson, and O. E. Williamson (eds.), *The Firm as a Nexus of Treaties*. London: Sage, 94–111.

Ritter, J. (1987). 'The Costs of Going Public'. *Journal of Financial Economics*, 19:269–81.

Rob, R. (1989). 'Pollution Claim Settlements under Private Information'. *Journal of Economic Theory*, 47(2):307–33.

Rock, K. (1986). 'Why New Issues are Underpriced'. *Journal of Financial Economics*, 15:187–212.

Roe, M. (1983). 'Bankruptcy and Debt: A New Model for Corporate Reorganizations'. *Columbia Law Review*, 83:527–602.

Ruback, R. S. (1988). 'Coercive Dual–Class Exchange Offers'. *Journal of Financial Economics*, 20:153–73.

Rydqvist, K. (1992). 'Takeover Bids and the Relative Prices of Shares That Differ in Their Voting Rights'. Working Paper 35, Northwestern University.

Sappington, D. E. M. (1991). 'Incentives in Principal–Agent Relationships'. *Journal of Economic Perspectives*, 5(2):45–66.

Scharfstein, D. (1988). 'The Disciplinary Role of Takeovers'. *Review of Economic Studies*, 55:185–99.

Schmidt, K. (1990). 'The Costs and Benefits of Privatization'. Mimeo, University of Bonn Discussion Paper A–287.

Segal, I. (1995). 'Complexity and Renegotiation: A Foundation for Incomplete Contracts'. Mimeo, Harvard University.

Shapiro, C., and Willig, R. D. (1990). 'Economic Rationales for the Scope of Privatization'. In E. N. Suleiman and J. Waterbury (eds.), *The

Political Economy of Public Sector Reform and Privatization. London: Westview Press, 55–87.

Shleifer, A., and Vishny, R. (1986a). 'Large Shareholders and Corporate Control'. *Journal of Political Economy*, 94:461–88.

—— —— (1986b). 'Greenmail, White Knights, and Shareholders' Interest'. *Rand Journal of Economics*, 17:293–309.

—— —— (1992). 'Liquidation Values and Debt Capacity: A Market Equilibrium Approach'. *Journal of Finance*, 47:1343–66.

—— —— (1994). 'Politicians and Firms'. *Quarterly Journal of Economics*, 109:995–1025.

Simon, H. (1951). 'A Formal Theory of the Employment Relationship'. *Econometrica*, 19:293–305.

Smith, C. W., Jr, and Warner, J. B. (1979). 'On Financial Contracting: An Analysis of Bond Covenants'. *Journal of Financial Economics*, 7:117–61.

Smollen, L., Rollinson, M., and Rubel, S. (1977). *Sourceguide for Borrowing Capital*. Chicago: Capital.

Spier, K. (1992). 'Incomplete Contracts and Signalling'. *Rand Journal of Economics*, 23:432–43.

Stein, J. C. (1988). 'Takeover Threats and Managerial Myopia'. *Journal of Political Economy*, 96:61–80.

Stigler, G. J. (1951). 'The Division of Labor is Limited by the Extent of the Market'. *Journal of Political Economy*, 59:185–93.

Stiglitz, J. (1974). 'On the Irrelevance of Corporate Financial Policy'. *American Economic Review*, 64(6):851–66.

Stuckey, J. (1983). *Vertical Integration and Joint Ventures in the Aluminum Industry*. Cambridge, Mass.: Harvard University Press.

Stulz, R. (1990). 'Managerial Discretion and Optimal Financing Policies'. *Journal of Financial Economics*, 26:3–27.

Tao, Z., and Wu, C. (1994). 'On the Organization of Cooperative R&D: Theory and Evidence'. Mimeo, Hong Kong University.

Thomas, J., and Worrall, T. (1994). 'Foreign Direct Investment and the Risk of Expropriation'. *Review of Economic Studies*, 61(1):81–108.

Tirole, J. (1986a). 'Procurement and Renegotiation'. *Journal of Political Economy*, 94(2):235–59.

—— (1986b). 'Hierarchies and Bureaucracies'. *Journal of Law, Economics and Organization*, 2(2):235–59.

—— (1988). *The Theory of Industrial Organization*. Cambridge, Mass.: MIT Press.

—— (1992). 'Collusion and the Theory of Organizations'. In J. J. Laffont (ed.), *Advances in Economic Theory*. Cambridge: Cambridge University Press, 71–155.

—— (1994). 'Incomplete Contracts: Where do we Stand?' Mimeo, IDEI.

Titman, S., and Wessels, R. (1988). 'The Determinants of Capital Structure Choice'. *Journal of Finance*, 43:1–19.

Townsend, R. (1978). 'Optimal Contracts and Competitive Markets with Costly State Verification'. *Journal of Economic Theory*, 21:265–93.

Tufano, P. (1993). 'Financing Acquisitions in the Late 1980s: Sources and Forms of Capital'. In Margaret Blair (ed.), *The Deal Decade: What Takeovers and Leveraged Buyouts Mean for Corporate Governance*. Washington: Brookings Institution.

Vancil, R. F. (1987). *Passing the Baton*. Cambridge, Mass.: Harvard University Press.

Warner, J. (1977). 'Bankruptcy Costs: Some Evidence'. *Journal of Finance*, 32:337–47.

Weber, M. (1968). *Economy and Society*. New York: Bedminster Press.

Weisbach, M. S. (1988). 'Outside Directors and CEO Turnover'. *Journal of Financial Economics*, 20:431–60.

Weiss, L. (1990). 'Bankruptcy Resolution: Direct Costs and Violation of Priority of Claims'. *Journal of Financial Economics*, 27:285–314.

—— (1991). 'Restructuring Complications in Bankruptcy: The Eastern Airlines Bankruptcy Case'. Mimeo, Tulane University.

Wernerfelt, B. (1993). 'The Employment Relationship and Economies of Scale'. Mimeo, Sloan School of Management, MIT.

White, M. (1989). 'The Corporate Bankruptcy Decision'. *Journal of Economic Perspectives*, 3:129–52.

Williamson, O. (1964). *The Economics of Discretionary Behavior: Managerial Objectives in a Theory of the Firm*. Englewood Cliffs, NJ: Prentice-Hall.

—— (1975). *Markets and Hierarchies: Analysis and Antitrust Implications*. New York: Free Press.

—— (1985). *The Economic Institutions of Capitalism*. New York: Free Press.

Zingales, L. (1995). 'Insider Ownership and the Decision to Go Public'. *Review of Economic Studies*, forthcoming.

—— (1994). 'The Value of the Voting Right: A Study of the Milan Stock Exchange Experience'. *Review of Financial Studies*, 7:125–48.

Zwiebel, J. (1995). 'Block Investment and Partial Benefits of Corporate Control'. *Review of Economic Studies*, 62(2): 161–86.

—— (1994). 'Dynamic Capital Structure under Managerial Entrenchment'. Mimeo, Stanford University Graduate School of Business.

Index

Note: The letter n following a page number indicates a reference in the footnotes.